Advising Mentally Disordered Offenders

SECOND EDITION

Related titles from Law Society Publishing:

Assessment of Mental Capacity (3rd edn)
A Practical Guide for Doctors and Lawyers
The British Medical Association and the Law Society

Criminal Defence (3rd edn)
Good Practice in the Criminal Courts
Roger Ede and Anthony Edwards

Mental Capacity (2nd edn)
A Guide to the New Law
Nicola Greaney, Fenella Morris and Beverley Taylor

Titles from Law Society Publishing can be ordered from all good bookshops or direct (telephone 0870 850 1422, email **lawsociety@prolog.uk.com** or visit our online shop at **www.lawsociety.org.uk/bookshop**).

ADVISING MENTALLY DISORDERED OFFENDERS

A Practical Guide

SECOND EDITION

Carolyn Taylor and Julia Krish

with Dr Frank Farnham

The Law Society

ISBN–13: 978-1-85328-634-6

First edition published in 2000

This second edition published in 2010 by the Law Society
113 Chancery Lane, London WC2A 1PL

Typeset by Columns Design Ltd, Reading
Printed by TJ International Ltd, Padstow, Cornwall

The paper used for the text pages of this book is FSC certified. FSC (the Forest Stewardship Council) is an international network to promote responsible management of the world's forests.

FSC
Mixed Sources
Product group from well-managed forests and other controlled sources
Cert no. SGS-COC-2482
www.fsc.org
© 1996 Forest Stewardship Council

Contents

Preface

In April 2009, Lord Bradley published the findings of his government-commissioned review of people with mental health problems or learning disabilities in the criminal justice system. He concluded in the executive summary, 'Evidence suggests that there are now more people with mental health problems in prison than ever before. Custody can exacerbate mental ill health, heighten vulnerability and increase the risk of self-harm and suicide.' Despite the development of mental health assessment teams attending police stations, mental health diversion schemes at magistrates' courts, and pilot mental health courts, a large number of people with mental health difficulties still find themselves within the criminal justice system.

This second edition of the book has been expanded to cover representation of mentally disordered offenders not only in the police station and magistrates' courts, but also the youth court and Crown Court. The Appendices have been extended to provide useful reference material for some of the more important procedural steps. It is aimed at all practitioners involved in this area of work and provides a comprehensive analysis of the law and procedures, from arrest until disposal at the Crown Court. It is also intended to help clarify the role of those practitioners and enable them to perform it effectively.

Dr Frank Farnham provided invaluable psychiatric expertise, contributing to the medical aspects of this area of law and in particular to Chapter 1, which includes a guide to identifying the main mental disorders that are met within the criminal justice system together with an overview of the Mental Health Act 1983 as recently amended by the Mental Health Act 2007. At the time of going to press, the Coroners and Justice Act 2009 has just received Royal Assent, but in respect of the provisions relevant to this book, there is no date fixed for them coming into force. When they do, they will amend the current defences of diminished responsibility and provocation, as well as the law on infanticide, and provide for the examination of an accused to be conducted through an intermediary.

We would like to express our thanks to the following who read, commented on or otherwise contributed to various parts of the text: Deborah Postgate (co-author of the first edition), Bryony Dean, Anthony Edwards, David James, Dr Guy Norfolk, Naomi Redhouse, Mark Studdert and Garden Court Chambers.

The law is as stated at 30 November 2009.

Carolyn Taylor
Julia Krish

Preface

Table of cases

Table of statutes

Table of statutory instruments

Abbreviations

AC	approved clinician
ADI-R	Autism Diagnostic Interview – Revised
ADOS-G	Autism Diagnostic Observation Schedule – Generic
AHCP	appropriate health care professional
AMHP	approved mental health practitioner
ASD	autistic spectrum disorder
BASW	British Association of Social Workers
CAMHS	Child and Adolescent Mental Health Services
CJA	Criminal Justice Act
CJPOA 1994	Criminal Justice and Public Order Act 1994
CP(I)A 1964	Criminal Procedure (Insanity) Act 1964
CP(IUP)A 1991	Criminal Procedure (Insanity and Unfitness to Plead) Act 1991
CPN	community psychiatric nurse
CPR	Criminal Procedure Rules
CPS	Crown Prosecution Service
CTL	custody time limit
CTO	Community Treatment Order
CYPA 1933	Children and Young Persons Act 1933
DPP	detention for public protection
DSCC	duty solicitor call centre
DSM-IV	Diagnostic and Statistical Manual of Mental Disorders Edition IV
DVCVA 2004	Domestic Violence, Crime and Victims Act 2004
DYOI	detention in a young offender institution
ECHR	European Convention on Human Rights
FME	forensic medical examiner
GMC	General Medical Council
GP	general practitioner
GPVTS	general practice vocational training scheme
HSE	Health and Safety Executive
ICD-10	International Classification of Diseases 10th Edition
IPP	imprisonment for public protection
LSC	Legal Services Commission
MHRT	Mental Health Review Tribunal
MHT	Mental Health Tribunal
PACE	Police and Criminal Evidence Act 1984
PCC(S)A 2000	Powers of Criminal Courts (Sentencing) Act 2000

PCMH	plea and case management hearing
PCT	Primary Care Trust
PD	Practice Direction
PER	prisoner escort record
PH	preliminary hearing
PSR	pre-sentence report
RC	responsible clinician
SCT	Supervised Community Treatment
SGC	Sentencing Guidelines Council
SOAD	second opinion approved doctor
WAIS	Wechster Adult Intelligence Scale
WISC	Wechster Intelligence Scale for Children
YJCEA	Youth Justice and Criminal Evidence Act 1999

CHAPTER 1

Medical and legal definitions

There is a disparity between the terminology used by statute and the terminology used in medical practice when defining mental disorder. This chapter examines the legal and medical definitions of mental disorder and describes the principal powers of detention available in England and Wales.

1.1 THE MENTAL HEALTH ACT 1983 AS AMENDED BY THE MENTAL HEALTH ACT 2007

1.1.1 The legislation through which mentally disordered offenders are detained and treated in hospital in England and Wales is the Mental Health Act 1983, as amended by the Mental Health Act 2007 (hereinafter referred to as 'the Act'). Scotland has a separate Mental Health Act (Mental Health (Care and Treatment) (Scotland) Act 2003). The solicitor in England and Wales is likely to encounter clients detained under both Part II and Part III of the Act.

Part II – Civil sections

1.1.2 Part II of the Act relates to what are commonly known as the 'civil' sections. The majority of people detained in psychiatric hospitals in England and Wales are detained under one of the following civil sections of the Act. These are set out in full at **Appendix 1**.

Section 2 – Admission for assessment

1.1.3 This section authorises the compulsory admission of a person to hospital for assessment (or assessment followed by medical treatment). It lasts for up to 28 days and cannot be renewed. If the person requires continued treatment in hospital and is unwilling to stay informally, then an assessment under s.3 of the Act is required (see **1.1.5** below). Section 2 requires a 'Mental Health Act assessment' to be performed by two registered medical practitioners and the application to be approved by an approved mental health professional (AMHP) or nearest relative. One of the registered medical practitioners must be approved under s.12(2) of the Act as having 'special experience in the diagnosis or treatment of mental disorder' (commonly referred to as a 's.12 approved doctor'). The other must usually be a doctor with previous acquaintance of the person under assessment, or must also be a s.12 approved doctor. However, in an emergency, where the person is not known to any available doctors and two s.12 approved doctors cannot be found, a doctor who is neither s.12 approved nor previously acquainted with the person under assessment can complete a recommendation. A Mental Health Act assessment can take place anywhere, but usually occurs in a hospital, at a police station, or in a person's home.

1.1.4 In order to make compulsory recommendations for detention in hospital under s.2, an AMHP or nearest relative together with two registered medical practitioners must agree that the person:

- is suffering from mental disorder of a nature or degree which warrants his detention in a hospital for assessment (or for assessment followed by medical treatment) for a least a limited period; and
- ought to be so detained in the interests of his own health or safety or with a view to the protection of other persons.

Written medical recommendations are completed by the medical practitioners but it is necessary for the AMHP or nearest relative to agree that there is no viable alternative to detaining the person in hospital for the section to be implemented.

Section 3 – Admission for treatment

1.1.5 An order under s.3 of the Act provides authority for compulsory admission to hospital for treatment. Initially, it may last up to six months. Thereafter, the order can be renewed, for six months in the first instance and subsequently for periods of one year. It is effected in a similar manner to s.2, i.e. following an assessment by two registered medical practitioners and approval by nearest relative or AMHP. Note that if the AMHP is making the application he must consult with the nearest relative and if the nearest relative objects to the admission then the AMHP cannot make the application. The two registered medical practitioners must agree that:

- the person is suffering from mental disorder of a nature or degree which makes it appropriate for him to receive medical treatment in a hospital; and
- it is necessary for the health and safety of the person or for the protection of other persons that he should receive such treatment; and
- it cannot be provided unless he is detained under this section; and
- appropriate medical treatment is available for him.

Section 4 – Admission for assessment in cases of emergency

1.1.6 Section 4 is implemented by one registered medical practitioner and an AMHP or nearest relative in an emergency where there is insufficient time to obtain a second suitably registered medical practitioner to conduct an assessment under s.2 or s.3 of the Act. The registered medical practitioner need not be approved under s.12 of the Act and so can be the appropriate health care professional (AHCP) at the police station, if the AHCP is a doctor. Once the person is in hospital, the order lasts up to 72 hours and can be converted to a s.2 order if a further medical recommendation is provided by a second suitably qualified registered medical practitioner.

Section 5 – Application in respect of a patient already in hospital

1.1.7 Section 5(2) can be used only on patients who have already been admitted to a hospital on an informal basis, but who then wish to leave. It can be implemented following an assessment by the registered medical practitioner or approved clinician (AC) or his deputy. It lasts up to 72 hours, during which time a further assessment may result in either discharge from the section or detention under s.2 or s.3.

1.1.8 Section 5(4) is a holding power which can be applied by a nurse on informal (i.e. voluntary) patients who wish to leave hospital in situations where no doctor is readily available to complete a s.5(2) detention form. An order under s.5(4) lasts up to six hours. It is rarely used in practice.

Section 7 – Guardianship

1.1.9 Under s.7 a person is received into the guardianship of the local social services authority or a named person who is acceptable to the authority. The application is made by either a nearest relative or AMHP and on the recommendation of two registered medical practitioners. The criteria are as follows:

- the person is suffering from mental disorder of a nature or degree which warrants reception into guardianship; and
- it is necessary in the interests of the welfare of the patient or for the protection of other persons that he should be so received; and
- he is over 16 years old.

1.1.10 The duration of the order is as for s.3 (see **1.1.5**). Under s.8 of the Act the guardian is given a number of powers to require the patient:

- to reside at a specified place;
- to attend at specified places and times for medical treatment, occupation, education or training;
- to allow access to any doctor, AMHP or other specified person.

Note that as a patient received into guardianship is not 'liable to be detained in hospital' he is not subject to the consent to treatment provisions in Part IV of the Act.

Section 17A – Supervised Community Treatment and Community Treatment Orders

1.1.11 Section 17A of the Act provides for Supervised Community Treatment (SCT) via a Community Treatment Order (CTO). It provides that a patient with a mental disorder, who is compulsorily detained in hospital for treatment, may be discharged from hospital subject to conditions to ensure that he continues to receive his treatment in the community. The criteria for imposing a CTO are as follows (s.17A(5)):

- patient is detained (i.e. not s.2);
- mental disorder is of a nature or degree appropriate to receive medical treatment in interests of health/safety or protection of others;
- patient can be treated without detention as long as he remains subject to recall;
- appropriate medical treatment is available;
- AMHP agrees with responsible clinician (RC)'s opinion.

1.1.12 There are two mandatory conditions that must be specified when putting a patient on a CTO (s.17B(2)). First, the patient must make himself available for a medical examination as to whether the CTO should be extended, and secondly, if a Part 4A medical treatment certificate is required to provide authority to treat, he must make himself available for that examination by the second opinion approved doctor (SOAD). Note that failure to comply with one of these conditions may in itself lead to recall.

1.1.13 Any number of discretionary conditions can be specified, such as the patient must make himself available at a particular time and place for medical treatment or must reside at a certain address. The RC and AMHP must agree conditions are necessary or appropriate to ensure the patient receives medical treatment and to prevent risk of harm to the patient's health or safety or protect other people. Note that failure to comply with any of the discretionary conditions is not in itself enough to justify recall but 'may be taken into account for the purposes of exercising power of recall'.

1.1.14 The recall lasts for 72 hours from the time when the patient is admitted to hospital. During the 72-hour period the patient can be treated with medication even if he refuses consent or is unable to consent. If the patient is discharged from hospital at any time during the 72 hours the CTO will continue. If, however, the RC believes that the patient has become so ill that he needs to be detained under section in hospital then, with the agreement of an AMHP, the CTO can be revoked and the patient will become detained in hospital under s.3. A CTO is renewable in the same way as a recommendation for detention under s.3 or s.37, i.e. after the first six months it can be renewed for a further six months and then for 12 months at a time.

Part III – Criminal sections

1.1.15 Part III of the Act applies to persons concerned in criminal proceedings including those who have been sentenced. Below is an outline of the relevant sections, considered in more detail later in the book.

Section	Description
Section 35	Allows *magistrates' court or Crown Court* to remand an accused defendant *(convicted and unconvicted)* to a hospital for a report on his mental condition.
Section 36	Allows for the *Crown Court* to remand an *unconvicted* defendant to a hospital for treatment.
Section 37 (hospital/ guardianship order)	Allows *magistrates' court or Crown Court* to authorise the admission to a hospital of a *convicted* defendant or to place him under the guardianship of a local services authority. It is a sentence. Once the order is made, the court has no further powers in the case.
Section 38 (interim hospital order)	Allows *magistrates' court or Crown Court* to authorise the admission to hospital of a *convicted* defendant for treatment and assessment for a s.37 order.
Section 41 (a restriction order)	Added to a s.37 hospital order by the *Crown Court* if it is considered necessary for the protection of the public from serious harm.
Section 45A	Allows the *Crown Court* to impose a prison sentence and make a hospital direction and a limitation direction (broadly similar to s.37/s.41). After the person no longer requires treatment in hospital the RC can seek his transfer to prison.
Section 47	Allows for the Ministry of Justice to issue a warrant directing a serving prisoner to be transferred to hospital for treatment.
Section 48	Provides powers for the Ministry of Justice to transfer a remand prisoner to hospital.
Section 49	Provides for 'restrictions' to s.47 and s.48, in the same way that s.41 provides for 'restrictions' on discharge to s.37.

Part X

1.1.16 Part X of the Act contains various miscellaneous and supplementary sections, two of which are particularly important and are discussed in **Chapter 2**.

Section 135: a warrant to search for and remove a person	Magistrates can issue a warrant giving a police officer the right to enter property and take a person to a 'place of safety' where an assessment under the Act is conducted.
Section 136: mentally disordered persons found in public places	Allows a police officer to take a person found in a public place, whom the officer considers to be mentally disordered and in need of care or control, to a 'place of safety' where an assessment under the Act is conducted.

Mental Health Tribunals (MHTs)

1.1.17 The First-tier Tribunal (Mental Health) is part of the Tribunals Service and used to be known as the Mental Health Review Tribunal. It is referred to throughout the book as the Mental Health Tribunal (MHT). The Tribunal is an independent judicial body that operates under the provisions of the Act. Its main purpose is to review the cases of persons detained under the Act and to direct the discharge of any persons where the statutory criteria for discharge are satisfied

1.1.18 Below is a table setting out a patient's rights of appeal to the MHT. A patient also has a right to apply at any time to the hospital managers for discharge.

Type of detention	When can person apply to MHT	Automatic reference
Admission for assessment (s.2)	Within the first 14 days of admission.	
Admission for treatment (s.3)	Within the first six months of admission, during the next six months and during each subsequent period of one year.	By hospital managers if MHT has not reviewed case within the first six months of admission; thereafter, every three years if MHT has not considered case within that period. (One year for child under age of 18.)

Type of detention	When can person apply to MHT	Automatic reference
Reception into guardianship (s.7/s.37)	Within the first six months of reception, during the next six months, and during each subsequent period of one year.	No automatic reference of guardianship cases to the MHT.
Hospital order without restrictions (s.37)	Between six and 12 months after the making of the order and during each subsequent period of one year.	By the hospital managers if a period of three years has elapsed since case was last considered by MHT. (One year for child under age of 18.)
Patient with restriction order or restriction direction who is in hospital (s.37/s.41)	Between six and 12 months after the making of the order or direction and during each subsequent period of one year.	Reference by Secretary of State at any time and in respect of any case not considered by MHT within the last three years (s.71).
Removal to hospital of persons serving sentence of imprisonment (s.47) with or without restrictions (s.47/s.49)	Within the first six months of detention, during the next six months and during each subsequent period of one year.	Reference by Secretary of State at any time and in respect of any case not considered by MHT within the last three years (s.71).
Removal to hospital of other prisoners with restrictions (s.48/s.49)	Within the first six months of detention, during the next six months and during each subsequent period of one year.	Reference by Secretary of State at any time and in respect of any case not considered by MHT within the last three years (s.71).
Restricted patient who has been conditionally discharged and is recalled to hospital (s.42)	Between six and 12 months after the recall and during each subsequent period of one year.	Reference by Secretary of State within one month after recall (s.75).
Restricted patient (s.37/s.41) who has been conditionally discharged and not recalled	Between one and two years after conditional discharge and during each subsequent period of two years.	Reference by Secretary of State at any time and in respect of any case not considered by MHT within the last three years (s.71).

Type of detention	When can person apply to MHT	Automatic reference
Supervised Community Treatment (SCT) via a Community Treatment Order (CTO). (s.17A)	Within the first six months of discharge, during the next six months and during each subsequent period of one year.	By the hospital managers if MHT has not reviewed case within the first six months of discharge; thereafter, every three years if MHT has not considered case within that period. (One year for child under age of 18.)

Mental disorder

1.1.19 Section 1(2) of the Act defines 'mental disorder' as:

> ... any disorder or disability of the mind

The term mental disorder is generic and is used throughout the Police and Criminal Evidence Act (PACE) 1984 and its Codes of Practice. This definition is a legal classification and should not be confused with medical and diagnostic terminology which is found in medical reports and records.

Learning disability

1.1.20 Section 1(4) of the Act defines 'learning disability' as meaning:

> a state of arrested or incomplete development of the mind which includes significant impairment of intelligence and social functioning

Note that a person with learning disability can only be made subject to the provisions of the Act if that person exhibits abnormally aggressive or seriously irresponsible conduct (s.1(2A)), except for admissions under s.2 of the Act.

Appropriate medical treatment

1.1.21 A treatment order cannot be made under the Act unless 'appropriate medical treatment is available'. Section 145 of the Act gives medical treatment a wide definition including 'nursing, psychological intervention and specialist mental health habilitation [learning], rehabilitation [relearning] and care'. However, in practice, medical treatment has been interpreted even more broadly.

(See *R (on the application of Munjaz)* v. *Mersey Care NHS Trust* [2005] UKHL 58 where Lord Hope held that treatment 'includes all manner of treatment under medical supervision of those suffering from mental disorders from cure to containment. It includes treatment under medical supervision which is designed to alleviate or prevent a deterioration of the patient's condition, even if it will have no effect on the disorder itself'.)

1.1.22 The Act stipulates that dependence on alcohol or drugs is not considered to be a disorder or disability of the mind and a person may not be treated as suffering from mental disorder by reason only of dependence on alcohol or drugs (s.1(3)). However, a person may suffer from a mental disorder as well as alcohol or drug dependency. In this case it is established in case law that compulsory treatment may be offered which deals with both disorders, which are often inextricably linked. For example, persons who suffer psychosis as a consequence of the abuse of drink or drugs may be compulsorily treated as suffering from mental disorder.

1.2 MEDICAL DEFINITIONS

1.2.1 Other than learning disability, the Act (since the 2007 revision) no longer defines individual categories of mental disorder. However, categories such as 'mental illness' and 'personality disorder' are terms used widely in day-to-day clinical practice.

1.2.2 The medical diagnoses are described in the two recognised manuals for the classification of psychiatric diagnosis: the International Classification of Diseases 10th Edition (ICD-10), which is produced by the World Health Organization; and the Diagnostic and Statistical Manual of Mental Disorders Edition IV (DSM-IV), produced by the American Psychiatric Association. Legal and medical terminologies concerning psychiatric problems are not necessarily compatible. For example, mental disorder is a legal term, with potentially very broad inclusion criteria, and is not a specific medical diagnosis. By contrast, schizophrenia is not referred to in the Act, but is a recognised medical diagnosis (ICD-10 F.20). The distinction between mental illness and personality disorder is important in clinical practice, but these terms are not used in the Act.

Mental illness

1.2.3 The term 'mental illness' is not now used in the Act, but is central to clinical practice. It is generally agreed that 'mental illness' covers disorders which have not always existed in the patient, but have developed in him to become a condition which overlays the patient's personality when well (his 'pre-morbid' personality). Contrast, for example, 'arrested or incomplete development of mind' in learning disability, which may well date from birth. The most commonly encountered types of mental illness in a criminal justice setting include schizophrenia, mood disorders, and manic episode and bipolar affective disorder.

Schizophrenia

1.2.4 Schizophrenia is a generic term for a group of diseases which have certain signs and symptoms in common, but do not necessarily have the same presentation or similar prognoses. Schizophrenia occurs in several clinical forms: simple, hebephrenic, catatonic, paranoid and residual. Some clinicians describe these as 'schizophrenic spectrum' disorders. If there is a large affective (mood) component, the expression 'schizo-affective disorder' may be used. Schizotypal and delusional disorders are often encountered. Schizotypal disorder is conceptualised as a form of 'mild' schizophrenia, often found in relatives of persons with full blown schizophrenia, involving difficulties with social interaction. Delusional disorders involve delusional beliefs, often paranoid and persecutory in nature, but with no associated perceptual abnormalities, such as hallucinations, and with an intact personality structure.

1.2.5 Paranoid schizophrenia is characterised by the person believing he is in a hostile environment, either as a result of a misinterpretation of the actions of others or as the result of a complex delusional system which may dominate his thinking and reactions. People with paranoid illnesses often get into trouble with the police and the solicitor is therefore likely to encounter persons with this form of schizophrenia. Typical symptoms include:

(a) Delusions – fixed false beliefs which cannot be altered in the face of incontrovertible evidence or reasoned argument, for example, believing that alien beings have you under observation and intend you harm.
(b) Hallucinations – false perceptions that are most commonly experienced in the form of voices (auditory) or visions (visual) perceived by the person, in the absence of any obvious source or without any basis in external reality.
(c) Incoherence of speech, flat or grossly inappropriate responses.

1.2.6 If someone suffers from schizophrenia he may become socially withdrawn, be regarded as eccentric, is more likely to be a victim of assault provoked by his own erratic behaviour, and be at risk of self-destructive and suicidal behaviour (one in 10 people who have schizophrenia die from suicide). He may also display anti-social and violent behaviour. Many people resist or refute the diagnosis of their condition. It is rare for a person openly to state that he suffers from schizophrenia, especially when detained in the police station. It may be possible to make an educated guess about someone's clinical diagnosis by establishing what medication has been prescribed for him. First-line medications for the treatment of schizophrenic illness include the 'atypical' antipsychotics. The most common of these are:

Drug	Trade Name
Amisulpride	Solian
Olanzapine	Zyprexa
Quetiapine	Seroquel
Risperidone	Risperdal
Aripiprazole	Abilify
Clozapine*	Clozaril Denzapine Zaponex

*Clozapine is licensed for the treatment of schizophrenia only in patients unresponsive to, or intolerant of, conventional antipsychotic drugs. It can cause blood disorders and its use is restricted to patients registered with a clozapine patient monitoring service. Regular blood tests are required (weekly initially).

Older antipsychotic medications which are still prescribed include:

Drug	Trade Name
Chlorpromazine	Largactil
Haloperidol	Haldol Serenace
Pimozide	Orap
Sulpiride	Dolmatil Sulpor
Trifluoperazine	Stelazine
Zuclopenthixol Acetate	Clopixol

Some patients are prescribed long-acting 'depot' (intra-muscular injection) antipsychotic medication. The most common of these are:

Drug	Trade Name
Flupentixol Decanoate	Depixol
Fluphenazine Decanoate	Modecate
Haloperidol Decanoate	Haldol Decanoate
Pipotiazine Palimitate	Piportil Depot
Zuclopenthixol Decanoate	Clopixol
Risperidone	Risperdal Consta

Mood (affective) disorders

1.2.7 Mood can be depressed as in depressive illnesses or elevated as in manic episodes or bipolar affective disorder (where the patient has a period of 'high' mood followed by a depressed phase). The typical symptoms of a depressive episode include lethargy, persistent depressed mood, loss of weight, disturbed sleep patterns, morbid and guilty thoughts including thoughts of self-harm and suicide. Severe depression may be associated with psychotic symptoms.

1.2.8 First-line pharmacological treatment for depression is often with one of the antidepressants called Selective Serotonin Reuptake Inhibitors (SSRIs):

Drug	Trade Name
Fluoxetine	Prozac
Paroxetine	Seroxat
Citalopram	Cipramil
Clomipramine	Anafranil

1.2.9 Older tricyclic antidepressants are still occasionally used. These include Amitriptyline and Imipramine. Electroconvulsive therapy (ECT) is an effective treatment which is used in highly selective cases of very severe depression. Effective psychological treatments are available for depression. The most well known and established of these is Cognitive Behavioural Therapy (CBT).

Manic episode and bipolar affective disorder

1.2.10 Manic symptoms include elevated, expansive or irritable moods, characterised by over-activity and restlessness, grandiose beliefs, flight of ideas, racing thoughts and speech. Physical treatment for manic disorders or bipolar affective disorder includes mood stabilising medications such as:

Drug	Trade Name
Lithium carbonate	Priadel Camcolit Liskonum
Lithium citrate	Li-Liquid Priadel
Carbamazepine	Tegretol
Sodium valproate	Epilim

Personality disorder

1.2.11 Personality disorders are chronic, enduring abnormalities in an individual's personality. ICD-10 defines these disorders as 'severe disturbances in the personality and behavioural tendencies of the individual; not directly resulting from disease, damage, or other insult to the brain, or from another psychiatric disorder; usually involving several areas of the personality; nearly always associated with considerable personal distress and social disruption; and usually manifest since childhood or adolescence and continuing throughout adulthood'.

1.2.12 ICD-10 F.60 describes a wide range of diagnosed personality disorders, including dissocial personality disorder (F.60.2), paranoid personality (F.60.0), emotionally unstable personality disorder (F.60.30, F.60.31) and borderline personality disorder (F.60.31). The disorder of dissocial personality must be longstanding and is inferred from evidence of persistent antisocial or culturally deviant behaviour, characterised by a lack of social responsibility, consideration for others, judgement and foresight. It can often result in irresponsible and aggressive behaviour. Personality disorders are generally apparent by late childhood or adolescence. They are not secondary to any organic cause or any other mental disorder although they can coexist with other disorders.

1.2.13 Treatments for personality disorder are primarily psychological although antidepressant and low-dose antipsychotic medications are sometimes used to help with symptoms of aggression or irritability.

Learning disability

1.2.14 The term 'learning disability' is generally used clinically to describe people in this category of mental disorder although the PACE Codes of Practice use the term 'mentally vulnerable'. Other terms which are sometimes used include mental handicap, learning difficulties, mental retardation, developmental disability and intellectual disability. Learning disability covers various conditions and manifestations. In some people, learning disability is the direct result of organic damage, such as malfunction of the nervous system during or shortly after birth. Others have a chromosomal abnormality such as Down's syndrome or have no known organic defects. Learning disability is sometimes qualified with the terms, 'mild', 'moderate', 'severe' or 'profound' according to the severity of the disability.

1.2.15 Assessment of learning disabilities combines assessment of intellectual, behavioural and social skills. People who have intellectual or cognitive deficit are measured by performance in IQ tests. Mental impairment generally covers those falling in the IQ range 50–70, while below 50 is taken to be severe impairment. However, note the Court of Appeal decision in the case of *R* v. *Silcott, Braithwaite and Raghip* (1991) *The Times*, 9 December where it was accepted that an IQ of 75 amounted to a mental handicap and this contributed to the exclusion of confession evidence. Stress was laid on the need to assess each individual's abilities, rather than the exact IQ figure. A guidance booklet produced by Voice UK, 'Competent to Tell the Truth', sets out very helpful advice on identifying people with learning disabilities and ways of assessing their competence as witnesses.

Autistic spectrum disorders

1.2.16 Autistic spectrum disorder (ASD) includes several distinct diagnoses such as classic autism, high-functioning autism, pervasive developmental disorder and Asperger's syndrome. Each one has its own identifying symptoms. They are lifelong disabilities, occurring from early stages of development, that affect how a person makes sense of the world, processes information and relates to other people. They are often described as 'spectrum disorders' because the conditions affect people in many different ways and to varying degrees. The three main areas of difficulty which all people with ASD share are sometimes known as the 'triad of impairments'. They are difficulties with social communication, social interaction and social imagination. The person may also be preoccupied with a particular subject of interest.

1.2.17 The DSM-IV describes distinct differences between Asperger's syndrome and other ASDs, stating that:

> The essential features of Asperger's Disorder are severe and sustained impairment in social interaction . . . and the development of restricted, repetitive patterns of behavior, interests, and activities . . . The disturbance must cause clinically significant impairment in social, occupational, or other important areas of functioning. In contrast to Autistic Disorder, there are no clinically significant delays or deviences in language acquisition (e.g., single non-echoed words are used communicatively by age 2 years, and spontaneous communicative phrases are used by age 3 years) . . . although more subtle aspects of social communication (e.g., typical give and take in conversation) may be affected.

1.2.18 The definition of mental disorder in the Act includes the full range of ASDs, including those existing alongside a learning disability or any other kind of mental disorder. These disorders are developmental in nature and are not mental illnesses in themselves. However, people with an autistic spectrum disorder may have additional or related problems, which frequently include anxiety. These may be related to social factors associated with frustration or communication problems or to patterns of thought and behaviour that are rigid or literal in nature. They may also occasionally experience psychotic symptoms. As with people with learning disabilities, people with autistic spectrum disorders may also have co-morbid mental illness, including mood disorders and, occasionally, personality disorders.

1.3 PRACTICAL CONSIDERATIONS

1.3.1 In practical terms, those with acute symptoms of schizophrenia or mania are usually admitted to hospital for treatment, on a compulsory basis if necessary.

It is realistic to expect that urgent Mental Health Act assessments can be arranged in police cells, at courts where diversion schemes operate or through remand prisons. Those with depression are unlikely to be admitted to hospital, unless the symptoms are severe or there is clear suicidal intent.

1.3.2 Personality disorder may be a mental disorder in terms of the Act. However, such cases are not often subject to disposal under Part III, and even less commonly under Part II of the Act. People with personality disorder may briefly be admitted to psychiatric hospitals when in crisis for a few days, but this is for treatment of associated adjustment disorders, not for treatment of the personality disorder itself. Treatment of personality disorder involves psychological therapies, often over a period of many years, although drug treatment may be useful for suppressing associated symptoms of depression and impulsivity. Psychiatric services have traditionally offered limited services for those with personality disorder, although there are some indications that this is changing with the establishment of dedicated Personality Disorder Units within some psychiatric hospitals.

1.3.3 Services for those with learning disability are generally based in the community, rather than hospital, except where the condition is severe or in cases of serious offending. Such services are separate from those for mental illness.

CHAPTER 2

Procedures in the police station

2.1 THE SOURCES OF LAW

2.1.2 The most important legislation is:

- Mental Health Act 1983 (as amended by the Mental Health Act 2007).
- Mental Health Act Code of Practice issued pursuant to s.118 of the Act.
- Police and Criminal Evidence Act 1984 (PACE).
- Police and Criminal Evidence Act Codes of Practice issued pursuant to s.66 of PACE.

2.1.2 Code C, Annex E of the PACE Codes of Practice summarises all the provisions relating to mentally disordered and otherwise mentally vulnerable people at the police station. Additional references are contained in Code C itself and in two other sections of the Codes.

2.2 DEFINITIONS

2.2.1 Unless otherwise stated, in this book 'the Act' refers to the Mental Health Act 1983 (as amended by the Mental Health Act 2007). 'PACE' refers to the Police and Criminal Evidence Act 1984. 'C', 'D', 'E' and 'F' are references to the Codes of Practice issued under PACE (e.g. C.1.10 is a reference to Code C, para. 1.10). 'NFG' is a reference to the 'Notes for Guidance' within the Codes. The term 'detainee' is used throughout the section on the police station procedure and refers to a person detained under the Act, someone who is arrested, and also someone who is attending the police station voluntarily. All references to 'solicitor' in the same section include accredited representatives who are also authorised to undertake police station work.

2.3 PUBLIC FUNDING

2.3.1 As with any detainee at the police station, a mentally disordered detainee is entitled to free legal advice, which is not means tested, and to be represented by a solicitor. Firms are paid a fixed fee, the amount depending upon whether telephone advice only is given or there is an attendance at the police station.

The fee varies from area to area around the country and only if it exceeds three times the fixed fee can the excess attract a fee payable on the number of hours worked.

2.3.2 Form CDS1 must be completed. It is also advisable to ask the detainee to sign Form CDS2 which is means tested. This will cover cases where it may be necessary to see a client in the office for further advice if he has been bailed to return to the police station at a later date. However if there has been an attendance at the police station there is no separate fee for the CDS1 work, but the value does count towards the 'three times' limit referred to in **2.3.1** above. If the detainee is too ill to sign Form CDS2, the Unified Contract (Crime) July 2008, para. A9 allows a solicitor to accept an application for work on behalf of a person lacking mental capacity under the Mental Capacity Act 2005, s.2(1), where:

> For the purposes of this Act, a person lacks capacity in relation to a matter if at the material time he is unable to make a decision for himself in relation to the matter because of an impairment of, or a disturbance in the functioning of, the mind or brain.

The form can be signed by his/her deputy or attorney under the 2005 Act or any other person where there is 'good reason' (para. A9.2) as long as there is sufficient connection between the person lacking mental capacity and the other person to ensure that the other person is likely to act responsibly in the interests of the person lacking mental capacity. The other person must have sufficient knowledge of the person lacking mental capacity, the problem and his financial circumstances (where relevant) to give proper instructions. Where the solicitor accepts an application under para. A9.1, the form should be completed in the name of the person lacking mental capacity but signed by the person who is applying on behalf of the person lacking mental capacity with an annotation to that effect.

2.4 REASON FOR DETENTION

2.4.1 There are three ways in which a mentally disordered person may find himself being detained at the police station. The first two are under ss.135 and 136 of the Act and the third is on arrest on suspicion of a criminal offence. Sections 135 and 136 should only be used by police as a stop-gap before transfer to hospital.

2.4.2 Section 135 of the Act provides for a magistrate, on receiving an information made by an AMHP, to issue a warrant authorising a police constable to enter any private premises for the purpose of removing to a place of safety, a person believed to be suffering from mental disorder. Any police officer may execute the warrant, as the meaning of constable is 'the office of a constable' and not the rank of constable (Police Act 1964, s.18 and Sched. 2). The person must either have been or is being ill-treated, neglected or kept otherwise than under proper control, or is living alone and unable to care for himself. When executing the warrant, the officer must be accompanied by an AMHP and a registered medical practitioner.

2.4.3 The removal to a place of safety is with a view to the making of an application in respect of the person under Part II of the Act (see **Chapter 1**) or of other arrangements regarding his treatment or care. The maximum length of time a person can be detained under s.135 is 72 hours from arrival at the place of safety.

2.4.4 Under s.135(2), a magistrate has the power to issue a warrant to enter and remove a person who is already liable to be detained under the Act, i.e. someone who has absconded from hospital while under section. In these circumstances the person is usually taken straight back to hospital. Sections 15 and 16 of PACE, which mainly set out the specific practice and procedure to be followed on issuing and executing warrants, apply to warrants issued under this section.

2.4.5 Section 136 of the Act provides that a police constable on finding a person in a public place, who appears to him to be suffering from mental disorder and to be in immediate need of care and control, may remove that person to a place of safety. No medical evidence is required to substantiate the diagnosis of mental disorder prior to the removal as the officer need only have a reasonable belief that the person is mentally disordered and that it is necessary to remove him in the interests of that person or for the protection of others. This section, unlike s.135, specifically requires the person, once detained at the place of safety, to be examined by a registered medical practitioner and interviewed by an AMHP and for any necessary arrangements to be made for his care or treatment.

Points to note in ss.135 and 136

2.4.6 (a) Detention under the Act has no age limit and thus children and youths of any age can be removed and detained under ss.135 and 136.

(b) Section 135(6) includes a police station in its definition of a place of safety. When the Act came into force it was envisaged that if the place of safety had to be a police station, then it should only be used in exceptional circumstances and for a few hours. This is reiterated in the Act's Code of Practice 10.21 which advises that 'a police station should be used as a place of safety only on an exceptional basis'. The police service should draw up suitable arrangements with local health authorities and social services departments for the detention and assessment of mentally disordered people. Both the Inter-Agency working document (issued with Home Office Circular 12/95) and the Bradley Report (Lord Bradley's review of people with mental health problems or learning disabilities in the criminal justice system, April 2009) point out that police stations do not have the facilities necessary for the welfare of such people and detention in them is likely to be damaging to their health. Solicitors should be aware of the local arrangements in existence for a place of safety. C.NFG.9D states that there is no power under the Mental Health Act 1983 to transfer a person detained under s.136 from one place of safety to another place of safety for assessment. However the Act's Code of Practice (10.34–38) allows for the transfer as long as the second place of safety is willing and able to accept the detainee.

(c) Even though a person detained under ss.135 and 136 is not under arrest, the PACE Codes of Practice apply (C.1.10). Detainees under both ss.135 and 136 have a right to consult a solicitor in private and receive independent free legal advice. In addition, s.26 of, and Sched. 2 to, PACE preserve the power to arrest under s.136 and hence the person has all the rights under PACE of a person arrested on suspicion of a criminal offence. The Act's Code of Practice (10.45) also confirms that although the Act uses the term 'remove', it is deemed to be an 'arrest' for the purposes of PACE. It follows, therefore, that a police constable who has detained a person under s.136 is empowered to search him.

(d) As the PACE Codes of Practice apply to a person detained under ss.135 and 136 the custody officer should also inform an appropriate adult of the person's detention and request that he attend the police station. Most custody officers are of the view that this obligation is fulfilled by calling the AMHP to the police station to interview and examine the person. However this is not the case and an appropriate adult should be called separately. If the detainee is also arrested in respect of a criminal matter then in any event the appropriate adult must be called to attend the station.

(e) Under C.3.6 there is an obligation on the police to ensure the person detained under s.136 be assessed as soon as possible. If that assessment is to take place at the police station then an AMHP and registered medical practitioner must be called to the station as soon as possible to interview and examine the detainee. This requirement absolves a custody officer from his obligation to call an AHCP under C.9.6 and Annex E.5. as long as the custody officer believes the assessment by a suitably qualified medical practitioner can be undertaken without due delay. Once this has been done and arrangements have been made for the detainee's treatment or care, he can no longer be detained under s.136. The Act's Code of Practice (10.50–53) states that where the police station has been used as a place of safety and the assessors are of the view that compulsory detention is indicated, then it is the responsibility of the doctor and AMHP to make any necessary further arrangements for the person's treatment and care.

(f) Paragraph 10.29 of the aforementioned Code confirms that if it appears that the person detained under s.136 has a learning disability, it is desirable for a consultant psychiatrist specialising in learning disabilities or an AMHP with experience of working with people with learning disabilities to be available to make a joint assessment.

(g) Paragraph 10.8 states that as soon as detention in a place of safety under both sections ends, the individual must be told that he is free to leave by those detaining him.

2.4.7 As a person detained under either of the sections can be brought to a police station and PACE applies, a solicitor may be asked to advise the detainee. This is more likely under s.136, as under s.135 people are usually taken straight to hospital. If the solicitor is contacted, on first speaking to the client the solicitor should try and establish if there is a history of contact with mental health services so that, where possible, contact can be made with either a treating doctor or care coordinator to ensure that an assessment takes place as soon as possible with knowledge of the patient being passed to the assessor. The solicitor's role is to ensure as far as possible that the police powers of arrest have been reasonably and properly exercised and that the detainee is being monitored appropriately. It is unlikely that the solicitor would attend the police station in these cases and telephone advice is normally sufficient.

2.5 THE ROLE AND DUTIES OF THE CUSTODY OFFICER IN RELATION TO MENTALLY DISORDERED DETAINEES

2.5.1 If a person has been arrested on suspicion of a criminal offence and the custody officer has any suspicion or was told in good faith that a person of any age may be mentally disordered or otherwise mentally vulnerable, then that person shall be treated as being a mentally disordered or otherwise mentally vulnerable person for the purposes of the Codes of Practice (C.1.4 and Annex E.1). NFG.1G confirms that where the custody officer has any doubt about the mental state or capacity of a person detained, the detainee should be treated as mentally vulnerable and an appropriate adult called. A mentally vulnerable person is defined within the Codes as 'any person who, because of their mental state or capacity' may not understand the significance of what is said, of questions or of their replies.

2.5.2 It is extremely important to establish as early as possible whether the detainee falls into one of the categories listed in **2.5.1** above. The custody officer can be informed by anyone including the detainee's solicitor. A relative or the detainee himself may tell the solicitor and if that is the case, as long as the client's authority to disclose this information is obtained, the solicitor may inform the police.

2.5.3 Once the custody officer authorises the detention of a person falling under C.1.4 he must, as soon as is practicable, ask an appropriate adult to attend the police station to see the person and inform the adult of the grounds for detention (C.3.15 and Annex E.3). Action to inform the appropriate adult must still be taken even if the detainee is being held on suspicion of having committed a serious arrestable offence and the provisions of Annex B to Code C (see NFG.B1), delaying the suspect's right to legal advice and the right to have someone informed of his arrest, apply.

2.5.4 *R* v. *Aspinall* (1999) *The Times*, 4 February held that a suspect who suffered from schizophrenia, but was exhibiting no symptoms and had been examined by the police surgeon and deemed fit for detention and interview, still required the presence of an appropriate adult at the police station. The fact that he was 'lucid in thought and oriented in time and place' did not negate the obligation on the custody officer to call an appropriate adult. The court held that the question which had to be determined was not whether the appellant's condition obviated the need for an appropriate adult to be present, but whether the admission of the evidence from the interview would have had such an adverse effect upon fairness that it should have been excluded.

2.5.5 C.9 covers the care and treatment of detained persons. C.9.5 and Annex E.5 set out the custody officer's obligation to call an AHCP when a mentally disordered person is brought to the station. A similar obligation arises to a person *already detained* who subsequently appears to be mentally disordered. The relevant criteria bringing this obligation into being are that the detainee:

(a) appears to be suffering from a mental disorder; or
(b) appears to need clinical attention.

C.9.13 obliges the custody sergeant to ask the AHCP about any risks or problems with continued detention, when to carry out the interview and the need for safeguards. However it is to be noted that *Aspinall* (**2.5.4** above) confirms that the custody officer should not rely on the advice of the AHCP as to the suspect's condition before deciding whether to call the appropriate adult. A decision by the AHCP that a suspect is fit to be detained and interviewed does not relieve the custody officer of his duty to call the appropriate adult.

2.5.6 C3.6–11 cover the obligation for risk assessments on detained persons. Home Office Circular 32/2000 also gives detailed guidance on risk assessments. Where necessary, the AHCP should be consulted and the risk assessment must follow a structured process. The custody officer is responsible for implementing the response to any specific risk assessment, e.g. reducing opportunities for self-harm, calling a health care professional or increasing the levels of monitoring or observation.

2.5.7 If the detainee has been prescribed any medication prior to his arrest, the custody officer must consult the AHCP before allowing the detainee to use that medication. Once authorised, the officer is then responsible for the safekeeping of any medication and for ensuring that the detainee is given the opportunity to take it (C.9.9). C.9.3 deals with the general rule on observations of detainees at a police station. They should normally be visited once an hour. If there is no foreseeable risk in the risk assessment, the detainee should not be woken up. However NFG.9B provides that wherever possible mentally vulnerable detainees should be visited more frequently.

2.6 APPROPRIATE ADULT

Who can be an appropriate adult?

2.6.1 In the case of a person who is mentally disordered or otherwise mentally vulnerable the appropriate adult is defined in C.1.7 as:

(a) a relative, guardian or other person responsible for his care or custody;
(b) someone who has experience of dealing with mentally disordered or mentally vulnerable people but who is not a police officer or employed by the police; or
(c) failing either of the above, some other responsible adult aged 18 or over who is neither a police officer nor employed by the police.

2.6.2 C.NFG.1D recommends that the appropriate adult is someone who has experience or training in the care of mentally disordered or vulnerable people. However, the wishes of the detainee as to who their appropriate adult is, should be respected.

2.6.3 C.NFG.1B states that a person, including a parent or guardian, should not be an appropriate adult if he is:

(a) suspected of involvement in the offence;
(b) the victim;
(c) a witness;
(d) involved in the investigation; or
(e) received admissions to the offence prior to attending to act as the appropriate adult.

A solicitor or independent custody visitor may also not act as the appropriate adult (C.NFG.1F and *R* v. *Lewis* [1996] Crim LR 260, CA).

2.6.4 The presence of an appropriate adult can be very important and the solicitor should satisfy himself that the person appointed is indeed 'appropriate'. It is apparent from the cases below that solicitors at the police station must take care to ensure that the detainee exercises his choice of appropriate adult and that the person chosen is suitable. If, for example, the alleged offence took place in a mental health hostel or psychiatric ward, then a worker from the hostel or nurse from the ward would be inappropriate.

2.6.5 The issue as to who should and who should not be appointed an appropriate adult has been considered in the following cases:

(a) *DPP* v. *Blake* [1989] WLR 432 upheld a defendant's right to choose who he wanted as his appropriate adult. The court took the view that an estranged parent who was willing to attend the police station could not be considered suitable as she was someone with whom the defendant had no empathy. This case also highlighted the policy of many local authorities to refuse to provide a social worker to act as an appropriate adult unless it is impossible to contact a 'suitable' person or that person has refused to attend.

(b) In *R* v. *O'Neill* (Birmingham Crown Court, 16 October 1990), the court had to consider whether the detainee's current probation officer could be considered by the police to act as an appropriate adult. The court held that a probation officer, particularly in relation to a mentally vulnerable person, is a person with some authority over him and should not really be the appropriate adult save in exceptional circumstances. It would also be difficult to prevent a jury from knowing the defendant had previous convictions if his current probation officer acted as appropriate adult. The defendant had in fact asked his common law wife to act and the police had refused to allow her to do so. The court held the police had no power to veto this request.

(c) In *R* v. *Morse and others* [1991] Crim LR 195, the defendant's father acted as his appropriate adult. He turned out to have an IQ between 60 and 70 and was virtually illiterate. There was doubt as to whether he was capable of appreciating the gravity of the situation in which his son found himself. The court held that since the purpose of an appropriate adult was to advise the defendant, if the appropriate adult was incapable of giving advice, he was not appropriate.

(d) In *R* v. *Jefferson, Skerritt, Readman and Keogh* [1994] 99 Cr App 1 R 13, it was held that an appropriate adult, as defined in C.1.7 who gave encouragement to a juvenile to tell the truth, did not fail in his duty to advise him under NFG.13C then in force, nor did it make him an 'inappropriate adult'. There was no duty to protect the juvenile from what the court decided was fair and proper questioning.

(e) In *R* v. *W and another* [1994] Crim LR 130, the mother of a juvenile appointed an appropriate adult was said to have a mental illness and be mentally handicapped. On appeal, it was submitted on behalf of the defendant that the mother was herself someone who would have required the protection of an appropriate adult had she found herself under arrest and in those circumstances the defendant's confession made in interview in mother's presence should not have been admitted. The court held that at the trial the judge based his decision to allow the interviews to be put before the jury on his own findings about the mother's capacity at the time of the interview. While she was psychotic at the time and suffering from some form of intellectual deficit, her paranoid delusions were confined to her neighbours. Her thought processes were rational in discussing her family and she was therefore capable of fulfilling the role of an appropriate adult at the time of the interview.

2.7 THE ROLE AND RESPONSIBILITIES OF THE APPROPRIATE ADULT IN RELATION TO MENTALLY DISORDERED DETAINEES

2.7.1 In 2003, the Home Office (now Ministry of Justice) issued a document 'Guidance for Appropriate Adults' for both those called upon to perform the role of the appropriate adult and the detained person benefiting from the appropriate adult's support. The Ministry of Justice recommends that the guidance document or similar local document be handed to an appropriate adult on their arrival at the police station. The Guidance sets out the rights of detained persons and the rights of the appropriate adult and summarises their roles and responsibilities.

2.7.2 The custody officer must advise all suspects that the appropriate adult is there to assist and advise them and that they can consult with the appropriate adult in private at any time (C.3.18).

2.7.3 The appropriate adult must be present when the provisions of C.3.1–3.5 (i.e. the detainee's right to have to someone informed of his arrest, to consult privately with his solicitor and to consult the Codes of Practice) are complied with. If the detainee has already been through these procedures they must be repeated in the presence of the appropriate adult.

2.7.4 An appropriate adult can exercise the right to legal advice even if the detainee has declined it (C.3.19 Annex E.4). However detainees cannot be forced to see a solicitor if they do not want to. It is possible for a solicitor to be called by the Duty Solicitor Call Centre at the request of the appropriate adult rather than the detainee. Some appropriate adults are unaware of this right so solicitors should draw their attention to it when dealing with people who act as appropriate adults.

2.7.5 The appropriate adult's rights are as follows:

(a) To be told why the detained person is being held.
(b) To speak to the detained person in private and at any time.
(c) To inspect the written record of the person's period in detention (the custody record) at any time.
(d) To see copies of the notices of rights and entitlements referred to above.
(e) To see a copy of the Codes of Practice setting out the powers, responsibilities and procedures of the police.
(f) To intervene in an interview if necessary and in the interests of the detained person to help them communicate effectively with the police.
(g) To ask for a break in any interview either to seek legal advice or to consult with the detainee (particularly if the interview is a lengthy one or if the detained person is distressed or ill).

2.7.6 If the suspect's detention is to be reviewed by a review officer or a superintendent, the appropriate adult must, if available at the time, be given an opportunity to make representations to the officer about the need for continuing detention (C.15.3 and Annex E.10).

2.7.7 An intimate or strip search of a mentally disordered or mentally vulnerable person may only take place in the presence of an appropriate adult of the same sex unless the detainee specifically requests the presence of a particular adult of the opposite sex. Except in cases of urgency, where there is a risk of serious harm to the detainee or to others, whenever the strip search involves exposure of intimate body parts there must be at least two people present other than the detainee and one must be the appropriate adult (Annex A.11(c)).

2.7.8 Any procedure requiring the consent of the person who is mentally disordered or mentally vulnerable is only valid if given in the presence of an appropriate adult. This covers identification by witnesses, finger prints and body samples and impressions as well as the taking of a photograph of the detainee by the police (D.1.11)

2.7.9 D.1.14 emphasises that any procedure involving the participation of a person, whether a suspect or a witness who is mentally disordered or mentally vulnerable, must take place in the presence of the appropriate adult; but the adult must not be allowed to prompt any identification of a suspect by a witness.

2.7.10 A mentally disordered or mentally vulnerable person must not be interviewed or asked to provide or sign a written statement (including comments recorded in an officer's notebook) in the absence of an appropriate adult. However if an urgent interview is authorised under C.11.1, for example because the delay would lead to interference with or physical harm to others, guidance requires the authorising officer to be satisfied that the interview would not cause significant harm to the detainee's physical or mental state. It can then take place without the appropriate adult. The interview may not continue once sufficient information to avert the risk has been obtained.

2.7.11 The appropriate adult must be present at charging or any other such action, e.g. bailed to return or caution. A copy of the charge sheet must also be given to the appropriate adult.

2.7.12 The case of *R* v. *Aspinall* referred to in **2.5.4** above emphasises the importance of the various duties of an appropriate adult at the police station. In particular the court held that 'an appropriate adult was necessary to provide protection for the suspect and to discharge the duties set out in the codes'.

2.8 THE ROLE OF APPROPRIATE HEALTH CARE PROFESSIONAL (AHCP)

2.8.1 AHCP is the term used throughout the PACE Codes for the medical practitioner called to see a detainee requiring 'clinical attention'. The previous Codes used the term 'police surgeon'. The Codes were amended in 2003 to provide for other medical professionals such as nurses or paramedics to administer health care in custody suites. In practice, they are referred to as forensic physicians, except for London where they are still known as forensic medical examiners (FMEs) and Northern Ireland where they are called forensic medical officers. As the Codes of Practice refer to them as AHCPs, this is the term adopted throughout the book.

2.8.2 The majority of police forces have outsourced the provision of forensic medical services to companies who offer a multi-professional delivery of care. In London most AHCPs are still general practitioners (GPs), whereas they tend to be nurses or paramedics in other parts of the country. They are now paid a sessional rate for the work rather than according to the number of detainees they are called to see.

2.8.3 Outsourcing has allowed police authorities to put in minimum contract requirements to ensure that AHCPs undergo induction and then follow-up training. Whilst GPs have the option to spend six months working in a psychiatric hospital as part of their training on a general practice vocational training scheme (GPVTS) and may come across mentally unwell patients in their 12 months' training in a GP practice, it is still possible for a GP to have no formal training in this area. Other professionals such as nurses may have gained their experience in A&E and may not have received any formal training on identifying and treating psychiatric illnesses. However they ought to be able to at least identify mental health issues and call in an appropriate expert for an opinion. Other professionals who might now be included under the general term AHCP may have even less experience in this area, but with the Faculty of Forensic and Legal Medicine and the companies themselves providing training, this should be improving.

2.8.4 In February 2009, the BMA Medical Ethics Department and the Faculty of Forensic and Legal Medicine issued a guidance document entitled 'Health care of detainees in police stations'. Its primary aim is to draw attention to the entitlement of detainees to standards of health care equal to those in the NHS and to set out the parameters of good ethical practice in relation to vulnerable detainees.

2.8.5 As set out in **2.5.5** it is the responsibility of the custody officer to call the AHCP to the station to examine the detainee. It does not expressly say in the Codes who should or should not be present when the detainee is examined. If the solicitor is of the view that it would be in the detainee's best interests to have either the appropriate adult or solicitor present, that should be discussed with the detainee and his consent should be obtained. The solicitor should then tell the custody officer and AHCP of the detainee's wishes. If they raise any objection or refuse the request, there is no reason why the solicitor cannot ask to see an inspector and make a complaint known to him and/or have it noted on the custody record.

2.8.6 There are three reasons why it may be advisable for the solicitor to be present at, or at least in earshot of, the detainee's examination by the AHCP. First, an officer is sometimes present if there is a perceived threat to the AHCP's safety. Secondly the officer, if present, may make notes of 'unsolicited' comments made by the detainee. Finally, AHCPs have been known to ask wholly inappropriate questions to which the solicitor might wish to raise objections. (See the case of *R* v. *McDonald* referred to in **3.6.8** below.) The AHCP has a duty to record his clinical findings on the custody record or note in the custody record where they are recorded. In practice, this will now be in a computerised record. The custody record will also note the length of time the detainee was out of his cell for the examination. An AHCP is obliged to keep his own contemporaneous notes so if the examination becomes an issue in any subsequent proceedings, the solicitor can ask for disclosure of these notes when preparing the defendant's case. However, information which is necessary to custody staff to ensure the effective ongoing care and well-being of the detainee must be recorded openly in the custody record (C.9.16).

2.8.7 If the AHCP is unsure whether the detainee is fit to be detained or interviewed, he can refer him to a hospital for a full psychiatric examination. It is more usual for police stations to have an arrangement with a local psychiatric team to attend the police station, so the AHCP may refer the detainee to that team. Some police stations operate a duty psychiatric nurse scheme. If the AHCP refers the detainee to the nurse, the nurse can then manage the immediate mental health needs of the detainee, including asking for a Mental Health Act assessment. The AHCP can provide one of the required medical recommendations for emergency admission to hospital under s.4 of the Act even if he is not a registered medical practitioner under s.12 of the Act (approved by the Secretary of State as having special experience in the diagnosis or treatment of a mental disorder). There is no reason why he, together with an AMHP or nearest relative, cannot sign section papers to admit the detainee to hospital. For all other sections, if an AHCP is to be used, he must be approved under s.12.

2.8.8 If the detainee is taken to hospital for examination, the PACE clock stops until he returns. If he is subsequently detained under section by the hospital, the custody officer also has power to bail him with or without conditions.

CHAPTER 3

Advice and assistance prior to interview

3.1 ROLE AND AIM OF THE REPRESENTATIVE

3.1.1 Before representing a mentally disordered suspect in the police station, the solicitor should be familiar with the Home Office Circular 66/90 (see **Appendix 4**). The purpose of the circular is to draw to the attention of the police and Crown Prosecution Service (amongst others) 'the desirability of ensuring effective cooperation between agencies to ensure that the best use is made of resources and that mentally disordered persons are *not* prosecuted where this is not required by the public interest'. Although due to new legislation the circular is in parts out of date, it confirms that alternatives to prosecution, such as cautioning by the police, and/or admission to hospital or support in the community, should be considered *first* before deciding that prosecution is necessary.

3.1.2 The solicitor's main aims are to ensure that the detainee is afforded all the rights under the PACE Codes of Practice pertaining to mentally disordered detainees and, where possible, to prevent a prosecution or to delay the decision to interview or prosecute pending a full medical examination of the detainee. This will also enable the solicitor, where appropriate, to make representations either to the police or to prosecuting authorities. Awareness of the law, circulars and other guidance will enable the solicitor to represent the detainee's interests.

3.1.3 Solicitors should also be familiar with or able to find out about, the local services and facilities available for mentally disordered people. Psychiatric services are provided via Primary Care Trusts (PCTs) and they should be able to provide information about the services in each locality. These facilities can include a dedicated psychiatric hospital with a mixture of closed and open wards or a general hospital with psychiatric wards. A local hospital may for example operate a 24-hour crisis intervention service enabling people who are mentally ill to be assessed in hospital or in the community at any time of the day or night. NHS patients may also be sent to private psychiatric hospitals under contractual arrangements with PCTs which purchase their services. Patients who are able to pay private hospital fees may of course be admitted at their own request or via a GP.

3.1.4 There are also a number of regional medium secure units which provide secure accommodation for patients whose behaviour constitutes a risk to others. The average length of stay in these units is 18 months to three years and people often come to these units via the courts. There are currently three special hospitals in England (Ashworth, Broadmoor and Rampton), which provide treatment under conditions of maximum security for patients subject to detention under the Act. To be detained at a special hospital the patient must exhibit 'dangerous, violent or criminal propensities' (National Health Service Act 1947, s.4). The special hospitals use the shorthand 'grave and immediate danger' to identify the type of risks their patients pose.

3.1.5 All hospitals operate a catchment area requirement and it is important therefore to know where the detainee lives or, if homeless, last lived. Occasionally the place where the alleged offence took place is used to identify the appropriate catchment area. Information regarding outpatient facilities such as mental health hostels, day centres and drop-in centres can be obtained from local social services departments as well as local advice agencies or agencies specialising in advice for people with mental health difficulties.

3.2 INITIAL REFERRAL

3.2.1 The initial request to a solicitor for advice is likely to come from one of the following sources:

(a) the detainee (own or duty client);
(b) the appropriate adult;
(c) a relative or guardian of the detainee.

3.2.2 If the first telephone call is from someone calling on behalf of the detainee (e.g. a relative), take the basic details: i.e. name and address of detainee, date of birth, location of detainee, reason for detention, relationship to relative. If the issue of mental health has been raised, ask for details of the nature and length of the illness, what treatment the person may be receiving or has received in the past and any current contact with a psychiatrist or social worker. It is essential to speak to the detainee to confirm he has not instructed anyone else to act for him, including the duty solicitor. If that is the case, then in order to receive payment, the solicitor will have to obtain a reference number from the duty solicitor call centre (DSCC). He must inform the DSCC that he has been instructed to act for the detainee even though the phone call has not come through the usual channels. The DSCC will give a reference number which can be quoted when making a claim for payment.

3.2.3 When speaking to the detainee on the telephone, it is important to try and obtain specific instructions on his mental health background as he must consent to the solicitor discussing this with the custody officer if the officer has not already received information to this effect. The detainee must also be asked if he consents to the solicitor continuing to communicate with the relative who made the initial contact and what information he authorises to be passed on.

3.2.4 In all circumstances it is important to ascertain from the custody officer if the detainee is being treated as a mentally disordered person under code C and whether or not he has already been examined by the AHCP. It might also be useful to ascertain if the detainee is able to speak on the telephone and give coherent instructions.

3.2.5 In any event a solicitor should always try and speak to the detainee as it is important to reassure him that the solicitor is independent from the police, his relative and/or the appropriate adult and to explain his role. If the issue of mental health has been raised before the telephone call, the solicitor may wish to advise the detainee that he is aware of some information relating to his mental health. If appropriate, further information regarding current contact with mental health services should be obtained as it may be useful at an early stage to make contact with a psychiatrist, social worker or care coordinator who may be able to provide more details of the nature and extent of the detainee's illness as well as the availability of care and treatment. If the detainee has stopped taking medication, that person may be able to give advice on how quickly the onset of symptoms can be expected to occur. Guidance may be obtained as to the detainee's ability to deal with the police interview. However, the person who is being asked to provide this information will need to be satisfied that he has the detainee's express consent to disclosure.

3.2.6 It is extremely important that the solicitor acts immediately if he is made aware that the detainee is at risk of harming himself. If the detainee is an established client and has a background of suicide attempts, it is vital that the solicitor informs the custody officer so that the detainee is kept under frequent observation by the police and any items in his possession are removed to prevent self-harm. If the solicitor is dealing with a new client, it is advisable when first talking to him on the telephone to ask him if he has a history of self-harm (e.g. wrist cutting) or attempted suicide. In all cases the solicitor will need the detainee's authority to pass on this information to the police. If the detainee is reluctant to give such information, reassurance should be given to him that the fact he is considered a risk to himself will not in any way prejudice the police investigation but rather should ensure that he receives the appropriate care and treatment during his detention. If the detainee mentions harming others, the solicitor should consider his position in accordance with the Law Society's guidance detailed at **3.4.4** below.

3.2.7 The initial advice on the telephone should also be to tell the detainee not to speak to the police about anything to do with the suspected offence nor to sign any document (including the officer's incident report book) until the solicitor attends the police station. If the appropriate adult is already at the police station or may arrive before the solicitor does, the detainee must be advised not to discuss details of the alleged offence with the appropriate adult. Owing to the difference in rules on confidentiality, any admission to the offence made in the presence of the appropriate adult could be passed on to the police (see **3.4** below). C.NFG.6B2 sets out when legal advice will be by telephone and when an attendance is more likely to be indicated. It should be noted that an attendance by a solicitor for an offence suitable for telephone advice can depend on whether the detainee is 'eligible for assistance from an appropriate adult' or 'whether the detainee is unable to communicate over the telephone'.

3.3 ARRIVAL AT THE POLICE STATION

3.3.1 On arrival at the police station, the solicitor is entitled to inspect the custody record (C.2.4) which records the medical and risk assessments. The solicitor is entitled to see all the clinical findings even if they are to be found elsewhere within documentation (C.9.16). If the detainee has not yet been examined, it is important to make sure the custody officer has made a telephone call to request attendance of the AHCP.

3.3.2 In the Metropolitan Police area, custody records include a continuation sheet entitled 'Appropriate Adult and Medical Care' (Form 57M) which records the need for an appropriate adult and the need for medical attention. At the end of the form it is noted that regardless of the answers, if there is any doubt about the arrested person's medical condition, action to secure medical attention should be taken in accordance with C.9 and current Metropolitan Police Service policy.

3.3.3 It is useful to check with the custody officer that the conditions of detention are appropriate. Although the Codes of Practice only advise that a juvenile should not be placed in a cell, if the detainee is being held in a cell and this is affecting his mental well-being, the solicitor should make representations to the custody officer that the detainee be transferred to a detention room or some other more suitable accommodation. Representation should particularly be made if the detainee has a history of self-harm or attempted suicide as the Code also advises that people at risk should be visited in their cell (or other place of detention) more frequently that the mandatory hourly visits for other detainees. Regard should be had also to C.8.2 and Annex E.13 which note that particular care must be taken when deciding whether to use handcuffs to restrain a mentally disordered or otherwise mentally vulnerable person in a locked cell.

3.4 CONFIDENTIALITY: SOLICITOR AND APPROPRIATE ADULT

3.4.1 It is extremely important that the solicitor spends some time, where possible, with the appropriate adult without the detainee present. The purpose of this meeting is to make sure that no issues will arise which will potentially raise the issue of confidentiality. Discussions will vary depending on whether the appropriate adult is a professional (e.g. social worker) or a lay person (e.g. relative or person appointed from a local panel of appropriate adults). Annex A to the Home Office 'Guidance for Appropriate Adults' (referred to in **2.7.1** above) specifically states 'your conversations with the detained person are not covered by legal privilege'. It also reminds the appropriate adult that they are 'not entitled to be present during private legal consultations between the detainee and their legal representative'.

Social worker

3.4.2 Guidance issued to social workers acting as appropriate adults advises them to see the detainee alone and before he sees his legal representative so that the social worker can explain the difference between the roles of the appropriate adult and the solicitor and they can explain that an admission of guilt to them may be passed on to the police. The guidance for social workers is set out in the British Association of Social Workers (BASW) Code of Ethics (2002) which contains a section specifically dealing with privacy, confidentiality and records. The most important parts are set out below.

(a) Respect service users' rights to a relationship of trust, to privacy, reliability and confidentiality and to the responsible use of information obtained from or about them;

(b) Observe the principle that information given for one purpose may not be used for a different purpose without the permission of the informant;

(d) Divulge confidential information only with the consent of the service user or informant, *except where there is clear evidence of serious risk to the service user, worker, other persons or the community, or in other circumstances judged exceptional on the basis of professional consideration and consultation, limiting any such breach of confidence to the needs of the situation at the time.* [emphasis added]

3.4.3 Not all social workers belong to BASW and so it is not clear what code of ethics they adhere to, if any. Some local authorities issue their own guidance whereas others have no policy on confidentiality. Most justify disclosure of personal information to a request from a senior police officer (e.g. Superintendent or above), if it can help 'to prevent detect or prosecute a serious crime'. If a solicitor has any doubts as to the individual social worker's position on confidentiality were the detainee to either make admissions in his presence or make remarks indicating a possible danger to other persons, it is important to ensure that the detainee is made fully aware of this.

3.4.4 The Law Society, in an effort to clarify the position, issued guidance to solicitors in May 1993 entitled 'Advising a Juvenile, Mentally Disordered or Mentally Handicapped Suspect in a Police Station when an Appropriate Adult is Present'. The main recommendation is that owing to the difference between the codes of conduct of solicitors and social workers and to ensure that a suspect has the opportunity of confidential consultation with his solicitor, the suspect must *first* be advised by the solicitor *in the absence of the appropriate adult* about the risk of disclosure.

3.4.5 *R* v. *Brown* (CA, 21 May 1999) highlighted the problem of a client admitting an offence to a social worker, believing that the information would go no further. Brown (aged 17) was arrested for causing grievous bodily harm. At the police station he had an appropriate adult who was a social worker. She had been his supervisor appointed by his local Youth Justice Team for the previous eight months. She attended the police interview together with his solicitor. After the interview, she was alone with the defendant and he admitted having committed the offence. She discussed the conflict between her duty of confidentiality to her client and her obligations to the public with her employer. Subsequently, she made a witness statement to the police recounting his admission. The Crown Court judge admitted her evidence. The Court of Appeal upheld the conviction on the grounds that the admission could not be excluded under ss.76 or 78 of PACE. It confirmed the trial judge's finding that the duties of social workers with regard to confidentiality are not relevant to the question he had to decide. It found that the fact that the defendant did not realise that the confession would be used against him did not render its admission in evidence unfair.

Other professionals

3.4.6 Other professionals may be given guidance by their own professional body, for example if the appropriate adult is a nurse, or it may be set out in their contract of employment. However they may have no guidance at all as to whether they owe a duty of confidentiality to the detainee. It is important therefore that the solicitor discusses with the appropriate adult the different roles and finds out the appropriate adult's own view as to what he would do if the detainee were to make admissions in his presence.

Lay person

3.4.7 If the appropriate adult is a non-professional (e.g. a relative), he will owe no duty of confidentiality to the suspect. The solicitor should carefully explain the role of appropriate adult to the person appointed particularly in relation to the interview and that he is there not to persuade the detainee to answer questions but rather to safeguard the detainee's welfare during the interview.

3.4.8 Code A.NFG.1 states that when a police officer is investigating an offence, he is entitled to question any person from whom he thinks useful information can be obtained and further that all citizens have a duty to help police officers 'to prevent crime and discover offenders'. If, therefore, a lay appropriate adult has received an admission of guilt the police could use this as evidence in any future prosecution. In the case of *R* v. *West* (*Rosemary*) [1996] 2 Cr App R 374 (not reported for this specific point) husband and wife Fred and Rosemary West were both arrested and charged with numerous murders and assaults. Fred West had a non-professional appropriate adult at the police station. Before trial he committed suicide. At his wife's trial, the prosecution called his appropriate adult to give evidence against her. This evidence was information obtained from the appropriate adult's conversations with Fred West when acting in that role. The judge allowed that evidence.

Solicitors

3.4.9 The guidance for solicitors in respect to confidentiality is set out in the Solicitors' Code of Conduct 2007. Rule 4.01 of the Code requires solicitors to keep the affairs of clients and former clients confidential except where disclosure is required or permitted by law or by the client (or former client).

3.4.10 The overriding principle is one of absolute confidentiality save in exceptional circumstances. Notes 12 and 13 of the Guidance to Rule 4 advise solicitors that they may reveal confidential information to the extent that the solicitor believes it necessary to 'prevent the client or a third party committing a criminal act that you reasonably believe is likely to result in serious bodily harm'. In considering what might constitute exceptional circumstances, a solicitor must consider what would be in the public interest. It also allows for cases where there may be exceptional circumstances involving children where the solicitor should consider revealing confidential information to an appropriate authority. This may be where the child is the client and the child reveals information which indicates continuing sexual or other physical abuse but refuses to allow disclosure of such information. Similarly, there may be situations where an adult discloses abuse either by himself or by another adult against a child but refuses to allow any disclosure. The Guidance advises that the solicitor must consider whether the threat to the child's life or health, both mental and physical, is sufficiently serious to justify a breach of the duty of confidentiality.

3.4.11 If, having considered the facts of a particular case, the solicitor takes the view that he may be entitled to disclose information received from the detainee, he should first consider if there is any other way of remedying the situation without revealing the information, and secondly if the information is or is not disclosed whether the solicitor would be able to justify his actions to the Solicitors Regulation Authority or to a court. The solicitor should always consult his principal on the appropriate course of action to take. If the solicitor is uncertain as to whether to report confidential information, he should consider seeking legal advice or contacting the professional ethics guidance team for advice.

3.4.12 The Practice Note issued by the Law Society's Mental Health and Disability Sub-Committee to solicitors representing patients at Mental Health Review Tribunals (PN 2009) advises solicitors that if clients disclose to the solicitor that they intend to do serious harm to themselves or to someone else, guidance should be sought from the Law Society's Professional Ethics Division. If disclosure is advised, the solicitor should inform the client that he has been professionally embarrassed and will cease to act.

3.5 FIRST CONSULTATION WITH DETAINEE

3.5.1 Prior to taking instructions from the detainee, advance disclosure must be obtained from the officer in the case. If the detainee is being treated as a mentally disordered person, it may be useful to obtain the view of the officer in the case on the seriousness of the alleged offence and whether the detainee's mental health has any bearing on the commission of the offence and to try and find out how the officer sees the case progressing e.g. taking no further action, caution, diversion or charge.

3.5.2 When acting for a detainee who is mentally disordered, the solicitor may be required to consider his own personal safety. Occasionally the custody officer will raise this if he has been told by someone else or has himself experienced that the detainee may be violent or has indicated that he may harm someone. If the client is known to the solicitor, the solicitor may be in a position to assess the likelihood of danger to himself if he is aware of any previous psychiatric history and diagnosis. If, on the other hand, this is a new client, the solicitor should be careful and ask the custody officer to allow facilities to take instructions which are within eyesight of a police officer. Steps should be taken to safeguard the confidential nature of a solicitor–client interview so ensure that the officer is just within calling range rather than being able to hear the consultation with the detainee. The solicitor should ask specifically that any room/cell not be locked.

3.5.3 As a result of a number of incidents which were brought to the attention of the Home Office and the Health and Safety Executive (HSE) highlighting the actual and potential risks faced by solicitors particularly when carrying out private consultations with their clients in the custody area, the HSE advised that the level of risk has on occasions been serious and of significant concern. As a result the Home Office issued guidance entitled 'Safety of Solicitors and Accredited and Probationary Representatives Working in Custody Suites at Police Stations' (Home Office Circular O34/2007). The guidance covers the role and responsibilities of both the solicitor and the solicitor's firm as well as the police. It is an extremely helpful document and all solicitors attending police stations should familiarise themselves with it. It states that the solicitor firm (as the employer) has a duty to assess the risks to its staff associated with working in custody suites. Whereas solicitors as employees:

- have a duty to review their own safety before each consultation with a detainee;
- should seek relevant information from police in order to assess the risks to their own safety before any consultation;
- should not expose themselves to unnecessary risk simply for the sake of expediency;
- should cooperate with police to ensure that their actions do not compromise the overall safety of those in the custody suite;
- should explain how any risk assessments they have carried out might affect their client suspect.

It emphasises that the custody officer is responsible for determining, in each case, the level of disclosure of details of the detainee's physical or mental condition and is responsible for disclosure of the risk, and should *not* withhold information that would place a solicitor at risk. It also confirms that the custody officer is required to seek information relevant to the risk assessment of a detainee from all available sources including the solicitor. The disclosure of this information will be subject to the solicitor's professional rules and obligations in relation to confidentiality but the guidance advises that 'the focus is on minimising risk for the detainee and those who come into contact with the detainee'.

3.5.4 The first consultation with the detainee should be without the appropriate adult for the reasons set out in **3.4** above. It is important to try and establish a rapport with the detainee as quite often those suffering from mental disorder have a distrust of professionals or people in authority. The difference between the role of solicitor and appropriate adult should be explained and the detainee should be asked at what point he would like the appropriate adult to be present. He may feel happier going through all the preliminary matters with the solicitor alone and the appropriate adult can then be brought in at the end to meet the detainee and have his role explained.

3.5.5 It is important to check with a detainee whether he would like anyone else informed of his arrest, such as a relative. This is a right which those with mental health problems or learning difficulties often do not take up on arrival at the police station yet it can be of great assistance to both the solicitor and the detainee to speak to someone who knows him well. It may also help to alleviate any anxieties detainees may have regarding the welfare or care of their children or other dependants.

3.5.6 If, during the private consultation, the detainee admits to a history of mental illness and/or that he is currently receiving treatment but specifically tells the solicitor not to inform the police, the solicitor must abide by these instructions. If the solicitor is strongly of the opinion that it is not in the detainee's interests to withhold such details from the police then there could be a conflict of interest. Home Office Circular 034/2007 gives further guidance on this (see **3.5.3** above). Before deciding whether to withdraw from the case, consideration should be given to requesting that someone else talk the matter over with the detainee. This could be a relative or the appropriate adult, who might be able to persuade the detainee that informing the police would afford him more protection in the police station and be of advantage to him in the long term.

3.5.7 Depending on how ill the detainee is, instructions should be taken with reference to the detailed checklists in **Appendix 8** which should assist in gathering information about the detainee's mental state and ability. It is also useful to have access to other source material such as Anthony Edwards, *Advising a Suspect in the Police Station* (Thompson/Sweet & Maxwell, 2009) which has a detailed general checklist.

3.5.8 If the detainee is suffering from a mental disorder it is helpful to try and assess its extent. This should become apparent when talking to the detainee – for example, he may not be able to concentrate for very long or may display paranoid ideas. If the detainee has stopped taking his medication, he may be experiencing new symptoms, making it difficult for him to communicate with people. The solicitor should try and find information about what medication the detainee is on and whether he is still taking it and in what dose, or if he has stopped taking the medication, when he stopped taking it.

3.5.9 It can often be difficult for the solicitor as well as the police and AHCP to identify a detainee with learning disabilities. He may be able to complete simple tasks easily (e.g. signing public funding forms), whilst finding complex and stressful situations requiring rapid thought and articulate response (e.g. the police interview) beyond his ability. He is unlikely to volunteer that he has specific difficulties and is less likely than a mentally ill person to have an active programme of mental health or social care.

3.5.10 If the detainee falls within the definition of 'learning disability', he is likely to have problems with comprehension and expressing himself. Some people with learning difficulties have difficulty recalling information as they may take longer to take in information as well as then to understand and categorise it. Some find it difficult to record details and remember events in a form that can be understood by others. Limited language ability can result in some people with learning difficulties having problems in understanding a question or conveying precisely what they mean to say. Further research by Gudjonsson and others has revealed other difficulties, including feeling intimidated during interactions with people in authority.

3.5.11 In order to try and establish the severity of the learning disability, seeking information about the detainee's educational background to establish whether he has attended a special school may be extremely helpful. If the solicitor has doubts about the detainee's ability to read or write it might be useful to test him. The Royal College of Psychiatrists and St George's Hospital have produced a series of booklets, 'Books Beyond Words', which explain police and court procedures to people with learning difficulties through pictures. The Home Office has encouraged the police to make the booklet 'You're Under Arrest' available at police stations.

3.6 EXAMINATION BY AHCP

3.6.1 By now the solicitor ought to be able to assess whether the detainee needs a full psychiatric examination before the investigation proceeds any further. If the solicitor is of the opinion that this would be in the detainee's best interests, the detainee's authority will be required for the solicitor to liaise with the AHCP with a view to discussing this option. If the detainee has already been examined by the AHCP, the custody officer can be asked to recall the AHCP to the police station if a solicitor is of the view that the detainee needs a further and more detailed examination/assessment. C.Annex G accepts that a detainee may be at risk in an interview if it is considered that 'conducting the interview could significantly harm the detainee's physical or mental state or anything the detainee says in the interview about their involvement or suspected involvement in the offence about which they are being interviewed *might* be considered unreliable in subsequent court proceedings because of their physical or mental state' (see Annex G.2(a–b)).

3.6.2 In assessing whether the detainee should be interviewed, the AHCP should consider how the detainee's mental state might affect his ability to understand the nature and the purpose of the interview, to comprehend what is being asked and to appreciate the significance of any answers given and make rational decisions about whether he wants to say anything. The extent to which the detainee's replies may be affected by his mental condition rather than representing a rational and accurate explanation of his involvement in the offence is also important. Annex G.4 states it is essential that AHCPs who are consulted 'consider the functional ability of the detainee rather than simply relying on a medical diagnosis, e.g. it is possible for a person with severe mental illness to be fit for interview'. AHCPs should advise on the need for an appropriate adult to be present (however, see **2.4.6(d)** above).

3.6.3 If the AHCP is of the view that the detainee requires a fuller psychiatric assessment, in some areas of the country police stations have arrangements with their local hospital whereby one or more members of the psychiatric team will attend the police station to make the assessment. In others, the detainee is usually taken by the officer in the case to the local hospital for a psychiatric assessment. There is no provision in the PACE Codes of Practice for the appropriate adult to go with the detainee and so detainees should be asked whether they would like the appropriate adult to attend. If they want the appropriate adult to attend, as discussed earlier it is important that the client is reminded not to discuss the case with the appropriate adult, or indeed the accompanying police officers.

3.6.4 There is no obligation on the detainee to agree to be examined by an AHCP or psychiatrist. Under General Medical Council guidelines entitled 'Consent: patients and doctors making decisions together' (2 June 2008), a doctor is required to obtain the person's valid and informed consent to examination. The detainee's consent should be obtained both to the examination and to the release of his notes to the police before the examination commences.

3.6.5 Doctors are advised that no one can give or withhold consent on behalf of a mentally incapacitated patient unless they have legal authority to do so or have been appointed to represent the patient. The doctor must first assess the person's capacity to make an informed decision about the investigation/treatment. If patients lack capacity, provided they comply, the doctor may carry out any investigation or treatment (which may include treatment for mental disorder) that the doctor considers to be in the patient's best interest (Part 3). If the detainee does not comply, the doctor may only compulsorily examine or treat him for any mental disorder within the safeguards laid down by the Act. If the solicitor is of the opinion however that it is in his client's interests to be examined because, for example, it might result in his being diverted and not being charged, then this should be explained to the detainee as clearly as possible.

3.6.6 If they receive certain information during the course of a medical examination, doctors (including psychiatrists) have a duty of confidentiality which is different from that of solicitors. The General Medical Council (GMC) publication entitled 'Confidentiality' (2009) contains its guidance on this subject. This should be read in conjunction with the BMA Guidance referred to at **2.8.4** above. The need for the Guidance arose specifically out of the confusion between forensic physicians' duty to disclose information to the police and their duty of confidentiality. It makes clear that reports prepared by doctors for criminal proceedings must be given to the police but any information obtained for therapeutic purposes is subject to the usual rules of confidentiality. Paragraph 4.3 of the BMA Guidance advises that 'Only forensic information and *other information likely to affect the outcome of the case* should be included in the statement prepared for the police' (emphasis added). Doctors are advised that they must respect requests by patients that information should not be disclosed to third parties, save in exceptional circumstances. These include where a failure to disclose information may expose the patient to risk of death or serious harm and where disclosure is necessary for the prevention or detection of a serious crime (GMC Guidance, para. 37).

3.6.7 Most doctors are aware of the difficulty that this places them in if a suspect does start to confess to a crime or admits to thoughts of harming someone else and they should take steps to avoid being put in that situation by not asking leading questions. The problem can arise when the AHCP is not a doctor but another health professional (e.g. a nurse, community psychiatric nurse or AMHP) as they may have different codes of practice. This may also arise at hospital when the examining doctor is making a psychiatric assessment at the request of the police.

3.6.8 In the case of *R* v. *McDonald* [1991] Crim LR 122, CA (Crim Div) the defendant, who was charged with murder, was examined by a psychiatrist for the purpose of determining fitness to plead, diminished responsibility and mental state in general. The doctor asked him about a piece of non-medical evidence and the defendant gave a reply which constituted an admission of the offence. The doctor's evidence on this point was allowed at trial and the defendant was convicted. Counsel for the defendant, in the Court of Appeal, conceded that the communication between the defendant and the doctor was not privileged and had not been obtained by oppression or inducement and further, that it was admissible for a doctor to give evidence on non-medical matters. The issue to be decided was whether the statement, once obtained, was used fairly. Earlier cases referred to by the court included *R* v. *Payne* [1963] 1 WLR 637 and *R* v. *Smith* (1979) 69 Cr App R 378 which held, *inter alia*, that there is no confidentiality in a doctor–patient relationship unless the defendant was expressly told that the content of the medical examination, for which his consent was required, would not be given in evidence. These decisions need to be considered together with both the GMC and BMA Guidance referred to above and the guidance issued to doctors who are preparing court reports (see **6.3.2** below).

3.6.9 If the solicitor is of the opinion that the detainee is *not* fit to be detained or interviewed, it is worth discussing this view with the appropriate adult to try and enlist his support. If the AHCP disagrees and certifies the detainee fit to be detained and interviewed, the solicitor should make his representations known to the custody officer. The appropriate adult should be encouraged to do the same. The role of the AHCP is an advisory one and the custody officer does not have to follow it. If that fails, the solicitor must address his representations to an inspector and have the objections noted on the custody record. Unfortunately once the AHCP has deemed a detainee fit to be detained and interviewed, the police invariably go ahead with an interview. A client may be fit to be interviewed and detained but still be vulnerable and it is important that both the solicitor and the appropriate adult are alert to his particular difficulties. See **4.5** below as to what to do in the interview in these circumstances.

3.6.10 If the solicitor has any worries or doubts about the seriousness of his client's illness he should try and speak to the client's treating doctor, social worker or a relative who knows him well as they may be able to advise on how the detainee is normally and the nature of his illness. C.9.4 expressly states that a detainee may, in addition to being examined by the police surgeon, be examined by a medical practitioner of his own choice at his own expense.

CHAPTER 4

Police interview

4.1 ADVICE BEFORE THE INTERVIEW

4.1.1 Once the solicitor has taken instructions on the detainee's background, he should go through the details of the prosecution case provided by the police. The detainee should be reassured that the allegations are not yet proven and he has an opportunity to deny them in interview. It is particularly important to listen carefully to his instructions, giving plenty of time for the details to emerge and, where the detainee has a learning disability, to use the interviewing techniques set out in **4.2.7**. One way of ensuring that the detainee's instructions have been recorded correctly is to read his account of events back to him.

4.1.2 With mentally disordered suspects it is particularly important to consider all the elements of the offence, taking into account any subjective element which forms part of the *mens rea*. A person's mental disorder may distort his understanding of events so that he has motives for his actions which are not based in reality. Sometimes his mood (e.g. depression or elation) may affect his judgement.

4.1.3 If the detainee says he has answered police questions before the solicitor's arrival at the police station or he has discussed the case with anyone else, e.g. the AHCP or appropriate adult, he must be prepared for any question about a 'significant statement or silence' which may be put by police at the beginning of the interview (C.11.2A). It will also forewarn the solicitor of any intervention he may wish to make during the interview as to the admissibility of evidence.

4.1.4 Once an account of events has been taken with which the detainee agrees, the solicitor must consider, as with any client, whether he should answer police questions, remain silent or make a prepared statement. As a starting point, when advising whether to advise the detainee to remain silent, the criteria set out in Ed Cape, *Defending Suspects at Police Stations* (LAG, 2006) p. 202 (hereinafter referred to as 'Ed Cape') should be considered:

- knowledge of the police case;
- apparent strength of the evidence;
- admissibility of the police evidence;
- legality of the arrest, detention and questioning;

- prior comments and/or 'significant silences' of the client;
- likely fairness of the interview;
- apparent intelligence of the client;
- apparent mental condition of the client;
- apparent physical condition of the client;
- strength of the client's defence;
- any reason for early statement of the client's defence;
- specific reasons for remaining silent (e.g. to protect others);
- possible advantages of early admission of the offence(s).

4.1.5 Whether the detainee is advised to answer questions in interview depends on the facts of each individual case (as with any other criminal client) but it is important to weigh up the nature and severity of the detainee's illness and ability to deal with and understand the questions in the interview, against the result it is hoped to achieve for him. Chapter 5 of Anthony Edwards, *Advising a Suspect in the Police Station* (Thompson/Sweet & Maxwell, 2009) contains very helpful guidance on this issue.

4.1.6 Consideration must be given as to whether the decision to advise the detainee not to answer questions will lay him open to the drawing of an adverse inference from his silence under ss.34, 36 and 37 of the Criminal Justice and Public Order Act (CJPOA) 1994. Guidelines set down by the courts in relation to adverse inference directions are contained in a number of cases including *Condron* v. *UK* (2000) 8 BHRC 290, *R* v. *Betts and Hall* [2001] EWCA Crim 224, and *R* v. *Beckles* [2004] EWCA Crim 2766. Two of these cases assist in considering advice to be given to mentally disordered or otherwise mentally vulnerable suspects. In *R* v. *Argent* [1997] Crim LR 346, CA the court held that a subjective test must be used for interpreting the circumstances which led to the client not answering police questions at the time. 'Circumstances' could include matters such as the time of day, the client's age, experience, mental capacity, state of health, sobriety, tiredness, knowledge, personality and legal advice. References to 'the accused' meant to the actual accused with such qualities, apprehensions, knowledge and advice as he was shown to have had at the time. In *R* v. *Howell* [2005] 1 Cr App Rep 1 the court held that the kind of circumstances which may be most likely to justify silence will be 'such matters as the suspect's condition including ill-health, in particular mental disability'. If the solicitor decides that it is not appropriate for the detainee to answer questions, he must make a comprehensive record of all the factors which have led him to that decision bearing in mind that if called to give evidence, for example in a *voir dire*, privilege may have to be waived.

4.1.7 In acting for detainees who are mentally vulnerable and less able to deal with the pressures of an interview, it is frequently appropriate to consider putting in a prepared statement at the start of the interview. If, however, there has already been a 'no comment' interview the statement could be submitted before charge. This method should be particularly considered if the detainee is so vulnerable that he would not do himself justice when asked questions.

4.2 SPECIAL CONSIDERATIONS ON INTERVIEWING PEOPLE WITH LEARNING DISABILITIES

4.2.1 Research confirms that the learning disabled are frequently vulnerable to making misleading statements in interviews (see especially Clare and Gudjonsson (1995), 'The vulnerability of suspects with intellectual disabilities during police interviews: a review and experimental study of decision-making', *Mental Handicap Research*, 8(2), 110–128). There is a greater tendency among learning disabled people when being questioned by police to go along with the story which is put to them, particularly if leading questions are put with a certain degree of force by the interviewer, which places pressure on the interviewee to comply.

4.2.2 The following tendencies have been noted in research:

(a) acquiescence, i.e. the tendency to answer questions in the affirmative regardless of their content;
(b) interrogative suggestibility, i.e. a tendency either to be (mis)led by leading questions or to change initial answers in response to negative feedback from the questioner to the first response;
(c) confabulation, i.e. when people unconsciously replace gaps in their memories or add to existing memories with distorted or fabricated material. This is a less common, but still significant, tendency, often driven by a desire to please the interviewer or to draw attention to oneself. This tendency is thought to be associated not so much with low intelligence as with personality abnormality and certain types of brain damage.

4.2.3 It is common for the learning disabled detainee to believe that because he is being interviewed he must have done something wrong. The sense in which the interview is an investigation to establish the truth may escape him; thus he is less likely to put his version of events across in the face of opposition.

4.2.4 The desire to make oneself the centre of attention by confessing to serious offences, without regard to the consequences, may prey on the mind of some suspects. A well-known example of this is the case of *R* v. *Ward* (1993) 96 Cr App R 1. Judith Ward, although of normal intelligence, suffered from a personality disorder. She 'confessed' to a large number of terrorist acts, some of which she could not possibly have committed, in order to bring 'interest and excitement to an otherwise lonely and friendless person', according to the psychologist Gudjonsson who gave evidence at her appeal. The same impulse, and the wish to be admitted to a psychiatric hospital, led a defendant of limited IQ (73–6), to admit offences which he could not have committed (*R* v. *McKenzie* (1993) 96 Cr App R 98).

4.2.5 The wish to extricate oneself from the immediate situation and put an end to questioning was a feature in *R* v. *Delaney* (1989) 88 Cr App R 338, in which a 17-year-old youth with an IQ of 80 was accused of sexual offences with a three-year-old girl. He initially denied the offences. During further questioning, the officers minimised the gravity of the offence and suggested to him that treatment, not punishment, was the likely outcome if he confessed, an approach they later justified by saying that they did not want to 'frighten him away from confessing his guilt'. The Court of Appeal allowed the appeal as unsafe and unsatisfactory remarking that the appellant was 'poorly equipped to cope with sustained interrogation and the longer the pressure was imposed on him the more confused he was likely to be in his own mind'.

4.2.6 Research into questioning witnesses who have learning disabilities has also shown that most are capable of giving reliable evidence if the questioning is done in a way that they understand and which does not encourage the tendencies to mislead set out in **4.2.1–4.2.5** above. Expert questioning of a mentally impaired suspect (or witness) can be a painstaking and lengthy process, requiring specialist knowledge and an awareness of the particular interviewee's difficulties. Ideally, the interviewer should have professional training and a full history of the interviewee before starting the interview. However, in the police station setting, this is not possible for the solicitor, appropriate adult or police officer.

4.2.7 The following suggestions are based on research into questioning witnesses who have learning disabilities (see the research paper by Bull and Cullen, 'Witnesses who have Mental Handicaps' (Crown Office, Edinburgh, 1992)). Note should be taken of these points when taking instructions and, as far as possible, they should be followed by police in the interview.

(a) Questions which demand only a 'yes' or 'no' answer should be avoided. People with learning disabilities frequently give the answer 'yes' wrongly, in a misguided attempt to 'help' the interviewer by falling in with his version of events, or to disguise the fact that the question has not been understood.

(b) Avoid 'upgrading' answers which have been given by the detainee, for example, by repeating back to him what he is understood to have said, even though it was incomplete and unclear. He may acquiesce in the new version of events and a crucial element of the story may be lost. Do not finish sentences for him even if he is struggling to express himself. Patience is essential.

(c) Try to break down an inconsistent answer into simpler phrases. If an answer is confusing and attempts to clarify it do not seem to work, leave it and move on. Insistence may easily force the detainee into a false agreement; returning to the question later when the sense of pressure has lessened may allow him to offer more detail.

(d) Be aware that many learning disabled people find it difficult to describe emotion with any clarity, especially the emotions of others. Concepts such as shame, surprise and anger may be hard for them to convey in words. Concentrate on descriptions of events if possible.

(e) Avoid leading questions where possible. This should reduce the risk of acquiescence.

(f) Legal terminology and difficult words should be avoided wherever possible. Sometimes a solicitor cannot avoid having to explain certain legal terms, for example the caution, but it is unwise to assume that the detainee correctly understands common words, such as bail or custody. Check that he understands these terms by asking him to explain them.

4.3 PREPARATION FOR INTERVIEW

4.3.1 The detainee must understand that evidence given in interview will form part of the case against him and that giving the police officers the answers they seem to want is not necessarily in his interests in the long term. It is good practice to go over the conduct of the interview with him so that he understands the routine procedures. He should be told about the people who will be in the interview room, the taping of the interview, and the fact that his answers have to be audible. It should also be explained to him that, although the solicitor is there to help him, he will have to answer the questions by himself and that no one can speak for him. He must be reminded that at any time during the interview he can ask for it to be stopped if he wants to speak to his solicitor privately and that either the solicitor or the appropriate adult will be able to intervene if necessary.

4.3.2 The form of the interview should be practised with the detainee so that he is aware of how it will be conducted. It is also helpful to identify the likely questions he will be asked, not so that he can be told what answers to give but rather to assist him in understanding the 'question–answer' format and to prepare him for the type and depth of questioning.

4.3.3 The pre-interview caution must be explained to the detainee and he should be asked to repeat it back in his own words to ensure that he understands it. If the solicitor thinks that the detainee does not fully understand the caution, he should inform the custody officer and the officer in the case before the interview starts. If they insist on the interview going ahead the solicitor can request that the AHCP is recalled or that the objection is noted on the custody record. The objection should be repeated in the interview. If it appears that a person does not understand the caution, the person giving it should explain it in their own words (C.NFG.10D).

4.3.4 If the solicitor thinks that detainee is capable of being interviewed but may have problems understanding long words, he should inform the custody officer and the officer in the case. There may come a point when the solicitor asks for the interview to be stopped, and it will be helpful to any argument that may arise later in court that this concern was raised at an earlier stage as well as in the interview. It might be helpful for the solicitor to discuss his views with the appropriate adult to enlist his support if necessary. Similarly, if the appropriate adult conveys to the solicitor that he has doubts about the detainee's intellectual capacity, that should be noted.

4.3.5 The detainee should be asked if he has any particular fears about the interview. He may be worried about something unconnected with the allegation against him, such as a child or a pet left unattended. It may be possible to make arrangements which will put his mind at ease. He may be frightened of being bullied by police officers. Reassurance can be given to him that the solicitor and the appropriate adult will be with him throughout the interview and will raise any objections if this occurs. It is also important to explore with the detainee at this stage what he expects to happen after the interview, to rectify any false impressions that he may have been given, for example about bail.

4.4 THE ROLE OF THE SOLICITOR IN THE INTERVIEW

4.4.1 Mentally disordered offenders are unusually dependent on their solicitor's advice and protection during police interviews. It is unlikely that admissions made in interview will be excluded if the detainee had a solicitor present (see *R* v. *Dunn* at **8.4.3**). It is therefore necessary to be able to monitor the detainee's behaviour during the interview. Some police officers will try to sideline the solicitor into a passive role once the interview has started. It should be made clear from the start by the solicitor that he intends to be active in his client's defence, in particular because of his vulnerability.

4.4.2 The seating arrangements in the interview room are important. If the solicitor is allocated a chair which prevents him from having effective eye contact with the detainee so that he cannot monitor the detainee's state of mind, he should move it. Ed Cape (p.287) makes the helpful suggestion that if the police officer objects, the solicitor should move the chair once the tape is running. The officer will find it much harder to challenge this while the tape is running, without sounding obstructive.

4.4.3 Consideration should be given by the solicitor as to whether it will be helpful to make an opening statement about his role at the beginning of the interview. It is a matter of practice and judgement in each case. If issue is being taken with the police officer on a particular point, for example, that the detainee is unable to understand the caution, this must be referred to in the statement so that it is recorded on tape. If representations have already been made to the police that the detainee is unfit for interview, it should be mentioned here as well as on the custody record. If the solicitor is advising the detainee not to answer questions for any reason, consideration should be given to stating those reasons at this point (see suggested defence lawyer's opening statement at Ed Cape, p. 295). The solicitor may be required to give evidence in court as to why he advised the defendant to make a 'no comment' interview so detailed notes are essential.

4.4.4 It is essential to monitor the detainee's mental state throughout the interview. Mentally disordered interviewees are often able to answer questions easily at the start of the interview but can become confused or aroused as the pressure of being in a long interview begins to take effect. The detainee may start to ramble incoherently or leave long pauses in his speech in such a way that it suggests that he may be responding to auditory hallucinations. If this occurs, the solicitor should consider stopping the interview with a view to making representations that the detainee is not fit to be interviewed and requires further examination by an AHCP.

4.5 INTERVENING DURING THE INTERVIEW

4.5.1 C.NFG.6D states clearly that the solicitor may intervene in order to seek clarification or to challenge an improper question to his client, or the manner in which it is put, or to advise his client not to answer particular questions or to give him further legal advice. It acknowledges that on occasion, this may require the solicitor to give advice which has the effect of his client avoiding giving evidence which strengthens a prosecution case. C.6.9 provides that a solicitor may only be required to leave the interview if his conduct is such that the investigating officer is unable properly to put questions to the suspect. Examples of unacceptable behaviour include answering questions on a suspect's behalf or providing written replies for the suspect to quote. The reasons for intervening, or for not intervening, in an interview must always be recorded by a solicitor in written notes which may be used later at trial.

4.5.2 The circumstances which require a solicitor to intervene will not differ essentially from those involving a client without any special vulnerability. In general these will be when he believes there has been a breach of PACE, ss.76–8 or the Codes of Practice, or that the questions put are unfair in either form or content. Situations where a solicitor should intervene in interview are discussed in Ed Cape, p. 298 and include domineering and bullying questioning, topic hopping (jumping from subject to subject without allowing the suspect time to gather his thoughts), and seeking to persuade the suspect to answer questions by maximising the advantages and minimising the disadvantages of confession. When representing a mentally disordered detainee, there should be a lower threshold of tolerance of questioning or behaviour which may fall into these categories. In particular, oppressive, bullying or pressurising interrogation is highly objectionable when used on mentally disordered detainees. Although, in *R* v. *Emmerson* (1991) 92 Cr App R 284, the court found that rude and discourteous questioning with some shouting and bad language was not oppressive within the meaning of s.76(2), it might be so if it could be shown that the suspect's nature was such as to make him particularly easily overwhelmed by such behaviour.

4.6 THE ROLE OF THE APPROPRIATE ADULT IN THE INTERVIEW

4.6.1 C.11 and 12 contain directions to officers on how to conduct the interview of any suspect. These paragraphs give specific directions on interviewing vulnerable or mentally disordered suspects and are also summarised in Annexes C and E.

4.6.2 A mentally disordered or otherwise mentally vulnerable suspect must not be interviewed or asked to provide or sign a written statement in the absence of the appropriate adult unless the provisions of C.11.1 or Annex C apply.

4.6.3 NFG.C.11C and Annex E.2 confirm that if there is any doubt about a person's mental state or capacity, an appropriate adult should be involved:

> Although juveniles or people who are mentally disordered or otherwise mentally vulnerable are often capable of providing reliable evidence, they may, without knowing or wishing to do so, be particularly prone in certain circumstances to provide information that may be unreliable, misleading or self-incriminating. Special care should always be taken when questioning such a person, and the appropriate adult should be involved if there is any doubt about a person's age, mental state or capacity. Because of the risk of unreliable evidence it is also important to obtain corroboration of any facts admitted whenever possible.'

4.6.4 Paragraph 11.1 permits emergency interviews of vulnerable suspects in the absence of an appropriate adult to be authorised by an officer of superintendent rank or above if delay would be likely:

(a) to lead to interference with or harm to evidence connected with an offence or interference with or physical harm to other people; or
(b) to lead to the alerting of other people suspected of having committed an offence but not yet arrested for it; or
(c) to hinder the recovery of property obtained in consequence of the commission of an offence.

4.6.5 An interview in the absence of the appropriate adult under the above provision may not continue once sufficient information to avert the risk has been obtained. Save in these circumstances the appropriate adult must also be present when the mentally disordered suspect is cautioned, and if not, the suspect must be cautioned again in the presence of the appropriate adult.

4.6.6 The appropriate adult present at the interview must be informed of the provisions of C.11.17 (Annex E.9):

> Where the appropriate adult is present at an interview, he must be informed that he is not expected to act simply as an observer; and also that the purposes of his presence are, first to advise the person being questioned and to observe whether or not the interview is being conducted properly and fairly, and, secondly to facilitate communication with the person being interviewed.

4.6.7 People acting as appropriate adults may interpret these guidelines in different ways and it is important to discuss them with the appropriate adult before the interview begins. If the appropriate adult is a professional, e.g. a social worker, he should be familiar with the process of 'facilitating communication with the client', which means enabling the detainee to tell his version of events as effectively as possible. It is not the appropriate adult's role to interpret this part of the Code of Practice as meaning that he is in a position to put pressure on the detainee to talk in the interview nor should he influence him to alter his account. If possible the solicitor and the appropriate adult should agree what their respective roles are in the interview so that they do not intervene at the same time. For example, it could be agreed that the appropriate adult will intervene on issues related to the detainee's health and welfare, while the solicitor will intervene, if necessary, on legal issues.

4.6.8 Some cases (particularly *R* v. *Lewis (Martin)* [1996] Crim LR 260, CA: see **2.6.3**) have suggested that although an appropriate adult may have greater insight into the difficulties of a person with a low IQ, the role of the appropriate adult and the solicitor during interview are essentially similar. This is to ensure that:

(a) the accused fully understands his rights;
(b) the interview is conducted correctly;
(c) the police do not abuse their position;
(d) the accused is able to make himself clearly understood; and
(e) the accused clearly understands what is being put to him.

4.6.9 In the *Lewis* case, the suspect had an IQ of 69 which was not recognised at the police station, nor raised at trial. Although a solicitor was present at the interview, no appropriate adult was called. The appeal was rejected because the confession, although obtained in breach of the Code, i.e. in the absence of an appropriate adult, was not unreliable as a solicitor was present. However, the court criticised the solicitor for failing to obtain evidence of his client's mental disorder which must have been apparent to him by the time of trial, since at the time of arrest he was on probation with a condition of psychiatric treatment.

4.6.10 Some non-professional appropriate adults, for example, family members, appear to think that part of their role is to press the detainee into making an admission. If the solicitor is concerned this may be the case, it is important to stress to them that it is for the solicitor to give advice on legal matters – their role is to ensure that their relative is not too distressed or under too much pressure in the interview. It is the role of both the appropriate adult and the solicitor to ensure that the police officer is aware of the suspect's particular difficulties and that special care is exercised throughout the interview.

4.7 ASSISTANCE AFTER THE INTERVIEW

Diversion

4.7.1 The detainee can be diverted from charge in a number of ways:

- no further action;
- warning/reprimand (under 18 only);
- caution/conditional caution;
- fixed penalty notice/penalty notice for disorder;

- bailed to return to the police station at a later date pending a decision to charge;
- sectioned under the Act.

4.7.2 In relation to the latter option, if the detainee has been assessed by a mental health practitioner, informal (i.e. voluntary) or compulsory admission to hospital under the civil sections of the Act may be appropriate. (See **Appendix 1** for the full text of these sections.) The only prerequisites for informal admission are that the patient does not resist admission or continued residence in hospital and that the hospital managers and the care team have made a bed available based upon the person's need for care and treatment. Compulsory admission may be indicated even though the detainee agrees to informal admission to hospital. This may be appropriate if his current mental state, together with reliable evidence of past experience, strongly suggests that he will change his mind about staying in hospital voluntarily with a resulting risk to his health/safety or protection of others. If the detainee is to be admitted to hospital, this can be done whether he is already at the hospital for a psychiatric examination or still at the police station. If the hospital where he is being examined arranges the admission, then the custody officer/CPS can decide either to take no further action on the case or the detainee could be bailed to return to the station at a later date. There is no need for him to be brought back to the station for this to be done.

4.7.3 Solicitors can make representations to both the officer in the case and the custody officer on whether or not the detainee should be charged. However, save where a caution might be indicated or in cases of very minor offences, the decision to prosecute lies with the CPS. CPS Direct operates at all police stations and is a statutory scheme whereby the CPS are involved in all stages of the charging and prosecution process. The CPS will look at the seriousness of the alleged offence and whether the incident can be shown to be an isolated event or whether it is part of a developing pattern of behaviour which may put the public at risk in the future.

4.7.4 If there is a decision not to charge and to take no further action, then that is the end of the matter. If the detainee has support in the community but is not taking it up, it might be appropriate to encourage him to cooperate with those concerned with his care, particularly if it will help to avoid further contact with the police.

4.7.5 Both the CPS and the custody officer have a duty to take into account alternatives (listed above) to prosecution (C.NFG.16A). Consideration must be had to Home Office Circular 30/2005 which contains cautioning guidelines. If the police/CPS are willing to caution, it is important that the solicitor explains to the detainee the full implications of the caution, including the fact that it will remain on his list of criminal convictions for three years and might be used against him if he finds himself in the same position again. Someone can only be cautioned if he understands the effect of his actions. This can cause difficulty with some clients, and so the solicitor must satisfy himself that the detainee is able to comprehend that what he has done is wrong and that effectively he is being given an official 'ticking-off '. The appropriate adult must be present when the caution is given.

4.7.6 Provision for conditional cautioning is one of the measures introduced by the Criminal Justice Act 2003 (Part 3, ss.22–27). A conditional caution is a new disposal available for adults and 16 and 17 year olds who are willing to admit their guilt. The scheme is aimed at cases where the public interest would be met more effectively by offenders carrying out specified conditions (which are attached to the caution) rather than being prosecuted. The conditions must help rehabilitate the offender and/or ensure that he makes reparation for the effects of the offence on the victim or the wider community. In respect of mentally disordered offenders, the person being cautioned must be well enough to be able to understand and where necessary undertake the conditions. Offenders who fail to comply with the conditions will usually be prosecuted for the original offence. There is no requirement that an admission be made by an offender in a cautioned interview under PACE before a conditional caution can be offered.

4.7.7 If the detainee is bailed to return to the police station at a later date it can be for a number of reasons. The police may need to make further inquiries into the alleged offence, or the CPS may require more time to decide whether the detainee should be charged and if a prosecution is in the public interest. This gives the solicitor the opportunity to consider making representations, at this stage, to the CPS not to charge. It will normally be advisable to obtain a psychiatric report to support the representations particularly when addressing the CPS Code of Practice (see **Appendix 6**). If the detainee is currently receiving outpatient treatment, then it might be advisable to instruct his doctor. Funding can be obtained by asking the detainee to sign Form CDS2 and requesting an extension to cover the cost of the report. See **Chapter 6** on how to instruct the psychiatrist.

4.7.8 If the report is helpful, consideration should be given to disclosing it (with the client's express agreement) to the police/Crown Prosecution Service with an accompanying letter highlighting the main points of the report which assist the representations to divert the client from the criminal justice process. It is useful to consider quoting the Home Office Circular 66/90 (see **Appendix 4**) as well as the CPS Code of Practice on whether it is in the public interest for the client to be prosecuted. If the CPS has been sent a psychiatric report by the solicitor it can ask to have the client examined by a psychiatrist instructed by the CPS. In this situation, the client is not obliged to attend such an appointment, but it is useful to do so if it could result in the client not being prosecuted. The same difficulty arises in relation to confidentiality as discussed in **3.6.6**. During the examination the client may be asked questions about the offence and he should be advised, where possible, not to make any admissions or discuss the evidence.

Charge and bail

4.7.9 If the CPS is of the view that the detainee should be prosecuted, the matter will be referred back to the custody officer for charge. This must be done in the presence of the appropriate adult, who is also given a copy of the charge sheet.

4.7.10 The detainee must be granted bail until his first appearance at court unless any of the following conditions apply:

(a) the information given regarding his name or address is unsatisfactory;
(b) detention is necessary for his own protection or other people's protection or to prevent loss or damage to property;
(c) there are reasonable grounds to believe he would fail to appear in court or interfere with witnesses/evidence;
(d) in the case of an imprisonable offence, the custody officer has reasonable grounds for believing that the detention of the client is necessary to prevent the commission of further offences.

If he is also a juvenile, he can be detained in his own interests (PACE, s.38(1)).

4.7.11 Bail can be granted subject to any conditions available to a magistrates' court save that the custody officer cannot bail someone to reside at a bail hostel. In cases involving mentally disordered suspects, the custody officer's usual objections are that the detainee may harm himself or others. If his current or previous behaviour appears to put others at risk, then it is unlikely he will be granted bail and he will be kept in custody to be produced at court the following morning. The solicitor must always address the issue of bail as continued detention may exacerbate the detainee's mental disorder. If the detainee is charged, it is advisable to complete legal aid forms for court so that legal aid can be applied for as soon as possible.

CHAPTER 5

First appearance in the magistrates' court

This chapter does not deal with the first appearance in the youth court although some of the considerations are common to both courts. For a full analysis of youth court procedure see Ashford, Chard and Redhouse, *Defending Young People in the Criminal Justice System* (LAG, 2009).

5.1 FUNDING

5.1.1 An application for a representation order should be made at the first available opportunity. Chapter 6 of Rodger Ede and Anthony Edwards, *Criminal Defence* (3rd edn, Law Society, 2008) provides a full analysis of practice and procedure in applying for a representation order. In respect of mentally disordered offenders, the important test under the interests of justice criteria is whether the defendant is able to understand the court proceedings or present his case. (See CDS14 Part B.4 – reasons for wanting representation.) It is important the solicitor includes information about the defendant's mental health history, current mental state and whether he has a learning disability, as these are all factors that can affect his participation in the court process.

5.1.2 There may be occasions where a defendant is too ill or does not have the capacity to sign the application form. If that is the case then the forms can be signed by:

- the applicant's attorney or deputy appointed under the Mental Capacity Act 2005;
- the nearest relative or guardian;
- a person acting as a litigation friend;
- any other person acting in the applicant's best interests and who has sufficient knowledge of the applicant's financial affairs to be able to sign the declaration on the applicant's behalf.

5.2 TAKING INSTRUCTIONS

5.2.1 Whether the defendant appears at court on bail or in custody, at the first meeting, the solicitor will need to take, as far as circumstances allow, full instructions including the details set out in the checklists in **Appendix 8**.

Consideration should be given to obtaining the defendant's consent to consult with all or any of the following:

(a) consultant psychiatrist (past or present);
(b) social worker;
(c) key worker;
(d) community psychiatric nurse (CPN);
(e) hostel staff;
(f) probation officer;
(g) family.

5.2.2 When discussing a defendant's previous contact with the mental health services, it is helpful to cover in detail his history of compliance with treatment, both in hospital and in the community, in particular the level of care in the community offered to him and whether he has accepted it. Patients often have a period of compliance after discharge from hospital followed by stopping medication and/or disengaging from the mental health services. This may lead to a deterioration in mental state. If the defendant is currently being prescribed medication, it is helpful to identify who has prescribed this medication and whether or not he has been taking it and, if not, the reason why he has stopped. Frequently people stop taking their medication because they believe they are 'better' and no longer need it or because they can no longer tolerate the adverse side effects which often occur when taking medication. The advocate must establish whether the defendant is willing to recommence treatment and, if so, whether an outpatient appointment can be obtained for him before the first hearing date or shortly thereafter.

5.2.3 Before being able to decide on the strategy to take in the case, it is important to ascertain the patient's attitude towards medical treatment generally and whether or not he would be willing to go to hospital (if indicated) or receive outpatient treatment in the community. As many clients are anxious to avoid any further treatment, the advocate must make sure that the defendant is willing for him to pursue a 'medical disposal' of his case. The advocate must respect his instructions in this respect and resist colluding with the court to effect a disposal of the case which the client opposes, even if the solicitor feels it is in his client's best interests. However, if the court orders an adjournment of the case to a date when the defendant can be assessed by psychiatric services, there is little that the defence advocate can do to resist this.

5.2.4 Members of the defendant's family may attend court. They can be an invaluable source of background information, especially in the case of defendants with learning difficulties. They can also offer practical support, for instance in connection with a bail application (see **5.6** below). Note however that frequently family members will have very strong and often justifiable concerns about the defendant's treatment by police and/or health or social services. They may well paint a much more serious picture of his illness, vulnerability or dangerousness than he is prepared to accept. It is essential the solicitor adheres closely to the defendant's instructions and explains his professional duty and role to the defendant's family.

5.2.5 When obtaining advance disclosure careful reading of it is required for evidence of unusual behaviour or responses by the defendant during the course of his arrest or detention, which is often an indicator that there may be mental health issues to be raised in case. The list of previous convictions should be checked for any previous Mental Health Act disposals. The examination report of the AHCP is not routinely disclosed with the custody record and the sooner it can be obtained the better. Similarly if there is any s.136 documentation, this is also helpful in providing an early assessment of the defendant's mental state on arrest. It should be included in any letter of instruction to an independent psychiatrist (see **Chapter 6**).

5.3 STRATEGY AND OPTIONS

5.3.1 After taking initial instructions, the solicitor will need to consider whether he wishes to obtain a medical report on the defendant. This will depend on a number of factors including the defendant's wishes as well as the probable outcome of the case. If the solicitor is proposing to make representations to the CPS on discontinuance he will undoubtedly need to obtain a medical report, ideally before the case comes before the magistrates on the next occasion (see **5.8** below).

5.3.2 If the case does not come within the CPS guidelines for discontinuance, the solicitor's decision on whether to obtain a medical report will depend on the defendant's likely plea and the purpose of a report in his case. The solicitor should decide whether a report will be helpful before plea or after plea and if so for what purpose. It may also need to be obtained to effect transfer from prison to hospital for treatment (see **6.5.1 (xii)**).

5.3.3 If the defendant is mute or otherwise incapable of giving instructions due to severe learning disability or due to persistent delusions which affect communication, it is more than likely that he will need to be seen by a psychiatrist before proceeding to plea. There is a possibility he may be deemed 'unfit to plead'. The solicitor should always instruct a psychiatrist to examine the defendant to address these points specifically. In most instances, if the defendant is unfit to plead he is also likely to be suffering from a mental disorder under the Act. The magistrates' court may proceed under the provisions of s.11(1) of the Powers of Criminal Courts (Sentencing) Act (PCC(S)A) 2000 and s.37(3) of the Act, or on a trial on insanity (see **Chapter 7**).

5.4 MENTAL HEALTH ASSESSMENT SCHEMES

5.4.1 Concern at the number of mentally disordered offenders remanded in custody for long periods while awaiting medical reports or a transfer to hospital has led to the establishment of a number of court Mental Health Assessment Schemes around the country, usually run by the local Primary Care Trust. The schemes vary widely from court to court. Some are staffed by an AMHP and two doctors, some by a single doctor, and others consist of a CPN or AMHP. The aim of these schemes is to provide the court with timely information regarding the defendant's mental state, reducing the need for psychiatric reports and effecting a quicker disposal of the case. Defendants can be referred to the schemes by anyone including the gaolers. Solicitors should acquaint themselves with their local schemes so they are aware of where and when they operate, the staff involved and the particular arrangements in place. The immediate assistance they can offer depends on the level of staffing because, for example, to detain someone under s.3 of the Act, an AMHP is needed to make the application together with two written opinions of s.12 doctors, whereas a remand to hospital under s.35 can be effected on the report of a single doctor.

5.4.2 If the defendant is examined by the staff available on the court scheme, the solicitor will be able to obtain an immediate assessment as to whether a Mental Health Act disposal of the case is a possibility, even if a further remand might be necessary. The assessment can offer invaluable advice about the defendant's mental state, the options available and the mechanics of effecting his admission to hospital where indicated. Most schemes deal principally with defendants remanded into custody or appearing in custody overnight on first appearance. It may well be easier and quicker for the defendant to be seen by the court staff than to obtain a report from the relevant catchment area psychiatrist who may not be available to visit the defendant in custody for a number of weeks. It also has the advantage that it is not necessary to apply for prior authority under the representation order to the Legal Services Commission. There can sometimes be a delay in the defendant being examined by a member of the Mental Health Assessment Scheme if it operates at court on a particular day. In that case the defendant may have to be remanded in custody to that specific date.

5.4.3 The defendant may insist that he is well and has no need to see a doctor. Even if the solicitor disagrees, he should not press the defendant to be examined. The defendant's behaviour may well make his mental health difficulties obvious to the court, in which case the court is likely to order a report on him whether or not he wishes it. The solicitor must advise him that the court has power to order reports notwithstanding his objections and although he does not have to speak to the doctor, it may be in his best interests to do so.

5.5 REPORTS

5.5.1 The court has various powers to order medical reports both before and after plea and to ensure the defendant's cooperation with their preparation. These are in addition to the power to ensure the defendant's cooperation with reports under s.3(6) of the Bail Act 1976.

5.5.2 The responsibility for payment to doctors for reports varies but generally reports ordered by the court to be obtained by the Probation Service are paid for by them, whereas reports provided by the defence must be paid for by the solicitor, with prior authority from the Legal Services Commission. It is important to clarify on each occasion which agency is responsible for requesting and paying for the reports.

5.5.3 Under s.54 of the Act a copy of any medical report prepared for the court must be given to the defendant's solicitor if he is represented. If the defendant is not represented the contents of the report must be explained to him. Either the court or the defendant may request the author of the report to attend to give oral evidence and the defendant may call evidence to rebut the contents of the report.

5.5.4 If the defendant is remanded into custody for the preparation of a report ordered by the magistrates' court, it is advisable to supply the prison psychiatrist (who is often a visiting consultant forensic psychiatrist) with detailed information about the defendant's history and background, particularly if there has been any recent inpatient treatment, as this will assist in a fuller report being provided to the court.

5.5.5 Most prison health care centres are visited at least weekly by a local catchment area psychiatrist with forensic experience and it may well be helpful to find out the details of this doctor so that the defendant's case can be discussed with him. If it appears that the defendant is in need of urgent treatment then contact should be made as soon as possible to try and effect a transfer to hospital under s.48 of the Act. Written reports from two doctors are needed to make the recommendation. A transfer direction made under s.48 automatically places the defendant on a restriction direction throughout the period of transfer.

5.5.6 Prison healthcare centres are not always staffed by trained psychiatrists and do not constitute a 'hospital' within the terms of the Act. Thus the rules in Part IV of the Act regarding medical treatment of detained patients do not apply to prisoners, and treatment cannot be given to a prisoner without his consent unless the common law emergency powers to treat apply. This can mean that floridly psychotic clients go untreated. It is acknowledged that a prison setting is the least appropriate option for care of a mentally disordered offender (see Home Office Circular 66/90, para. 7, **Appendix 4**).

5.5.7 Under section 33.6 of the Code of Practice of the Act, the Primary Care Trust should provide courts, in response to a request under s.9 of the Act, with comprehensive information on the range of facilities available for the admission of defendants subject to the criminal justice process. They should appoint a named person to respond to requests for information and ensure that prompt medical assistance is provided for defendants to assist in the speedy completion of the trial process and the most suitable disposal for the offender.

5.5.8 Under PCC(S)A 2000, s.11(1) the court is obliged to order a report after conviction or after hearing evidence sufficient to establish that the act or omission charged was done if the defendant is or appears to be mentally disordered (see **Chapter 7**).

5.5.9 Under s.157 of the Criminal Justice Act (CJA) 2003, in any case where the offender is or appears to be mentally disordered, the court must obtain and consider a medical report before passing a custodial sentence other than one fixed by law.

5.5.10 Section 35 of the Act allows the convicted or unconvicted defendant to be remanded to a hospital for the preparation of reports. The single medical authority necessary to effect the remand to hospital for a fuller assessment can, if necessary, be provided by the court duty psychiatrist if suitably qualified. It is important to note that this power may be used prior to any indication of plea, if the defendant consents. Remand to hospital under s.35 has the advantage to the defendant of ensuring that he receives care in hospital, undoubtedly clinically preferable to a prison setting. The court may be reluctant to make the order as the section contains no stipulation about where the defendant is held, e.g. on a locked or open ward. The court may think that the hospital wing of a remand prison protects the public more effectively and sometimes tries to obtain assurances of secure conditions from the admitting doctor before making a decision. A hospital can sometimes be reluctant to admit a highly disturbed defendant under s.35, as the Act provides no power under this section to treat the patient without consent, save for common law emergency powers.

5.5.11 Paragraph 33.29 of the Act's Code of Practice recommends that where a patient remanded under s.35 is in need of medical treatment which cannot otherwise be given, the patient should be referred back to court by the clinician in charge of his care as soon as possible, with an appropriate recommendation and written assessment of whether he is in a fit state to attend court. If there is a delay in securing a court date, consideration should be given to whether the patient meets the criteria for detention under Part 2 of the Act (i.e. s.2 or 3 civil admission sections) to enable compulsory treatment to be given. This will be concurrent with, and not a replacement for, the remand made by the court. If the defendant is willing to enter hospital by this method and he is detained under s.2, or more likely s.3, the task of persuading the CPS that the public interest will not be served by continuing to prosecute him can be made easier as there is little difference in practice between the civil treatment under s.3 and a hospital/guardianship order under s.37 of the Act.

5.6 BAIL

5.6.1 A mentally disordered defendant has the same general rights of bail under the Bail Act 1976 (with the exceptions under CJPOA 1994) as any other offender and the general presumption in favour of bail operates. However the solicitor must consider not only the usual general objections under Sched. 1, Part 1, para. 2 (failure to surrender to bail, commission of further offences, interference with witnesses, etc.) but also whether the court may find that a remand in custody is necessary for the defendant's own protection (Sched. 1, Part 1, para. 3). Before the case is called the solicitor should have explored thoroughly the various means of providing treatment to the defendant outside prison either in the community or in hospital.

5.6.2 The bail conditions particularly appropriate to mentally disordered defendants may include:

(a) **Residence at an address**

The court may impose a condition of residence to ensure that the defendant stays in the community and receives outpatient treatment. Information about what arrangements there are for regular visits by a CPN or Assertive Outreach Team or Crisis Resolution Team from the local Primary Care Trust should be investigated and if possible this should be offered to the defendant. This will assure the court that the defendant's mental state is being regularly monitored by professionals.

(b) **Keep appointments for medical treatment**

If the solicitor has been able to make contact with the community team and appointments have been fixed, then offering the court the defendant's agreement to keep to such a condition might also assist in the bail application, as consistent support from outside agencies will also be helpful in reducing other objections to bail such as likelihood of commission of further offences and failure to surrender to bail.

(c) **Cooperation with the preparation of a medical report**

The court may use its power under s.3(6) of the Bail Act 1976 to impose a bail condition to cooperate with the preparation of such a report. This power may be exercised at any stage of the proceedings.

(d) **Residence at bail or other hostel**

Most bail hostels are unwilling to accept actively mentally ill residents, but hostels specialising in clients with mental health difficulties do also exist. Key workers at such hostels are able to remind defendants to keep appointments and to supervise medication as well as to monitor their mental state. In the case of people with learning disabilities who require a measure of social support and guidance, a highly staffed hostel may be an appropriate bail address. Sometimes the defendant will be already residing at such a hostel and obviously confirmation that he can return there is essential. Otherwise assistance from the Probation Service and bail support schemes may be able to identify a suitable placement.

(e) **Residence at psychiatric hospital**

The defendant may be admitted to hospital on remand in a number of ways. If he is already an informal patient and the treating doctor agrees, a condition of residence may be imposed requiring him to reside at a particular hospital. If, during a period of remand to a hospital, the hospital wants to discharge the defendant as no longer needing treatment, this will obviously place him in breach of bail. It is important to liaise regularly with the hospital to ensure that a bed is still available for the defendant before each remand date. If they wish to discharge him, the solicitor should find out the arrangements that have been made for his accommodation and aftercare, the names and details of those who will provide this, and the full address of the accommodation to assist in an application to vary the defendant's bail. This should obviously be done before he is discharged.

Otherwise, the defendant could be admitted to hospital under a civil section of the Act, i.e. s.2 or s.3. The criminal proceedings can then be adjourned for as long as the court thinks fit whilst he is receiving treatment under that section. At this stage the solicitor should consider whether or not to make representations to the CPS to discontinue the proceedings (see **5.8** below).

5.7 PROTECTION OF DEFENDANT AND OTHERS

Protecting the suicidal defendant

5.7.1 Representing a defendant in custody who is expressing an intention to harm himself may place the solicitor in a difficult and worrying position, particularly when there is no report available to the court and the defendant is likely to be refused bail. It is sometimes difficult to assess the seriousness of such threats and therefore all threats, whether explicit or implicit, must be taken seriously. The prisoner escort record (PER) form accompanies all prisoners from the police station to court and prison. It includes a record of the examination of the defendant by the AHCP, psychiatrist or CPN. This should alert the jailors to any suicide or self-harm risk and they should make frequent checks on the defendant in the cells. If there is a mental health assessment scheme at the court, the defendant may have already been referred to the scheme by the jailors. If not, the solicitor should consider making the referral sooner rather than later. In the absence of a court scheme, the solicitor can ask the custody officer in charge of security at the magistrates' court to call the AHCP to examine the defendant.

5.7.2 The defendant may say that a remand in custody will make him harm himself. A bail application based on this assertion may well be refused on the basis that he should be in custody for his own protection unless a suitable alternative package can be arranged where remand to hospital is possible. If the defendant's application for bail fails and a hospital bed is available, the solicitor should ask the court to make clear on the warrant to the prison any concerns about the defendant's mental state. A similar note must be made on the PER which accompanies the prisoner. After the hearing, it can be helpful for the solicitor to discuss his concerns about the defendant with the prison medical officer so as to obtain appropriate care for him in custody. It is of course possible for a prisoner to be transferred to hospital for treatment under s.48 of the Act (see **Appendix 1**).

Protection of others

5.7.3 The solicitor may be placed in a difficult position if the defendant makes clear and, apparently serious, threats against other people. Generally the duty of confidentiality is paramount, although in extreme circumstances it may be overruled (see **3.4.10**).

5.7.4 More frequently, the defendant's behaviour may be intimidating to a point where the solicitor is concerned for his own safety. This is a particular problem for a duty solicitor when he and the defendant have no previous knowledge of each other. Gaolors often give warnings about how dangerous the defendant is, most of which turn out to be well intentioned. If a solicitor is worried about being locked in a cell or an interview room with a defendant, then he should bring this to the jailor's attention to ensure that appropriate interview facilities are provided for protection of the solicitor.

5.8 THE ARGUMENT FOR DISCONTINUANCE

5.8.1 The solicitor must consider whether or not discontinuance of the charges is a possibility, taking into account a number of factors including the seriousness of the charge and the Code for Crown Prosecutors (see **Appendix 6**). If the solicitor decides that such a strategy is possible, he will undoubtedly need to obtain a medical report, ideally before the case comes before the magistrates' court on the next occasion (see **Chapter 6** for full details on how to instruct the expert).

5.8.2 Once the medical report has been obtained, it must be discussed with the defendant and his authority must be obtained to disclose it to the CPS if appropriate. The particular criteria to be considered by the CPS as to whether the case should be discontinued are set out in 'The Full Code Test' at para. 5 of the Code for Crown Prosecutors. It sets out two stages. The first stage is consideration of the evidence. If the case passes the evidential stage, the CPS must proceed to the second stage and decide if a prosecution is in the public interest. The particular criteria relating to mentally disordered offenders are found in para.5.10g of the Code:

> A prosecution is less likely to be needed if . . . the defendant is elderly or is, or was at the time of the offence, suffering from significant physical or mental ill health, unless the offence, is serious or there is real possibility that it may be repeated. The Crown Prosecution Service, where necessary applies Home Office guidelines about how to deal with mentally disordered offenders. Crown Prosecutors must balance the desirability of diverting a defendant who is suffering from significant mental or physical ill health with the need to safeguard the general public.

Crown Prosecutors are reminded by the Code to apply the principles of Home Office Circulars, the most relevant being 12/95 and 66/90 (see **Appendix 4**).

5.8.3 The arguments put forward by the solicitor in the letter of representation must follow these criteria and should show a realistic understanding of the seriousness of the offence and the likely sentence as well as a regard for the victim (where relevant). If the defendant has previous convictions for similar offences or there is an apparent risk of repeat offences (e.g. offences involving neighbours about whom the defendant has developed delusional beliefs) the question of future risk must be dealt with as far as possible. If it is clear that the offence is due to a short-term lapse in compliance with medication after a long period of stability in the community and that the previous status quo can be or has already been restored, the argument for discontinuance will be strengthened. The CPS will generally consult with both police and witnesses in the case so they need to receive the representations in reasonable time before the next hearing.

5.8.4 If the defendant has been admitted to hospital under s.3, this provides a good reason for arguing that the prosecution is unnecessary as if the likely disposal is s.37 (without s.41), the end result is effectively the same.

CHAPTER 6

Instructing the expert

6.1 GENERAL CONSIDERATIONS

6.1.1 It is very unusual in cases involving mentally disordered offenders not to instruct an expert to assist in the case. When and whom to instruct, as well as the purpose of obtaining a report, will depend on a number of factors, as advice might be sought on any of the following:

- diagnosis;
- mental state at time of the offence;
- insanity;
- *mens rea*;
- current mental state;
- fitness to plead;
- diminished responsibility;
- duress;
- provocation;
- ability to participate effectively in trial process;
- admissibility of interview (s.34 inferences) or other confessions;
- issues on giving evidence (s.35);
- transfer from prison to hospital;
- disposal;
- risk assessment; and
- discontinuance.

6.2 CHOOSING THE EXPERT

6.2.1 Psychiatrists specialise in different areas of psychiatry such as learning disability, forensic, children and adolescents, old age and general psychiatry. Solicitors need to consider what expertise is required for each individual case in order to instruct a psychiatrist in that field. The majority of patients in psychiatric hospitals are treated by general psychiatrists and within that there are specialisms, e.g. rehabilitation. The general psychiatrist may often be best placed to write a report as he will know the patient well; however it should be born in mind that in more complex cases a forensic psychiatrist is to be preferred as they have more experience of writing reports in the criminal justice system. There is a statutory requirement for psychiatric evidence in fitness to plead, insanity cases and in certain disposals and interim orders under the Act. In respect of the majority of admissions under the Act, at least one doctor must be 's.12 approved'.

6.2.2 If it is likely that the defendant will be sentenced to some form of psychiatric disposal, e.g a. s.37 hospital order, instructing his existing or recent RC or the catchment area consultant, with a view to finding a local bed for him, would be more appropriate. Even if the defendant is receiving treatment from a consultant, the solicitor may need to obtain a report from an independent doctor for a second opinion on diagnosis and/or treatment. When a defendant is accused of a violent or sexual offence a full 'risk assessment' prepared by a forensic psychiatrist will be necessary (see **Chapter 11**). This should make a prediction about the risk of future danger, based on all that is known about the defendant including his history, psychological make-up and current mental state.

6.2.3 Whom to instruct obviously depends on the facts of the individual case. An informal approach to a psychiatrist for advice on the case is sometimes useful to help point the solicitor in the right direction as to whom to instruct and what reports might be required. Sometimes the psychiatrist, after he has read the papers, may advise that the solicitor obtains a psychologist's report too. Psychologists deal with the defendant's functionality and personality structure whereas the psychiatrist tends to deal with diagnosis, mental illness and capacity. Thus they may be instructed not only in cases of learning disability but also where the diagnosis is personality disorder and a detailed assessment of the defendant's personality structure is required.

6.2.4 There may be some overlap between reports. For example, in the case of a defendant with a learning disability, where his low intelligence may be a factor in the court's decision as to whether evidence should be excluded or fitness to plead is an issue, a clinical psychologist would be instructed to carry out the initial formal psychometric testing. The results produced will help form the basis of instructions to the psychiatrist. As clinical psychologists also specialise in different areas of work it is important to only instruct someone who is a chartered psychologist and, depending on the facts of the case, who has one of the following specialisms: clinical, forensic, neuropsychology, health, occupational or education. In some cases the opinion of a psychologist alone will be sufficient, e.g. on adaptations for trial or admissibility of interview. A psychologist may also be instructed where the defendant is diagnosed with an autistic spectrum disorder (ASD). Examination or assessment of someone with ASD should be carried out where possible by a psychologist with experience and training in working with people with these disorders.

6.3 PROCEDURE/GUIDANCE ON EXPERT EVIDENCE

6.3.1 Schedule 5 to the Criminal Procedure (Amendment) Rules 2009, SI 2009/2087 incorporates and simplifies Part 33 of the Criminal Procedure Rules

2005, SI 2005/384 in respect of the procedure relating to expert evidence in the magistrates' and Crown Courts as well as the Court of Appeal. The Rules are set out in full at **Appendix 9** and give very helpful guidance on the content of an expert's report. They summarise what information the expert must provide in particular, regarding his expertise, the information relied upon to prepare the report and the reasons for his opinion. The Rules also give guidance on service of expert evidence, pre-hearing discussion of expert evidence and the court's power to direct that evidence is only given by a single joint expert. In the latter situation, where the court gives a direction under Rule 33.7 for a single joint expert to be used, each of the co-defendants may give instructions to the expert. It is important that the solicitor sets out clearly the particular questions he wants dealt with in respect of his client. In *R* v. *Redbridge Magistrates' Court* (see **7.3.5(b)**) the court criticised a report which entirely failed to comply with the requirements of Part 33(3), which should be a basic condition of admissibility.

6.3.2 The Act's Code of Practice also gives guidance to doctors who are asked to assess the defendant for the court. They are advised to explain to the defendant the limits of confidentiality in relation to the report and that any information disclosed and the medical opinion could be relevant not only to medical opinion by the court but also to the imposition of a punitive sentence or to its length. In cases of sentencing, if the doctor cannot say whether a hospital order will be appropriate, he should recommend an interim hospital order under s.38 so that the court can reach a conclusion on the most appropriate and effective disposal. Further guidance is given as to the contents of the report (para. 33.16 of the Code). It should set out:

- the material on which the report is based;
- how that material relates to the opinion given;
- where relevant, how the opinion may relate to any other trial issue;
- factors relating to the presence of mental disorder that may affect the risk that patients pose to themselves or to others, including the risk of re-offending; and
- if admission to hospital is recommended what, if any, special treatment or security is recommended and whether the doctor represents an organisation that is able to provide what is required.

It is specifically stated that the report should not speculate about guilt or innocence.

6.4 THE LETTER OF INSTRUCTION

6.4.1 The letter of instruction to the expert should be as detailed as possible, particularly where he has no prior knowledge of the defendant. It is essential to establish that the expert will be able to see him and write the report in good time so that, if appropriate, it can be submitted to the CPS for their consideration before the court date. If this cannot be done, an adjournment may need to be sought. Solicitors must also agree a fee for the report which is acceptable to the LSC so it is advisable to apply for prior authority (Form CDS4) before instructions are sent. If the solicitor has been asked to obtain the report by the court, it is rare for the LSC to refuse the request. The solicitor should consider carefully the purpose for which the opinion is sought before deciding whether to send the psychiatrist the defendant's instructions (if any have been obtained).

6.4.2 Even though the questions put to the expert will vary according to the advice the solicitor is seeking, the documents that should be sent will be broadly the same. Below is a list of items that should, depending on their relevance, be enclosed with the letter of instruction:

- previous psychological assessments/reports;
- previous psychiatric assessments/reports;
- GP records;
- school records/correspondence particularly if the defendant has received a statement of special educational needs;
- Child and Adolescent Mental Health Services (CAMHS) notes (under 18s);
- medical records;
- indictment;
- transcript of interview;
- depositions (relevant to mental state/behaviour);
- custody record;
- case summary;
- transcript of taped interviews;
- record of AHCP's examination of defendant at police station;
- list of previous convictions.

Special consideration should be given to whether the defendant's instructions are to be sent to the psychiatrist because the psychiatrist is likely to refer to them in the report, and they would then cease to be privileged and be available to the prosecution.

6.5 INSTRUCTING A PSYCHIATRIST

6.5.1 The letter of instruction should set out the brief facts of the case and then the issues on which advice is sought and at which the report is to be directed. These may include any of the following:

(i) **Diagnosis**
In some cases it will not be clear if the defendant is suffering from a mental disorder or, if he is, the type, nature and degree of that disorder. The psychiatrist should be instructed to confirm, where possible, the diagnosis.

(ii) **Mental state at the time of the offence**

Having made a diagnosis, he should be asked if the nature or degree of the disorder at the material time of the offence is such as to enable the defendant to rely on one of the defences at (iii)–(iv) below, i.e. insanity or lack of *mens rea*.

(iii) **Insanity**

The test for insanity is in the *M'Naghten* Rules (see **Chapter 10** for full text) and should be put in the letter. The psychiatrist must be asked to comment on whether at the time of committing the act:

(i) the defendant was acting under such a defect of reason, from disease of the mind
(ii) that he did he not know the nature and quality of the act he was doing or
(iii) if he did know it, that he did not know that it was wrong.

If the psychiatrist advises that insanity is not available as a defence, he should then be asked to advise if, as at the time of the offence, the defendant could have been capable of forming the necessary *mens rea*.

(iv) ***Mens rea***

It is important to know if the defendant's mental state at the time of the offence was such as to make him incapable of forming *mens rea*. The elements of each offence that the defendant is charged with should be set out in the letter. Consideration should be given to sending the doctor the relevant section(s) of the particular Act the defendant is charged under to ensure that the psychiatrist understands the *mens rea* for that offence. Some crimes require a 'specific intention' on the part of a defendant to commit an offence, whereas others require a basic intention or recklessness. For example, the case of *DPP* v. *Majewski* (1977) AC 443 held that intoxication can negate crimes of specific intent but not of basic intent. Those with an ASD may not be able to form specific intent as they often have no appreciation of the consequences of their actions or an intention that those consequences occur. In some cases therefore, psychiatric reports can have a critical role in showing the degree of specific intent or recklessness possessed by a disordered defendant at the time of the allegation arising. Identifying the *mens rea* required to commit a particular offence and applying that to the defendant with his particular mental disorder is very important. It is sensible to request that the psychiatrist's opinion on *mens rea* is put in a separate report if he is being asked to advise additionally on fitness to plead.

(v) **Current mental state**

Under this head the psychiatrist may be asked to address the effect of the continued prosecution on the defendant's mental state, particularly if the solicitor is considering making representations to the CPS to discontinue proceedings (see xv below). If a psychiatric disposal is indicated, the court will also want information on the defendant's current mental state. In other cases, it may be important for the solicitor to obtain an assessment of his current mental state in order to know whether or not the defendant is fit to plead.

(vi) **Fitness to plead**

The traditional legal test for fitness to plead was set out by Alderson B in *R* v. *Pritchard* (1836) 7 CP 303 (see **Chapter 10** for the full criteria). Other cases have approved and expanded the test over the years and are helpful when it comes to formulating questions for the psychiatrist to deal with. The solicitor should ask some or all the following questions:

- Has the defendant sufficient intellect to comprehend the proceedings so as to make a proper defence?
- Does he understand the charges?
- Can he decide whether to plead guilty or not?
- Can he instruct his solicitor/barrister (he must be able to give instructions on what any person in the witness box is saying in court)?
- Is he capable of exercising his right to challenge a juror (indictable offences)?
- Does he understand the details of the evidence? Note that he must be able to listen to the evidence, understand the words used by the witness and the import of them and then to be able to respond if the witness says something untrue or different from his own memory. Clearly the consequence of the defendant not being able to instruct his advocate on the evidence and issues as they arise throughout the trial is that he might not receive a fair trial.
- Can he give evidence in his own defence?

It is not sufficient for the psychiatrist to conclude that the defendant is fit to plead to the charges if he simply demonstrates that he, in some general sense, knew right from wrong, or if he believes he should plead guilty if he thinks he has 'done wrong'. It will be necessary for the psychiatrist to go through with the defendant the specific counts on the indictment.

(vii) **Ability to participate effectively in the trial process**

If the psychiatrist considers that the defendant is fit to plead, advice should be sought on what modifications to the trial process might be needed to ensure that the defendant can participate effectively in the trial process. He should be asked to advise whether there are any psychological factors which would impair the defendant's ability to understand the proceedings and participate effectively in the trial process. Reference might need to be made to any results and conclusions of psychological testing. For example, the defendant's level of functioning may be such that he can only cope with day-to-day needs, i.e. familiar concepts with limited options, but does not have the sophisticated ability to deal with variable and multi-optional situations. If this is the case, the psychiatrist should recommend what adaptations to the trial process should be put in place 'to assist a vulnerable defendant to understand and participate in' proceedings with reference to *Practice Direction (Criminal Proceedings: Consolidation)* para. III.30 (as inserted by *Practice Direction (Criminal Proceedings: Further Directions)* [2007] 1 WLR 1790) which is set out in full at **Appendix 7**. The Practice Direction (PD) applies to defendants before the adult or youth court who suffer from a mental disorder under the Act or who have any other significant impairment of intelligence or social functioning. The questions to be put to the psychiatrist might include whether the defendant requires:

- frequent breaks;
- assistance in understanding the meaning of language used;
- special seating arrangements;
- a supporting adult present;
- use of an intermediary (see **Chapter 9**); and
- to give his evidence by live link (see Youth Justice and Criminal Evidence Act (YJCEA) 1999, s.33A).

The issue of effective participation more commonly arises in cases of defendants with a learning disability rather than those with mental illness, although someone who is floridly psychotic could also be impaired in this situation.

(viii) **Ability to testify**

Section 35 of the Criminal Justice and Public Order Act 1994 allows the drawing of inferences from the failure of a defendant to testify at his trial. Section 1(b) states that such inferences should not be drawn if it appears to the court that the physical or mental condition of the accused makes it undesirable for him to testify. The psychiatrist should be asked to identify any possible psychological or psychiatric factors which would impair the defendant's ability to give coherent testimony or affect the reliability of his evidence.

(ix) **Diminished responsibility and provocation**

Both these defences arise in relation to charges of murder only. In the case of diminished responsibility the test is set out in s.2 of the Homicide Act 1957 (see **Chapter 10** for full discussion of this defence). However experienced the psychiatrist might be, the solicitor must set out the elements of the test to be addressed in the report:

- was the defendant suffering from such abnormality of mind
- as to substantially impair his mental responsibility for his acts/omissions
- in doing or being a party to the killing.

The psychiatrist must also be asked to comment on the defendant's conduct before, during and after the killing in the context of his abnormality of mind.

The defence of provocation can be found in the Homicide Act 1957, s.3 and is discussed fully in **10.6**. Psychiatric evidence might be relevant and the following questions for the letter of instruction should be considered:

- Does the defendant's mental disorder make it more or less likely that he lost self-control?
- Did the mental disorder affect the gravity of the provocation to the defendant?

(x) **Duress**

This can be an important defence available to mentally disordered defendants as they can be more vulnerable to pressure from others to commit offences. The issues the psychiatrist should be asked to consider are whether in the light of the defendant's mental disorder, he might be more susceptible to pressure and threats than the ordinary person. He should be asked to look at the characteristics of a person with the same difficulties as the defendant, as confirmed in the guidance set out in *R* v. *Bowen* (see **10.7.3**) which held that it was relevant in applying the test for duress if the accused belonged to a category of persons less able to resist pressure than people not within that category.

(xi) **Admissibility of interviews or other confessions**

Applications to exclude evidence, in particular interviews, of mentally disordered suspects conducted by the police in the absence of the suitable safeguards, are usually based on a combination of the grounds set out in PACE, ss.76–78. The effective use of suitable expert evidence of the defendant's mental condition at the time of interview is crucial in such cases to demonstrate to the court precisely why the nature of his mental disorder and the circumstances of his interview made it unreliable, oppressive or unfair. Most of the case law turns on three key factors:

(a) the level of the suspect's intelligence;
(b) whether effective legal representation was available; and
(c) whether there was a helpful and alert appropriate adult.

A psychiatrist, often with the assistance of a report from a psychologist, should be asked to make a functional analysis of the interview and to give his opinion on e.g. whether the suspect was 'led' in his interview or had the capacity to comprehend the questions.

(xii) **Transfer from prison to hospital (s.48)**

If the defendant is mentally unwell in prison and is in urgent need of treatment, he can be transferred to hospital (see **9.10.4**). A psychiatrist may need to be instructed to assist in effecting the transfer and advising on the current need for treatment. If the psychiatrist advises that the defendant should be admitted to hospital, he should be asked if he can assist in effecting the admission and arranging the second doctor's opinion, where necessary, for detention under the Act.

(xiii) **Disposals**

All the disposals appropriate to mentally disordered defendants are set out in **Chapter 11**. The solicitor will need to consider the applicability of each sentencing option to the individual case. For example, the doctor may need to be asked to advise on whether it is likely that the defendant will need long-term inpatient care under s.37 (with or without restrictions). If, on the other hand he only requires outpatient treatment, the doctor should be asked to confirm the services provided by the local community mental health team. The psychiatrist should always be asked to give his opinion on the impact of custody on a defendant's mental state. If a s.41 order is a possibility, the court usually requires some form of risk assessment to be done (see xiv below). A risk assessment might also be relevant to the court's deliberations regarding sentencing for certain offences e.g. arson.

(xiv) **Risk assessment**

A risk assessment for the court should assess the extent to which the defendant possesses risk factors which are associated with a risk of violence and/or re-offending in the future. This assessment is often done by both a psychologist and psychiatrist using various assessment tools. If a s.41 restriction order is being considered the test to ask the psychiatrist to consider is, 'is it necessary for the protection of the public from serious harm' that he be made subject to the special restrictions set out in the section. In practice most psychiatrists will consider the defendant's antecedents, both criminal and 'clinical', the nature of the index offence, his response to treatment and an assessment of the risk of further offending. The psychiatrist should also be asked if the defendant could be adequately managed in the community after discharge from hospital without the additional safeguards afforded by s.41.

In respect of sentencing dangerous offenders under CJA 2003, ss.224–236, the court held in the case of *Lang* (see **11.14.8**) that where 'mental abnormality' may be an issue, it might be appropriate for a medical report to be obtained before a sentence is passed 'which is based on significant risk of serious harm to members of the public'. In practice, similar considerations as for s.41 apply. The psychiatrist should also be instructed to confirm what treatment may be available in the community, as the court in *R* v. *C* (see **11.14.11**) confirmed that if the overall sentencing package provides appropriate protection for the public, an IPP (imprisonment for public protection) should not be imposed.

(xv) **Discontinuance**
The letter of instruction should refer to all the relevant elements of the Code for Crown Prosecutors dealing with the grounds where a prosecution 'is less likely to be needed' (see **Appendix 6** for full Code and **5.8**). The psychiatrist will need to be instructed to advise particularly on:

- whether at the time of the offence the defendant was suffering from 'significant mental ill health';
- whether there is a real possibility the offence may be repeated (the psychiatrist may need to do a risk assessment); and
- the effect on the defendant's mental state of a continued prosecution.

6.6 INSTRUCTING A PSYCHOLOGIST

6.6.1 The psychologist will administer a number of psychometric tests including the WAIS (Wechsler Adult Intelligence Scale) which is designed for those aged 16–74 or the WISC (Wechsler Intelligence Scale for Children). These are a series of standardised tests used by psychologists to assess the cognitive and intellectual abilities in children and adults. Wechsler defined intelligence as, 'The global capacity of a person to act purposefully, to think rationally and to deal effectively with his/her environment.' The current version of both tests is number IV and was published in 2008. The WISC comprises a number of sub-tests designed to measure different aspects of a child's cognitive functioning and these sub-tests combine to form five composite scores one of which measures overall intellectual ability, in the form of a full-scale IQ. The others measure intellectual functioning of four specific cognitive domains namely, verbal comprehension index, perceptual reasoning index, working memory and processing speed index. The WAIS involves similar testing with 10 core sub-tests comprising the full scale IQ. WAIS-IV was standardised on a sample of 2,200 people in the age range 16–90 years. The average full scale IQ is 100 with a standard deviation of 15. In a normal distribution, the IQ range of one standard deviation above and below the average (i.e. between 85 and 115) is where approximately 68 per cent of all adults would fall. However, about 50 per cent of the population have IQs between 89 and 111, and about 80 per cent of the population have IQs ranging between 80 and 120, with 10 per cent lying below 80, and 10 per cent falling above 120. People therefore with an IQ of 75 would come within the bottom 10 per cent of the population and are likely to be functioning below the scale of normal average intelligence. Those with an IQ of 55–69 are described as having a 'significant impairment of intellectual functioning'.

6.6.2 The tests used to diagnose ASD include the Autism Diagnostic Observation Schedule – Generic (ADOS-G) and Autism Diagnostic Interview – Revised (ADI-R). The ADOS-G is a semi-structured standardised assessment of communication, social interaction and language and is intended to be used with the standardised interview (ADI-R) of the parent/carer.

6.6.3 It is helpful, if the solicitor already knows the diagnosis of the client, to read the relevant section in DSM-IV to enable the letter of instruction to address particular symptoms that might have a bearing on the charges and proceedings. The psychologist can advise on a number of areas including whether the defendant is suggestible, acquiescent or has a tendency to confabulate.

6.6.4 As with the psychiatrist, the letter of instruction to the psychologist should set out the brief facts of the case and the issues on which advice is sought and at which the report is to be directed. These may include any of the following:

- Where appropriate, a request for a full psychometric testing.
- Is the defendant intellectually impaired?
- Will he have any difficulty in following the trial process?
- Will he be able to give instructions?
- Does he need any special adaptations to the trial process e.g. frequent breaks or assistance in understanding the meaning of the language used? (Consider sending a copy of the Practice Direction in **Appendix 7**.)
- Will he be able to testify?
- Has he shown tendencies to acquiescence, suggestibility or compliance?
- If so, will this affect the veracity of the interview?

6.6.5 The psychologist will need to interview the defendant to perform the necessary testing. That is often done at the solicitor's office and care must be taken to provide a private space where there will be no distraction and to allow the defendant suitable breaks. It is rare for a psychologist to allow another person to be present as this can alter the performance of the person being tested. Psychologists will advise that no tests are ever totally precise in their measurements due to the fact that people perform slightly differently on various occasions. However an experienced psychologist will evaluate and interpret an individual's performance on the scales' sub-tests and make recommendations on these findings. From these, conclusions can be drawn about the defendant's general level of intellectual functioning and his ability to give instructions, testify, participate in the trial process, etc. Sometimes a psychologist's report is sufficient to proceed with the case e.g. where representations are being made to the CPS for discontinuance on the grounds of intellectual impairment or to the court on trial adaptations.

CHAPTER 7

Summary trial

7.1 OVERVIEW

7.1.1 This chapter covers both the youth and magistrates' courts. The youth court is part of the magistrates' court and whilst it has different powers in relation to jurisdiction, secure remands and sentencing, in most other aspects it is procedurally the same as the adult magistrates' court. The rules of evidence are no different from those of any other criminal court.

7.1.2 Preparing for the trial of a mentally disordered offender (whether in the magistrates' court, youth court or Crown Court) presents a number of challenges. In some cases it will have been possible to obtain instructions; in others it will not. Any instructions obtained will, in any event, have to be considered in conjunction with the psychiatric and/or psychological assessments which have been undertaken. The nature and degree of a defendant's mental disorder will dictate to a large extent the form that contested proceedings will take.

7.1.3 A defendant assessed as 'unfit to plead' or unable to participate effectively in proceedings will be dealt with quite differently, depending upon whether he is a defendant in a summary trial or in a trial on indictment. In the Crown Court, as will be seen in **Chapter 10**, the fitness to plead procedure is a two-stage process governed by the Criminal Procedure (Insanity) Act (CP(I)A) 1964 (as amended). It involves first a finding by judge alone as to whether a defendant is fit to plead according to the *Pritchard* criteria. If he is fit, a trial in the usual way will follow; if he is not, a jury will be sworn to consider whether the *actus reus* of the offence(s) charged is proved. If the jury finds the *actus reus* to be proved, a number of disposals under the CP(I)A 1964 are available to the court.

7.1.4 The CP(I)A 1964 does not apply to summary proceedings. Instead, in cases where a defendant is 'unfit', the court applies the statutory procedures set out in s.11(1)(a) of the Powers of Criminal Courts (Sentencing) Act (PCC(S)A 2000 and in s.37(3) of the Act.

7.1.5 In summary proceedings, unlike the Crown Court, there is no 'special verdict' of not guilty by reason of insanity (the 'special verdict' is a finding that the defendant has done the act or made the omission charged, but was insane at the time of the commission of the offence: see **10.3**). In the Crown Court, the CP(I)A 1964 provides for a choice of disposals which follow upon such a verdict. There is no such equivalent in summary proceedings. In summary proceedings, a finding of insanity prevents conviction.

7.1.6 It follows that in summary proceedings there are four different scenarios which could arise:

(i) Where a defendant cannot participate in summary proceedings, under PCC(S)A 2000, s.11(1) the court may proceed in certain circumstances to a finding that the accused did the act or omission charged (referred to throughout this chapter as a fact-finding hearing).The court can then make a hospital/guardianship order under s.37(3) of the Act without convicting him, adjourning for reports if not already available.

(ii) A defendant can raise a defence of insanity.

(iii) A defendant who suffers from mental disorder or from some other significant impairment of intelligence may be able to participate in criminal proceedings if necessary with adaptations to the trial process tailored to suit his particular needs (see *Practice Direction (Criminal Proceedings: Consolidation)* para. III.30 (as inserted by *Practice Direction (Criminal Proceedings: Further Directions)* [2007] 1 WLR 1790) (hereinafter referred to as the Practice Direction)).

(iv) Finally, there will always be a few defendants whose illness/disability is so severe that they are unable to participate in any way in their trial and where consideration will have to be given to applying for the case to be discontinued or, exceptionally, stayed on the grounds of abuse of process. The court can of its own volition adjourn the case *sine die* where the CPS is unwilling to discontinue.

7.2 EXPERT EVIDENCE

7.2.1 It will most often be the case that obtaining a report at an early stage will enable advice to be obtained on the most appropriate form the proceedings should take. The solicitor will have to consider whether this can be achieved by asking the court to order the report if, for example, the defendant has been referred to a court mental health assessment scheme, otherwise it will fall to the solicitor to instruct the expert. Each case will be different, and the issues upon which expert evidence is sought will inevitably vary. The most important question to be addressed is whether a defendant is able to participate effectively in criminal proceedings at all. A defendant who is incapable of giving instructions, whether because of learning disability or serious mental illness, such that he cannot follow or take part in criminal proceedings, will not be able to participate effectively in the proceedings. Such a defendant is almost invariably assessed by a psychiatrist in accordance with the '*Pritchard* criteria' (see **Chapter 10**). Even though they have no application to summary proceedings they are a useful diagnostic tool for assessing a defendant's mental state and ability.

7.2.2 In order to proceed to a finding of fact hearing or to try a defence of insanity the court will need evidence, prior to the hearing, that such a procedure is indicated. If it appears that the outcome of the case is likely to be an order under s.37(3) of the Act, consideration may also have to be given to whether a second report should be obtained before the finding of fact hearing. The availability of a second report would enable the court to proceed to fact finding and disposal in a single hearing.

7.2.3 Any psychiatric evidence relied upon must be served upon the court and CPS within the appropriate time frame in accordance with the current Criminal Procedure Rules (CPR). It is perfectly proper to amend a report before service upon the CPS and the court, but obviously any editing or amendments must not be misleading, and must be discussed and agreed with the author of the report and an amended version signed by him. If the evidence is contested, and the CPS instruct an expert of their choosing, the defence expert must be provided with a copy of the prosecution's expert report in good time before the hearing. He should be asked to comment on it, if necessary in the form of a short addendum report which, if it is going to be relied upon, will need to be served on the CPS, again prior to the hearing, in accordance with the CPR.

7.2.4 Prior authority should be obtained from the LSC to instruct the expert, as well as to cover the attendance of the expert at court if required to either give or listen to others give evidence. The expert must be notified of the date to attend.

7.3 FACT-FINDING HEARING

7.3.1 If it is clear that the defendant will be dealt with by way of a s.37(3) hospital order, an assessment will still need to be made of the prosecution case for the fact-finding hearing. It is important to remember that at a fact-finding hearing the court will not be concerned with *mens rea*, so the advocate should be ready to address the court as to which elements of an offence constitute the *actus reus*, as opposed to the *mens rea*. This is normally fairly straightforward – however the analysis must always be done.

7.3.2 The advocate will also have to consider (as he would in any trial) whether a prima facie case is disclosed, or whether it is possible that by testing the prosecution evidence, a submission of no case to answer could be made, in the usual way, at the close of the prosecution case. A successful submission of no case to answer in respect of the *actus reus* of the offence charged will conclude the proceedings as the case will be dismissed. It is important to note that the burden of proof to the criminal standard applies to these hearings. The court should adopt the same rules of evidence as in a criminal trial. Thus if, at the conclusion of the evidence, 'the court is not satisfied to the requisite standard that the act/omission was done or made, an unqualified acquittal must follow whatever the anxieties may be about the accused's mental state of health' (*R (on the application of Singh)* v. *Stratford Magistrates' Court* [2007] 1 WLR 3119, see **7.4.1** below). However, it should be noted that if a hospital order has been indicated, the defendant may well find himself detained under the appropriate civil section of the Act instead.

7.3.3 If the advocate considers that the elements of the *actus reus* of the offence are made out, there may be little purpose in testing the evidence by cross-examination, unless there is a positive case which can be put on the basis of evidence to be given by defence witnesses. A defendant himself would not be expected to give evidence at a finding of fact hearing. However, consideration should also be given to any applications that might be made to exclude evidence such as a defendant's interview, or admissions made at the scene (see further **Chapter 8**). If there can be no realistic challenge to the prosecution's case, and no defence evidence is to be called whilst technically the prosecution can be put to proof, a more realistic option (and one in accordance with the CPR) will be to agree that the evidence can be read in s.9 statement form or summarised in s.10 admissions.

7.3.4 In practice, PCC(S)A 2000, s.11 and s.37(3) of the Act are most often used by the court as a shortcut procedure which allows a hospital order to be made with the least possible delay once medical opinion is obtained supporting it. It is typically used in the case of a defendant who is suffering from mental illness (as opposed to any other form of mental disorder such as learning disability or personality disorder), who is very unwell as at the date of the criminal proceedings, whose illness is treatable but who cannot (at least until his condition improves) be treated in the community.

7.3.5 Despite what would appear to be a fairly straightforward procedure, in reality some magistrates' courts (and some prosecutors) are still unfamiliar with what the requirements are in such proceedings, and will need leading through the relevant provisions and authorities. Two recent cases illustrate this:

(a) In *Blouet* v. *Bath & Wansdyke Magistrates' Court* [2009] EWHC 759 (Admin) the magistrates' court had before it two psychiatric reports, one of which concluded that the defendant was fit to plead and another which concluded that he was not. Instead of adjourning the matter for a fact-finding hearing to determine whether the defendant had done the act, the court adjourned the case for trial. In ordering the case to be re-listed in the magistrates' court, the Administrative Court directed that:

> the approach which the District Judge should have followed is this. First there should be up-to-date medical evidence before him. If there is a possibility of a s.37(3) order being made, he will then try the issue in accordance with s.11 PCC(S)A. If thereafter there arises the obligation to adjourn for further reports then that was what had to happen. It may be of course that given the up-to-date reports which he will then have – only a short adjournment will be needed or, if everyone agrees that in the circumstances it is not, the matter can proceed under s.37(3) if that be appropriate.

(b) In *R (on the application of V)* v. *Redbridge Magistrates' Court* (QBD Admin, 11 March 2009) the defence had obtained medical evidence that the defendant was unfit to plead. The Crown produced a report prepared in relation to other criminal proceedings faced by the defendant, the conclusion of which was that the defendant was fit to plead, and submitted that the matter should proceed to trial. The defence objected and produced four reports to the contrary but the court proceeded to summary trial and conviction. The Administrative Court quashed the conviction and remitted it for the magistrates 'to determine whether the claimant did the acts alleged against him and then, in the light of such medical evidence as they have before them, to make such orders if any, as they think fit under s.37(3) of the Act'.

7.3.6 Although the provision is confined to summary proceedings, the court can proceed under s.37(3) in either way matters in circumstances where a defendant's mental disorder is such that he is unable to understand what it means to consent to summary trial: *R* v. *Lincoln (Kesteven) Magistrates' Court ex p. O'Connor* [1983] 1 WLR 335, DC.

7.3.7 The court's powers in relation to s.37(3) were further considered in *R* v. *Ramsgate Justices ex p. Kazmarek (*1985) 80 Cr App R 366, DC and in *R* v. *Chippenham Magistrates' Court ex p. Thompson* (1996) 160 JP 207. In *Kazmarek* it was held that even in a case where a defendant had elected trial by jury, the magistrates were entitled to adopt the s.37(3) procedure because they 'would have power, on convicting him of that offence' to make a hospital order. In contrast, in *Thompson*, the subsection could not apply where the offence in question was triable only on indictment, because in such a case the magistrates could not convict an offender of that offence.

7.4 INSANITY

7.4.1 The law in relation to insanity in the Crown Court is dealt with in **10.3**. Insanity is a common law defence which, if there had been any previous doubt on the issue, is and always has been available in summary proceedings: see *R (on the application of Singh)* v. *Stratford Magistrates' Court* [2007] 1 WLR 3119 in which the relationship between, s.11 of PCC(S)A 2000, s.37(3) of the Act and the insanity defence in summary proceedings was considered.

7.4.2 In *Singh*, defendant was charged with assaulting a police constable in the execution of his duty. He pleaded not guilty. He formally admitted the facts but served a report saying that at the time of the offence he was labouring under such defect of reason from a disease of the mind as not to know the nature and quality of his act. He was not unfit to stand trial. The district judge adjourned the trial for a second psychiatric report to be prepared under PCC(S)A 2000, s.11 with a view not to investigating insanity but rather to proceedings under s.37(3) of the Act in order to consider making either a hospital or guardianship order without convicting the defendant.

7.4.3 The court held that if it is clear that no s.37(3) order is indicated on the medical evidence, then, in the absence of some other compelling factor, the case must proceed to trial so that if the accused was insane, he is acquitted, and if not, he is convicted. It follows that a magistrates' court has the power, in an appropriate case, to try the issue of insanity and if established by the accused, this prevents conviction.

7.4.4 However, if the court is satisfied that there is no purpose in resolving the issue of insanity, and if a s.37(3) order is going to be made, the court can deal with the case without trying that issue. Before embarking on a case in which s.37(3) may be applied, magistrates should make it clear that it is a possibility and should invite submissions from the parties upon the course to be adopted. In particular, careful consideration must be given to any reasons advanced as to why the issue of insanity should be tried. Such an application should be resolved having regard to the interests of justice, which include, but are not limited to, justice to the accused. The court accepted that it might be very important for the accused that it be established that he was insane, rather than malicious. It might also be of real concern to others involved, or to the public, that it be known that he was legally insane at the time of the acts charged.

7.4.5 It is therefore clear that in a case in which both an insanity defence is available, and a s.37(3) disposal is a possibility, the advocate will need to give careful consideration as to why an insanity trial should be pursued in circumstances where the court is likely to find the interests of justice are better served by the making of an order under s.37(3), which would ensure that the defendant obtained medical treatment. Such an order is not likely to be indicated where the defendant was unwell at the time of the offence but has made a recovery to the extent that he could not satisfy the criteria for admission to hospital/guardianship under s.37.

7.4.6 There appears to be no statutory provision so far as medical evidence is concerned in support of an insanity defence in summary proceedings. Under CP(I)A 1964 the written or oral evidence of two or more registered medical practitioners, at least one of whom is approved under s.12, is required before a jury can return the special verdict of insanity. This does not apply in summary proceedings, although at the very least it would seem advisable, if an insanity defence is to be mounted, that the advocate should be in a position to call or read (if agreed) the evidence of two doctors in support of the defence.

7.5 ORDER UNDER S.37(3)

7.5.1 Section 11(1)(a) of PCC(S)A 2000 gives the court power to remand a defendant in custody (for up to three weeks) or on bail (for up to four weeks) for a medical examination and preparation of a report *provided* that it is satisfied that the accused did the act or made the omission charged. The court should apply the Bail Act criteria to the decision as to bail or custody. If the court remands on bail, s.11 requires the court to impose a bail condition requiring that the defendant cooperates with those preparing the reports.

7.5.2 If the court is of the view that it would be impracticable for a report to be prepared if the defendant were remanded on bail, s.35 of the Act gives the court power to remand to a hospital for the preparation of the report once it is satisfied he did the act or made the omission charged. A bed must be available within 28 days (see **Appendix 1** for full text).

7.5.3 The conditions for making an order under s.37(3) are that:

- the defendant is suffering from mental disorder of a nature or degree which makes it appropriate for him to be detained in hospital for appropriate medical treatment which is available for him; and
- the defendant did the act or made the omission charged;
- the offence is imprisonable; and
- the order is the most suitable method of disposing of the case.

7.5.4 Points to note in respect of all orders made under s.37(3) are as follows.

(a) The provisions of the Rehabilitation of Offenders Act 1974, s.1 apply to a defendant made the subject of an order under s.37(3). Whilst the defendant is not 'convicted', s.1(4)(b) confirms that references to a conviction include also references to 'any finding (other than a finding linked with a finding of insanity) in any criminal proceedings that a person has committed an offence or done the act or made the omission charged'.

(b) Such a defendant is also an 'offender' for the purposes of the Magistrates' Courts Act 1980, s.142, which enables a magistrates' court to vary or rescind an order made by it when dealing with an 'offender'. This would enable the court to re-open a finding in appropriate circumstances. This might be appropriate if, for example, it became apparent that the defendant did not in fact suffer from a mental disorder, or might not have done the acts complained of, or that arrangements could not in fact be made for his admission to hospital (*R* v. *Thames Magistrates' Court ex p. Ramadan* [1999] 1 Cr App R 386). It might also apply in circumstances where, a finding having been made, the defendant recovered sufficiently to be able to give instructions and wished the charge to be tried so that he could defend it (*Bartram* v. *Southend Magistrates' Court* [2004] EWHC 2691 (QB)).

(c) Section 45 of the Act provides a right of appeal to the Crown Court for a person who has been made the subject of a hospital or guardianship order under s.37(3). The Crown Court has the same powers as if the appeal had been against conviction and sentence. This provision enables the Crown Court on such an appeal to re-hear and re-determine both whether the defendant did the act/omission and the disposal, if found to have done the act/omission (s.45(1)).

(d) An appeal by a child or young person in respect of whom such an order is made may be brought by that child/young person or by his parent or guardian on his behalf, whether the appeal is against the finding or the order (s.45(2)).

7.6 EFFECTIVE PARTICIPATION IN SUMMARY PROCEEDINGS

7.6.1 It is a common experience in both the youth and adult courts to represent those who have a history of learning difficulties, low IQ, and/or other significant impairment of intelligence. The difficulties experienced by such defendants in understanding and participating in the criminal process can be considerable. Just as in the case with the defendant who suffers from mental illness, it is essential to have obtained expert evidence which is likely, in the first instance at least, to come from a clinical psychologist in order to establish the extent (if at all) to which such a defendant will be able to participate in a conventional trial.

7.6.2 The report may conclude that the defendant, by reason of his disability, cannot participate effectively in the trial process or it may be that, given adaptations to the trial process in accordance with the Practice Direction he will be able to do so (see **Chapter 9** for full discussion of the Practice Direction, which is also set out at **Appendix 7**). Given the presumption that even a defendant who is young or vulnerable, within the meaning of the Practice Direction, should be able to participate in criminal proceedings, the number of cases in which the court will find that effective participation is not possible are likely to be rare.

7.6.3 Any expert report to be relied upon should be served on the CPS and the court. If the report concludes that a defendant will be able to participate effectively at trial subject to modifications, approval of such modifications (particularly those requiring directions, such as the use by the defendant of live link: see **Chapter 9**) may need to be sought well in advance of the trial.

7.6.4 If it is contended that a defendant is unable to participate effectively at all, consideration should be given as how this is to be dealt with at trial (see below as to the proper approach). The court may wish to approach the case as a fact-finding exercise set out above, but if there is no available disposal (that is, if neither a hospital or guardianship order are applicable) there may be little purpose in proceeding with a trial of the facts. In those circumstances, the solicitor should consider (before the hearing) making representations that the proceedings should be discontinued. Alternatively, at trial, it may be appropriate to make an application to stay proceedings (although see *DPP* v. *P*, **7.7.7** below), or to invite the court to adjourn the proceedings *sine die*. In the cases below the courts have considered at some length the way forward in this difficult area of law/practice.

7.6.5 *R (on the application of P (a juvenile))* v. *Barking Youth Court* [2002] 2 Cr App R 19 deals with the correct procedure to be followed in summary proceedings (including in the youth court), when it is contended that a defendant is 'unfit to plead'. P (a minor) applied for judicial review of a youth court decision that he was fit to stand trial in respect of a number of summary offences. A report from a chartered educational and forensic psychologist concluded that he would not be able to understand or reply rationally to the indictment and would not be able to challenge jurors on any rational basis.

The bench rejected the psychologist's evidence and found that the defendant was fit to plead, having adopted the procedure set out in the CP(I)A 1964, and basing its conclusion upon the defendant's appearance and behaviour in the dock.

7.6.6 The Divisional Court held that the justices had erred in following the CP(I)A 1964 procedure; such procedure was specific to the Crown Court and had no application in summary proceedings. The correct procedure was set out in s.37(3), taken together with PCC(S)A 2000, s.11(1)(a). The court held that the two provisions, taken together, provide a 'complete statutory framework' for the determination of all issues that arise in cases of defendants who are or might be mentally disordered in the context of offences which are triable summarily only, whether that be in the magistrates' court or the youth court. The justices' finding was accordingly quashed and the matter remitted for the youth court to proceed in accordance with the machinery provided by the 1983 and 2000 Acts.

7.6.7 In reality, as anyone with any experience of the day-to-day representation of mentally disordered defendants in summary proceedings will appreciate, these two provisions do not provide a ready answer in many situations. The subsequent case of *DPP* v. *P* [2007] 4 All ER 628, DC acknowledged that s.37(3) and s.11(1) 'do not provide the solution to all of the problems which may confront a youth court before which a young person of doubtful capacity appears'.

7.6.8 In this case, the defendant P had faced trial in the Crown Court when he was aged 11. Psychiatric reports had concluded that he was unfit to plead. The prosecution had accepted the conclusions, and the proceedings were stayed. A year later he was brought before the youth court in respect of further offences. At the start of the hearing, the district judge stayed the proceedings on the application of the defence, as an abuse of process on the basis of the previous reports, and an additional report in similar terms. The CPS appealed. The Divisional Court held:

- The fact that a court of higher authority had previously held that a person was unfit to plead did not make it an abuse of process to try that person for subsequent criminal acts. The issue of a child's ability to participate effectively at trial had to be decided afresh, on the basis of all the information available at the time of the decision.
- Where the court decided to halt the criminal trial and switch to an enquiry into whether the defendant had done the acts alleged, the latter proceedings were not criminal and as such, Article 6 of the European Convention on Human Rights (ECHR) was not engaged.
- If, in criminal proceedings, the defence raises an issue relating to the capacity of the young person before any evidence is heard, the court should stay the proceedings as an abuse of process in only exceptional cases.
- In most cases, the medical evidence concerning capacity should be considered as part of the evidence in the case and not as the sole evidence in a free-standing application.

- The court has a duty to keep under continuing review the question of whether the criminal trial ought to continue. If at any stage the court concludes that the child is unable to participate effectively in the trial, it may decide to call a halt. If the trial is halted on this ground, the court should then consider whether to switch to a consideration of whether the young person has done the acts alleged (the fact-finding process) under the procedure referred to in the *Barking* case (see **7.6.5**).
- If there was a possibility of making an order under the Act, the court should usually find the facts.
- Even if a hospital order seemed unlikely it might still be appropriate to find the facts with a view to alerting the local authority to the position with a view to the commencement of care proceedings.
- Proceedings should be stayed as an abuse of process before fact-finding only if no useful purpose at all could be served by finding the facts.

7.6.9 The issues of effective participation and the minimum requirements for a fair trial arose again in *R (on the application of TP)* v. *West London Youth Court* [2006] 1 Cr App R 25. T was a 15-year-old boy who faced trial in the youth court on charges of robbery and attempted robbery. He had been assessed by a clinical psychologist as having a IQ of 63 and the intellectual capacity of an 8-year-old. An application for a stay of proceedings in the youth court (on the basis that he would not be able to participate effectively in the proceedings) was rejected by the district judge.

7.6.10 The Administrative Court upheld the district judge's ruling, reiterating the well-rehearsed principle that staying proceedings as an abuse of process was a power to be employed in exceptional circumstances only. The court found there to be no violation of Article 6 and the youth court (on the facts of this case) could adapt its procedure so that the defendant would be able to participate effectively in the proceedings, particularly as he was represented by an experienced youth court advocate.

7.6.11 The court noted that the district judge had directed himself correctly as to the minimum requirement for a fair trial for the defendant:

- He had to understand what he is said to have done wrong.
- The court had to be satisfied that the defendant when he had done wrong by act or omission had the means of knowing that was wrong.
- He had to understand what, if any, defences were available to him.
- He had to have a reasonable opportunity to make relevant representations if he wished.
- He had to have the opportunity to consider what representations he wished to make once he had understood the issues involved.
- The fact that a young person cannot take an effective part in the fact-finding process does not infringe his rights under Article 6 ECHR.

CHAPTER 8

Breaches of the PACE Code of Practice and other trial issues

8.1 LEGAL FRAMEWORK

8.1.1 The PACE Code of Practice provisions covering interviews of mentally disordered or otherwise vulnerable suspects are considered earlier in this book and the provisions themselves can be found in **Appendix 3**. Breaches of these provisions can form the basis of applications to exclude evidence under ss.76–78 of PACE in the magistrates' court, youth court and Crown Court. This chapter is applicable to proceedings in all three jurisdictions. Applications to exclude evidence, in particular interviews of mentally disordered suspects conducted by the police in the absence of the suitable safeguards, are usually based on a combination of the grounds set out in ss.76–78.

8.1.2 Section 76(2) of PACE provides that the court must exclude any confession if it was or may have been obtained:

(a) by oppression of the person who made it; or
(b) in consequence of anything said or done which was likely in the circumstances existing at the time to render unreliable any confession which might be made by the accused in consequence thereof, unless the prosecution can prove beyond reasonable doubt that the confession (notwithstanding that it may be true) was not obtained in such circumstances.

8.1.3 Section 77 of PACE is concerned with the court's proper approach where there has been a confession by a 'mentally handicapped' suspect in particular circumstances. It provides that a jury must be warned of the special need for caution where a case against a mentally handicapped defendant rests wholly or substantially on a confession made in the absence of an independent person. Where such circumstances exist, it may be appropriate to make an application to exclude the confession under the provisions of ss.76–78 as appropriate; to make a submission of no case to answer if the conditions for doing so are met (see *R* v. *Mackenzie* (1992) 96 Cr App R 98) or, if these have failed, to invite the judge to give the jury the appropriate directions and warning. In summary proceedings, the court itself must treat the case as one in which there is a special need for caution before convicting the defendant on his confession.

8.1.4 It should be noted that s.77 covers not merely a confession in interview or to police officers (for example on or before arrest) but also confessions made to others outside the context of the arrest or interview (see *R* v. *Bailey* [1983] 1 WLR 760).

8.1.5 For the purposes of s.77, an 'independent person' cannot be a police officer or a person employed for, or engaged on, police purposes. Furthermore, confessions made to a friend are not made 'in the presence of an independent person' under s.77. Such a person has to be independent of the person to whom the confession is made, not least because a mentally handicapped person might have difficulty in recalling what he or she said and independent evidence of the emotional and mental state of that mentally handicapped person might be desirable (see *R* v. *Bailey* [1983] 1 WLR 760). A solicitor can be an independent person even though he cannot be an appropriate adult under the Codes of Practice.

8.1.6 The definition of mental handicap/learning disability in s.77(3) of PACE and s.1(4) of the Act (as amended) is the same, that is a 'state of arrested or incomplete development of mind which includes significant impairment of intelligence and social functioning'. In contrast, C.AnnexE is broader in its definition as it covers suspects who are not only mentally disordered but those who are 'otherwise mentally vulnerable' and those mentally incapable of understanding the significance of questions put.

8.1.7 Section 78 of PACE provides that in any proceedings the court may exclude any prosecution evidence if it appears, having regard to all the circumstances (including the circumstances in which the evidence was obtained) that the admission of the evidence would have such an adverse effect on the fairness of the proceedings that the court ought not to admit it.

8.1.8 These provisions of PACE aim to protect mentally disordered suspects in the police station, especially in the interview. The advocate must be aware of the case law which demonstrates how inappropriate questioning of mentally disordered suspects, particularly learning disabled people, may lead them to give unreliable evidence.

8.2 APPLICATIONS TO EXCLUDE CONFESSIONS: CASE LAW

8.2.1 The success or otherwise of an application to exclude the confession of a mentally disordered suspect (whether 'mentally handicapped' within the terms of s.77 or more generally within the provisions of Code C) is likely to turn on three key factors:

(a) the nature and degree of the defendant's mental disorder;
(b) whether effective legal representation was available; and
(c) whether there was a helpful and alert appropriate adult.

8.2.2 Expert evidence as to the nature and degree of the defendant's mental disorder will be crucial in such cases to demonstrate to the court precisely why the defendant's confession is unreliable, or obtained oppressively rendering the admission of it unfair.

8.2.3 In *R* v. *Cox* [1991] Crim LR 276, the defendant, who had an IQ of 58, was interviewed by police without an appropriate adult present and admitted his part in two burglaries. He was illiterate but signed the note of interview after it was read for him. During the 'voir dire' the judge rejected the evidence of an officer who said he did not know that Cox was 'simple or backward'. However, the defendant himself admitted the burglaries in the course of the voir dire, leading the judge to admit the interview on the basis that it was likely to be true. The appeal was allowed on the ground that there had been a breach of the Code (absence of appropriate adult). The issue to be considered in relation to s.76(2) is whether the breach of the Code makes the confession unreliable, not whether the contents of it are true.

8.2.4 In *R* v. *Silcott, Braithwaite and Raghip* (1991) *The Times*, 9 December the Court of Appeal considered the admissibility of the interview of the defendant, Raghip, who had an IQ of 74. The court rejected the argument that the judicial approach to submissions under PACE should be governed by which side of an arbitrary line, whether 69 or 70, the IQ fell. The proper approach was to assess in each case what effect the learning disability might have on the suspect's conduct in interview.

8.2.5 The principle stated by the Court of Appeal in *Silcott & Others* (above) was applied in *R* v. *Kenny* [1994] Crim LR 284 in which it was said that the court should not take IQs from one case and apply them 'slavishly' to another.

8.2.6 In *R* v. *Walker* [1998] Crim LR 211, admissions had been made by the defendant who suffered from a severe personality disorder. Psychiatric evidence suggested these confessions were likely to be unreliable. The trial judge limited himself to consideration of whether the defendant was 'mentally impaired' in the sense of the case of *Silcott & Others* (above) and refused to exclude the evidence. The Court of Appeal held that the trial judge had erred in doing so as although most reported cases dealt with suspects of low intelligence, nothing in those cases limited or defined the particular form of mental or psychological condition or disorder upon which the defendant could rely to show that his confession was unreliable and thus should be excluded.

8.2.7 The importance of the court making a finding as to whether or not a defendant is 'mentally handicapped' within the meaning of s.77 was emphasised by the Court of Appeal in the case of *R* v. *Ham* (1997) 36 BMLR 169, CA. In that case the defendant, who had 'borderline' mental impairment with an IQ of 70 to 80, had made admissions in the absence of a solicitor or appropriate adult. The trial judge had heard evidence from a police officer that the defendant was 'streetwise, cocky and unremorseful' and that he had had no difficulty in answering the questions in interview. The judge made no explicit finding as to whether the appellant was mentally handicapped and the Court of Appeal criticised him for not doing so. Similar criticism of a judge's approach can be found in *R* v. *Everett* [1988] Crim LR 826 in which it was held that the defendant's mental state should be assessed with the help of medical evidence rather than the judge's own view of the defendant's performance in interview.

8.2.8 In *R* v. *O'Brien* [2000] Crim LR 676, CA it was held that the disorder must not only be of a type which might render a confession unreliable but that there must be a significant deviation from the norm shown. There must also be a history pre-dating the making of admissions which is not based solely on a history given by the defendant and which points to or explains the abnormality or abnormalities. Solicitors should note that medical evidence obtained in support of an application to exclude a confession must address these issues.

8.2.9 In *R* v. *Moss* (1990) 91 Cr App R 371, CA a 'borderline' mentally handicapped suspect was kept in custody for seven days during which he was interviewed nine times about alleged sexual offences against four young children, two of whom were his own. He was refused access to a solicitor for 36 hours and subsequently after his assigned solicitor withdrew, he was interviewed without an appropriate adult or solicitor. He denied all allegations until the fifth interview when some admissions were made. After six days and in the eighth interview he made admissions which formed the only evidence against him at his trial. The trial judge directed the jury under s.77 that special caution should be exercised, but refused to exclude the interview evidence. The Court of Appeal held that the defendant's mental disability, the length of the period in custody, the prolonged police interrogation, the fact that no admissions were made until the fifth interview and no solicitor or independent person was present, made the conviction unsafe and unsatisfactory.

8.2.10 The defendant in *R* v. *Campbell* [1995] Crim LR 157 was convicted of conspiracy to rob and murder. His first interview, in which he made significant admissions, took place without a solicitor. He was then examined by the police surgeon who said that he was mentally handicapped. In a subsequent interview with a solicitor and appropriate adult present, he denied the offences but indicated some involvement. Later, in another interview with only the appropriate adult present, he made further admissions. The judge refused to exclude any interview although it was accepted that there had been a breach of the Code because of the defendant's IQ. He found that the police had no reason to know of the handicap before the medical examination and that it was speculation to suggest that he would not have made admissions if he had had an appropriate adult and a solicitor with him. His findings were upheld on appeal.

8.3 ABSENCE OF APPROPRIATE ADULT: CASE LAW

8.3.1 In *R* v. *Law-Thompson* [1997] Crim LR 674, the Court of Appeal dismissed an appeal based upon the trial judge's refusal to exclude confession evidence under either s.76 or s.78 of PACE. The defendant, who had Asperger's Syndrome, made admissions on arrest (after caution) and further admissions in interview which was conducted without an appropriate adult but with a solicitor. The court found there to be nothing to suggest that the confession was obtained because the appropriate adult was absent or that such absence was likely to render the confession unreliable; nor would the admission of the evidence be unfair. The crucial factors were the presence of the solicitor, the intelligence of the defendant in spite of his abnormal social functioning and the independent evidence of his guilt.

8.3.2 In contrast, in the cases of *R* v. *Aspinall* (1999) *The Times*, 4 February and *R* v. *Haroon Ali* (see below), the Court of Appeal emphasised the importance of the role of the appropriate adult in the interview process in ensuring the fairness of the process. Mr Aspinall, a schizophrenic, was interviewed in the absence of an appropriate adult or a solicitor and made admissions. The court remarked that the appropriate adult played a significant role in respect of a vulnerable person whose condition rendered him liable to provide information which was unreliable, misleading or self-incriminating. A further important function of the appropriate adult was to act as a 'gateway' to other safeguards, especially in advising the suspect when to obtain legal advice. The admissions should have been excluded.

8.3.3 In *R* v. *Haroon Ali* (DA, No. 98/04160/X2) an 18-year-old defendant had made extensive admissions to large-scale drug supply. This was after he had been interviewed for nine minutes without an appropriate adult, having declined legal advice. There was no other evidence against him apart from these admissions. By the time of the trial it was established that the defendant's IQ range was between 66 and 72. An application to exclude the confessions under s.78 on the basis that neither an appropriate adult nor solicitor was present failed. The Court of Appeal, in allowing the appeal, held that there was no rule that a confession made by a mentally handicapped person in the absence of an appropriate adult and solicitor would lead automatically to the exclusion of that confession. Each case must be considered in the light of its individual circumstances. In this case, the court considered that, had an appropriate adult been present, there would have come a point when he would have 'intervened to establish from the defendant privately whether he meant what he was saying, whether he was boasting and whether he wanted to suspend the interview so that a solicitor could give him further advice'.

8.4 PRESENCE OF LEGAL REPRESENTATIVE: CASE LAW

8.4.1 In general the courts have treated the presence of a solicitor as being sufficient protection for the suspect even in the absence of an appropriate adult (see **Chapter 4**). Cases in which a solicitor, with or without an appropriate adult, has been present at the interview and the court has found nevertheless that the confession evidence should be excluded, are rare.

8.4.2 However in the case of *R* v. *Paris, Abdullahi and Miller* [1994] Crim LR 361, known as the 'Cardiff Three', the defendant, Miller, who was later discovered to have an IQ of 75, was subjected to interviews over five days which took up

19 tapes. In all but two of the interviews he was with a solicitor who, despite mounting bullying, shouting and pressure by the police, did not intervene. Having denied involvement over 300 times, Miller made 'admissions' on tapes 18 and 19. Allowing his appeal, the Court of Appeal criticised both the police, whose behaviour amounted to 'oppression' within the meaning of s.76(2), and the solicitor. The police were wrong to assume that their behaviour was within the Codes because the solicitor did not intervene. However it was equally important that the solicitor assisting the suspect in interview should discharge his functions responsibly and courageously as otherwise his presence might actually render a disservice to the client.

8.4.3 In *R* v. *Dunn* [1990] Crim LR 572, it was made clear that a lawyer is expected to intervene to prevent breaches of the Code and failure to do so, if justified at the time of the interview, would deter the trial court from excluding evidence even if improperly obtained.

8.5 CRIMINAL JUSTICE AND PUBLIC ORDER ACT 1994

Section 34

8.5.1 The decision as to whether to advise the detainee not to answer questions in interview can lay him open to the drawing of an adverse inference under CJPOA 1994, s.34. See **4.1.6** above for a fuller discussion and **Appendix 10**.

Section 35

8.5.2 Advising a mentally disordered defendant as to whether or not he should give evidence in court can be difficult. A number of factors have to be taken into account. As with any case, the strength of the prosecution evidence will be a matter for primary consideration. Otherwise, the defendant's ability to give a proper account and withstand cross-examination notwithstanding his mental disorder will have to be weighed in the balance. If a decision is taken that the defendant should not give evidence, it should not be assumed that even if medical evidence is called on the issue, the judge would direct the jury that no adverse inference should be drawn.

8.5.3 Section 35(1)(b) provides that where 'it appears to the court that the physical or mental condition of the accused makes it undesirable for him to give evidence' no adverse inference may be drawn from the defendant's failure to give evidence. It has been considered in the following cases.

8.5.4 In *R* v. *Friend* [1997] 2 All ER 1011 it was held that there was no misdirection by a judge in summing up to the jury by telling them that it was open to them to draw an adverse inference from the fact that the 15-year-old defendant in a murder trial had failed to testify even though his mental age was assessed at nine years old. The court had heard evidence from the psychologist to that effect. The Court of Appeal noted that 'no abnormality of mind has been suggested' and the trial judge did not have to treat the defendant as a nine year old.

8.5.5 In *DPP* v. *Kavanagh* [2005] EWHC 820 (Admin) it was held that for the court to properly exercise its discretion under s.35, there had to be an evidential basis as to why it was undesirable for a defendant to give evidence. In this case the defendant's mother had given evidence that the defendant had at one time suffered depression. It was held that it was not sufficient that the defendant suffered from a physical or a mental condition, as the condition had to render it undesirable for him to give evidence. The evidence of his mother was insufficient for the purposes of s.35(1)(b).

8.5.6 In *R* v. *Tabbakh (Hassan)* [2009] EWCA Crim 464 a conviction for the preparation of terrorist acts was upheld as although the defendant had mental health problems (post-traumatic stress disorder and he had self-harmed) the trial judge was entitled to take the view that neither condition was sufficient to make giving evidence undesirable. All the circumstances in the case had to be taken into consideration. The trial judge had properly explained the history and medical evidence to the jury and it was a matter for them as to whether or not to draw an adverse inference from the defendant's silence.

CHAPTER 9

Pre-trial issues in the Crown Court

9.1 PUBLIC FUNDING

9.1.1 It is common practice now for the magistrates' court to grant a 'through' representation order covering proceedings in that court and the Crown Court. If the defendant has somehow slipped through the net and has not had public funding in the magistrates' court, a full application dealing with the interests of justice test can still be made. The defendant should also complete Form B within 14 days of the case going up to the Crown Court. Until recently, unlike in the magistrates' court, no evidential proof of income or outgoings has been required in the Crown Court. However it is proposed to change this and introduce means-testing for representation in the Crown Court in 2010.

9.1.2 As far as the mentally disordered offender is concerned, unlike in the magistrates' court (see **5.1**), the court, judge of the court or the registrar of criminal appeals may grant a representation order at any stage of the criminal proceedings whether or not an application has been made for such an order. (Criminal Defence Service (General) (No.2) Regulations 2001 as amended by Criminal Defence Service (General) (No.2) (Amendment) Regulations 2006). It is unclear if an application form needs to be completed, but it is unlikely.

9.2 FIRST APPEARANCE IN THE CROWN COURT

General considerations

9.2.1 As with any other defendant, the mentally disordered defendant will first appear before the Crown Court following committal, transfer or sending for trial or having been committed for sentence. In respect of the first three, this will either be at a preliminary hearing (PH) or a plea and case management hearing (PCMH). These procedural hearings will be the first opportunity for the advocate to inform the court of issues arising in any contested case where the defendant's mental disorder is such as to affect any aspect of the trial process.

9.2.2 A committal for sentence may have been specifically with a view to the making of a hospital order with a restriction order pursuant to s.37 or s.41 of the Act, or may have been under the court's other powers to commit for sentence. The latter will be familiar to the practitioner, and are not dealt with here. Hospital orders and restriction orders are dealt with in **Chapter 11**.

9.3 COMMITTAL FOR SENTENCE

9.3.1 Neither the magistrates' court nor the youth court has the power to make a restriction order under s.41 of the Act. If the court is satisfied that the conditions exist upon which a hospital order under s.37 of the Act could be imposed, but is of the view that, having regard to the nature of the offence, the antecedents of the offender and the risk of his committing further offences if set at large, a restriction order should be attached to the hospital order, the court can commit an offender aged 14 or over to the Crown Court (s.43).

9.3.2 The magistrates may direct that the offender be detained in a hospital, pending the hearing of the case by the Crown Court (s.44). If the Crown Court decides not to make a hospital order, it can deal with the offender in any way in which the magistrates' court could have dealt with him or can remand him under s.35 or s.36 of the Act (see **9.10**), or it can make an interim hospital order under s.38 (see **Chapter 11**) in respect of him.

9.4 PRELIMINARY HEARINGS

9.4.1 A PH is not required in every case sent for trial under s.51 (see the *Practice Direction (Criminal Proceedings: Consolidation)* para. IV.41 (as substituted by *Practice Direction (Criminal Proceedings: Further Directions)* [2007] 1 WLR 1790)). Such a hearing should however normally be ordered by a magistrates' court or Crown Court in particular circumstances. These include:

- where the likely length of trial is three to four weeks or more;
- any case where it is desirable to set an early trial date;
- where the defendant is a child or young person;
- where a guilty plea is anticipated and the defendant could be sentenced.

9.4.2 The Practice Direction highlights the following potentially relevant issues for identification at a PH:

- fitness to plead;
- psychiatric reports where a guilty plea is anticipated;
- directions re expert evidence;
- whether fixing a trial date at this stage is possible and desirable because of a number of factors, including the health and vulnerability of the defendant.

9.4.3 Where it is clear that a defendant wishes to enter a guilty plea at the preliminary hearing, arraignment can take place provided that a valid indictment is in existence (if it is not, the prosecution advocate can usually settle an indictment on the day in a straightforward case). Provided that the advocate is satisfied that the defendant is fit to plead, and wishes to plead guilty, this course can properly be followed, and the court can then adjourn for sentence, ordering such reports as are appropriate (see further at **Chapter 11**).

9.5 PLEA AND CASE MANAGEMENT HEARINGS

9.5.1 Notwithstanding the above, the more usual course is for arraignment to take place at the PCMH. The advocate should always aim to be ready for arraignment at that hearing or to be in a position to inform the court that the defendant is not fit to plead. If reports are awaited and will not be ready for the PCMH date, the court and the CPS should be notified as it may be possible for the PCMH date to be moved administratively (and therefore without the need to attend) and for the hearing to be re-listed for a date on which the reports will be ready.

9.5.2 When the case is ready for an effective PCMH, the standard form PCMH questionnaire will have to be completed (see **Appendix 5** for the form together with the accompanying Guidance). Amongst the many boxes on the form which have to be completed, there are a number which are of potential significance to the trial of a mentally disordered offender. It is crucial to be as fully prepared as possible for the PCMH hearing and to be in a position to assist the judge with the case management issues which arise in each defendant's particular circumstances.

- Box 9 must be completed where issues arise as to a defendant's fitness to plead or stand trial. The advocate will be expected to assist the judge to fix a timetable for the service of experts' reports and for the issue to be tried (see PCMH form Guidance, para. 9).
- Box 12 relates to expert evidence likely to be relied upon, including the reasons why it is required and when it is reasonably practicable to serve the evidence. Realistic time estimates are expected for the service of outstanding reports (see Guidance, para. 12).
- Box 17 deals with special measures applications and should be completed where there is an application for a defendant to give evidence by live link. The written application should have been made prior to the PCMH in accordance with CPR 29 (see further below).
- Box 18 deals with young defendants and whether any arrangements are needed. It is clear from para. 18 of the Guidance that this box is intended to be completed in the cases both of young *and other vulnerable defendants*. The Guidance states that the needs of such defendants must be identified in advance of the trial so that the necessary arrangements can be made, in accordance with the PD (see **9.7**).
- Box 21 relates to the admissibility of interviews.

- Box 29 deals with admissibility and legal issues generally. The Guidance states that such issues should be identified where possible before trial, so that skeleton arguments can be exchanged and the judge can properly prepare for the hearing.

9.6 DEFENDANT UNFIT TO PLEAD AT PCMH

9.6.1 Where, at the date of the PCMH, a defendant has been assessed as unfit to plead, the judge is likely to raise the question of whether, given appropriate treatment, he may become fit to plead and stand trial, and if so, when that is likely to be. In such a case, the court has the option either to fix a date for a determination of the defendant's fitness to plead, followed if unfit by a trial of the facts (see **Chapter 10**), or to adjourn the PCMH so as to allow time for the defendant to recover sufficiently. If the court adopts the former course, the defendant may in any event become fit by the date of the hearing, in which case the matter can proceed to trial in the usual way.

9.6.2 Which course is followed depends on a number of factors:

- the nature of the defendant's mental disorder;
- the extent to which treatment will be able to address the issue if at all – a defendant suffering from severe intellectual impairment will be not be 'treatable' so as to allow him to become fit to plead if he has been assessed as unfit by reason of his mental impairment;
- the timescale involved;
- whether the defendant is currently receiving treatment either in the community or in hospital or is awaiting a transfer from custody for such treatment; and
- where the defendant is in custody, the custody time limit (CTL) implications of such a course.

9.6.3 Given the problems and delays frequently encountered in obtaining expert evidence, it is unfortunately more common than not to experience difficulties in being ready for trial within the CTL period. For the unfit defendant in custody, particular problems may arise because he is unwell and in need of treatment which is initially unavailable; or the treatment itself may extend of necessity beyond the expiry of CTLs.

9.6.4 Where a case cannot come to trial within the CTLs because of delays encountered by the defence in obtaining expert evidence within the relevant time frame, then, assuming that the Crown has met its obligations, there is unlikely to be any realistic prospect of objecting to the Crown's necessary application for the extension of CTLs.

9.6.5 The question of delay occasioned by the prosecution in responding to defence medical evidence was considered in *R (on the application of Alexander)* v. *Isleworth Crown Court* [2009] EWHC 85 (Admin). In that case, the defence (within the CTLs) had obtained and served two reports, both of which concluded that the defendant was unfit to plead. The Crown instructed its own expert, who fell ill without producing a report, which meant that an application for an extension of CTLs had to be made. The application to the trial judge was opposed, but succeeded. The Administrative Court held that the judge had been entitled to extend the CTLs and to find that the Crown had acted with due diligence and expedition. It was observed that it was common practice for the Crown to wait until the defendant had served the two medical reports required before instructing its own expert, and there was a potential considerable saving in cost in adopting that practice.

9.7 PRACTICE DIRECTION (CRIMINAL PROCEEDINGS: CONSOLIDATION)

9.7.1 The Practice Direction (Criminal Proceedings: Consolidation) para. III.30 (as inserted by Practice Direction (Criminal Proceedings: Further Directions) [2007] 1 WLR 1790) set out in full at **Appendix 7**, incorporates provisions introduced in 2000 in response to the decision of the European Court of Human Rights in the Thompson and Venables case (*T* v. *UK*; *V* v. *UK* 30 EHRR 121). It has been expanded to include not just young defendants, but adults suffering from a mental disorder or some other significant impairment of intelligence or social functioning.

9.7.2 The purpose of the PD set out in para. III.30.1, is to extend to proceedings in relation to such persons in the adult courts procedures analogous to those used in youth courts. The overriding principle is to ensure that:

> All possible steps should be taken to assist a vulnerable defendant to understand and participate in those proceedings. The ordinary trial process should, so far as necessary, be adapted to meet those ends. Regard should be had to the welfare of a young defendant as required by section 44 of the Children and Young Persons Act 1933, and generally to Parts 1 and 3 of the Criminal Procedure Rules (the overriding objective and the court's powers of case management). (III.30.3)

9.7.3 The PD applies to proceedings in the Crown Court and in magistrates' courts on the trial, sentencing or (in the Crown Court) appeal of:

(a) children and young persons under 18; or
(b) adults who suffer from a mental disorder within the meaning of the Act or who have any other significant impairment of intelligence or social functioning ('vulnerable defendants').

9.7.4 Both solicitors and advocates preparing for the trial of a young or vulnerable defendant and/or representing such a defendant at trial will need to be familiar with the contents of the PD at all stages of the proceedings. It should be noted that the pre-trial issues (which include pre-sentence or appeal) are dealt with at paras. III.30.4–30.8 and issues relating to the trial, sentencing or appeal hearing itself are dealt with at III.30.9–30.18. Below is a summary of the principal provisions of the PD with the focus on those paragraphs which are most likely to be of practicable application. It is not exhaustive and the PD itself should always be considered in its entirety, if only to discount such paragraphs as are irrelevant in the circumstances of the case.

Before the trial, sentencing or appeal (III.30.4–30.8)

9.7.5 The court will consider the following, as appropriate, at the PCMH, although inevitably any adaptations required and available will be different in each case:

- Whether it is appropriate to order joint or separate trials, where a vulnerable defendant is jointly charged with a non-vulnerable defendant.
- Where a vulnerable defendant, particularly one who is young, is to be tried jointly with one who is not, the court should consider whether the vulnerable defendant should be tried on his own, and should so order unless the court is of the opinion that a joint trial would not be in accordance of with Part 1 of the Criminal Procedure Rules (the overriding objective) and the interests of justice. If a vulnerable defendant is tried jointly with one who is not, the court should consider whether any of the modifications set out in the PD should apply and, so far as practicable, be given effect to (III.30.4).
- Whether a pre-trial court visit by the vulnerable defendant would be appropriate, to enable him to familiarise himself with the court setting out of court hours (III.30.6).
- Whether the assistance of the police is required to try to ensure that a defendant whose case has attracted or may attract widespread publicity or media interest is not, when attending court, exposed to intimidation, vilification or abuse (III 30.7).
- Whether Children and Young Persons Act (CYPA) 1933, s.39 reporting restrictions need to be made, if relevant and if not already ordered (III.30.8).
- Whether to give directions, and to make such directions, as far as practicable, for the full hearing on matters covered in paras. III.30.9–III.30.17 of the PD (III.30.5).

The trial, sentencing or appeal hearing (III.30.9–30.18)

9.7.6 The need for any of the following adaptations and the availability of such adaptations should be considered by the court both at the PCMH and at the start of the effective hearing, whether that hearing be a trial, a sentence or an appeal.

9.7.7 A judge at a PCMH hearing is likely to leave issues as to seating arrangements (III.30.10) and whether wigs and gowns are to be worn (III.30.14) to the trial judge. So far as the trial timetable is concerned (III.30.12), the judge at the

PCMH is very unlikely to make specific directions as to this, again usually preferring to leave it to the trial judge. The advocate should consider raising some matters – for example, if there will be a need for regular breaks to ensure the defendant has understood the evidence – as this will affect the trial time estimate. It often falls to the advocate to remind the trial judge of this requirement.

Effective participation at trial

9.7.8 The principal measures to ensure effective participation, in accordance with the overriding principle of the PD, include the requirement that, subject to appropriate security arrangements, the proceedings should, if practicable, be held in a courtroom in which participants are on the same or almost the same level (III.30.9). Seating arrangements in court for a vulnerable defendant, especially if young, should enable them to sit with family members or others in a like relationship, and with some other suitable supporting adult such as a social worker, in a place which permits easy, informal communication with his legal representatives. The court should ensure that a suitable supporting adult is available throughout the course of the proceedings (III.30.10).

9.7.9 At the beginning of the proceedings the court should ensure that the proceedings have been explained to the defendant in terms that he can understand, and remind those representing the defendant and the supporting adult of their responsibilities throughout the hearing to explain each step as it takes place, including the consequence of a guilty verdict. Throughout the trial the court should continue to take an active role in ensuring the defendant has understood what is happening and what has been said by the bench, advocates and witnesses (III.30.11).

9.7.10 The trial should be conducted according to a timetable which takes full account of a vulnerable defendant's ability to concentrate. Frequent and regular breaks will often be appropriate. The court should ensure, so far as is practicable, that the trial is conducted in simple, clear language that the defendant can understand and that cross-examination is conducted by questions that are short and clear (III.30.12).

9.7.11 In respect of the defendant's evidence, the court should consider whether a direction should be made so as to enable a vulnerable defendant to give evidence by means of live link in accordance with YJCEA 1999, s.33A and, if so, the practical arrangements to be made (III.30.13) (and see further below at **9.8**).

9.7.12 The presumption is that robes and wigs will not be worn unless the court, for good reason, orders that they should, although for sentencing in grave cases it may be appropriate for the court to be robed even where the trial has been conducted without robes and gowns. Security officers (where a defendant is in custody) should not be in uniform, and there should be no recognisable police presence in court, save for good reason (III.30.14).

9.7.13 Other provisions relating to the restriction of attendance of members of the public, reporting facilities, including the limitation of numbers of reporters in the courtroom, are dealt with at III.30.15–30.17.

9.8 SPECIAL MEASURES FOR DEFENDANTS/LIVE LINK

9.8.1 'Special measures directions', introduced in Part II of YJCEA 1999, applied originally only to vulnerable and intimidated witnesses (including defence witnesses), i.e. not to defendants. As a result of s.47 of the Police and Justice Act 2006, which inserted a new Chapter 1A into Part II of the Act as above, there is now provision for a vulnerable defendant to give evidence by live link.

9.8.2 An application for the use of live link by a vulnerable defendant may be appropriate for a number of reasons. Such a defendant may simply be facing trial alone and his ability to participate effectively be improved by giving evidence in that manner. Equally, where the court has declined to order separate trials, there are obvious advantages to a vulnerable defendant in his being able to give evidence by live link, either where he is jointly charged with a non-vulnerable defendant or defendants, and/or where the trial is being conducted on a 'cut-throat' basis, whether or not his co-defendant/s is/are vulnerable too.

9.8.3 Under s.33A of YJCEA 1999, a defendant aged 18 or over may apply to give evidence by live-link in the magistrates' court, youth court or Crown Court where the following conditions are met:

- he suffers from a mental disorder within the meaning of the Act or otherwise has a significant impairment of intelligence and social functioning; and
- he is for that reason unable to participate effectively in the proceedings as a witness giving oral evidence in court; and
- use of a live link would enable him to participate more effectively in the proceedings as a witness (whether by improving the quality of his evidence or otherwise (YJCEA 1999, s.33A(5) as inserted by Police and Justice Act 2006, s.47); and
- the court is satisfied that it is in the interests of justice for the defendant to give evidence through a live link.

9.8.4 A defendant under the age of 18 may give evidence in criminal proceedings, in those courts using a live link, if his ability to participate effectively in the proceedings as a witness giving oral evidence is compromised by his level of intellectual ability or social functioning provided that his ability to participate effectively would be improved by giving evidence over a live link (YJCEA 1999, s. 33A(4) as inserted by the Police and Justice Act 2006, s.47).The court must be satisfied that it is in the interests of justice for the youth to give evidence through a live link.

9.9 DEFENCE INTERMEDIARY AND OTHER ADAPTATIONS

9.9.1 In *R* v. *SH* [2003] EWCA Crim 1208, the Court of Appeal considered the position of an adult defendant with a significant learning difficulty, which meant he had limited communication skills. The court approved the use of a 'facilitator' (as being within the court's inherent powers) to assist the defendant in giving evidence in circumstances where the judge or counsel have difficulty in making themselves comprehensible to the defendant. It noted that in such a case, a person with understanding of the defendant's problems may be in a position where he can act as an interpreter, to make clear by putting into language which the defendant will understand, the nature of the question that he is being asked. The court also approved two possible courses of action where a defendant had a poor memory and this was hampering his ability to give evidence. First, the defendant's defence statement may be read to the jury so that the defendant's evidence could be understood in the light of that document. Second, the defendant may be permitted to refer to his proof of evidence or, if he cannot read, the court may permit leading questions to be asked from a document identified by him.

9.9.2 The function of a 'facilitator' as envisaged by the Court of Appeal (see **9.9.1**) is clearly very similar (if not identical) to that of an 'intermediary' within the terms of YJCEA 1999, s.29(2):

> (1) The function of an intermediary is to communicate –
>
> (a) to the witness, questions put to the witness, and to any person asking such questions the answers given by the witness in reply to them, and
>
> (b) to explain such questions or answers
>
> so far as necessary to enable them to be understood by the witness or person in question.

Hitherto, a defendant has not been not eligible for assistance from an intermediary under the terms of s.29, although the 'overriding principle' has enabled courts to appoint such an individual where it is justified, so as to ensure effective participation.

9.9.3 The lack of statutory provision for a defendant in these cases is now remedied by s.104 of the Coroners and Justice Act 2009. When this section comes into force (no fixed date) it will add a new s.33BA to YJCEA 1999, allowing for the examination of an accused to be conducted through an intermediary to ensure that he receives a fair trial:

> (6) Where the accused has attained the age of 18 when the application is made the conditions are that –
>
> (a) the accused suffers from a mental disorder (within the meaning of the Mental Health Act 1983) or otherwise has a significant impairment of intelligence and social function, and
>
> (b) the accused is for that reason unable to participate effectively in the proceedings as a witness giving oral evidence in court.

If the application is made on behalf of an accused under 18, the conditions are different; it has be shown that the ability of the accused to participate effectively in the proceedings, as a witness giving oral evidence in court, is compromised by his level of intellectual ability or social functioning. The function of an intermediary is to communicate to the accused questions put to him; to communicate his answers to any person asking such questions; and to explain such questions or answers so far as necessary to enable them to he understood by the accused or the person in question (s.33BA(4)).

9.9.4 In appropriate circumstances, the court may permit other more far-reaching adaptations to the trial process so as to secure effective participation. Such a situation arose in *R* v. *Ukpabio* [2008] 1 Cr App R 6, CA. In that case (decided prior to the earlier amendment of YJCEA 1999, which enabled the use of live link by a defendant), it was said that there is no limit on a court's power when it comes to securing the defendant's participation in his trial. Where, therefore, a defendant was unable to participate properly by being present, there was a power, exceptionally, to permit him not to be present and to stay in touch by live link or some other means. This exercise of the court's power or discretion thus goes beyond the statutory power under s.29 which allows a defendant to give evidence by live link, extending in exceptional circumstances to enable him to participate in the overall proceedings remotely.

9.10 INTERIM ORDERS UNDER THE MENTAL HEALTH ACT 1983

9.10.1 The court has the power to make a number of interim orders before deciding on either how a case is to proceed, or a defendant is to be sentenced. These are set out in full at **Appendix 1**.

Remand for reports

9.10.2 Section 35 gives the Crown Court (as well as the magistrates' court, see **Chapter 5**) power to remand any person awaiting trial at the Crown Court or post conviction (save in the case of a person convicted of murder) to hospital for the preparation of a report on his mental condition. The court must be satisfied on the written evidence of one s.12 approved registered medical practitioner that there is reason to believe that the accused is suffering from mental disorder and that it would be impracticable for a report to be prepared if he were on bail; and, based on written or oral evidence of a doctor or other representative of the admitting hospital, that a bed will be available for the accused within seven days. The remand in the first instance is for 28 days, and may be extended (in the absence of the defendant) for further 28-day periods, up to a maximum of 12 weeks, if the court has evidence from the doctor responsible for preparing the report that such further remands are necessary for completing the assessment.

Remand for treatment

9.10.3 Section 36 gives the Crown Court power to direct the remand to hospital for treatment of an accused person who is awaiting trial or during the course of a trial, i.e. an unconvicted defendant only. He must be charged with an offence punishable with imprisonment, other than murder. The court must have written or oral evidence of two registered medical practitioners that the accused is suffering from a mental disorder of a nature or degree which makes it appropriate for him to be detained in a hospital for medical treatment and appropriate treatment is available for him. The maximum period of detention is 12 weeks and, as under s.35 above, the defendant does not need to be produced at the subsequent renewal hearings which take place every 28 days.

Removal to hospital of other prisoners

9.10.4 Section 48, set out in full in **Appendix 1**, empowers the Secretary of State for Justice to direct the removal from prison to hospital of an unsentenced defendant where that defendant is suffering from mental disorder of a nature or degree which makes it appropriate for him to be liable to be detained in hospital for medical treatment. The Secretary of State must be satisifed that the defendant is in urgent need of treatment and such treatment is available for him. It should be noted that the power operates wholly independently of the court as it is the Secretary of State, on the appropriate medical recommendation, and not the judge or magistrate, who makes the order.

9.10.5 This power is particularly useful where a defendant is unable to give instructions owing to mental illness, is not receiving treatment in custody and is accordingly deteriorating. A s.48 direction can be made at any stage prior to sentence (there is an equivalent power under s.47 in relation to defendants who have been sentenced and are serving a term of imprisonment). If a defendant transferred under this section ceases to be a prisoner on remand, either because he is bailed or because the case collapses, the s.48 powers cease with immediate effect. In those circumstances, if he is still in need of treatment in a hospital, he can be detained under a civil section of the Act (see **Chapter 1**).

CHAPTER 10

Crown Court defences

10.1 OVERVIEW

10.1.1 The Domestic Violence, Crime and Victims Act (DVCVA) 2004 made a number of amendments to legislation governing fitness to plead and insanity. In particular, that Act amended the Criminal Procedure (Insanity) Act (CP(I)A) 1964 as already amended by the Criminal Procedure (Insanity and Unfitness to Plead) Act (CP(IUP)A) 1991. This legislation applies only to proceedings in the Crown Court although magistrates' courts have a role to play in reviewing, revoking or amending supervision orders made under these provisions.

10.1.2 Fitness to plead proceedings and insanity trials on indictment are different in nature from each other, although there is some overlap. Fitness to plead involves a consideration by a judge alone of the defendant's mental state at the time of trial. If a determination is made that he is unfit, a jury will be sworn to consider whether he did the act or made the omission charged (the *actus reus* of the offence). If the jury find he so did, the court will proceed to impose one of the disposals under CP(I)A 1964, ss.5 and 5A, as amended.

10.1.3 In contrast, in an insanity trial, a jury will consider the defendant's mental state at the time of the offence as part of the overall evidence in the case. The issues for the jury in such a trial are twofold: they must consider first whether they find the defendant to have done the act or made the omission charged (*actus reus*); if they so find, they then consider whether they find the defendant to have been insane at the time of the offence. If the jury are satisfied of both, they will return the 'special verdict' of not guilty by reason of insanity. The court will also then proceed to disposal under CP(I)A 1964, ss.5 and 5A, as amended.

10.1.4 Sections 4, 4A, 5, 5A of, and Sched. 1A to, CP(I)A 1964 are set out in **Appendix 2**. It is notable that these provisions just deal with the *procedures* to be followed in such cases, whereas the *criteria* by which fitness to plead and the test of insanity are determined are to be found in *R* v. *Pritchard* (1836) 7 C&P 303 and *M'Naghten's Case* (1843) 10 CL&F 200 respectively.

10.1.5 Many of the problems arising from both the *Pritchard* and *M'Naghten* tests relate to the fact that they were devised when psychiatry was in its infancy. The law is set out as it is now, but it should be noted that the Law Commission is currently working on a project, which, using empirical evidence and comparative jurisdictions, will attempt to identify more appropriate contemporary legal tests and rules for determining both fitness to plead and legal insanity.

10.2 UNFIT TO PLEAD

10.2.1 There are three situations in which a defendant, on arraignment, may fail to plead to the indictment:

- whcre he is unfit to plead;
- where he is mute of malice, i.e. he has deliberately chosen to stay silent;
- where he is 'mute by visitation of God' – this will include a defendant who is deaf and dumb (*R* v. *Pritchard*, see **10.2.2**) or so deaf he cannot hear the indictment when read.

Legal test of unfit to plead

10.2.2 The test of unfitness to plead is to be found in the leading case of *R* v. *Pritchard* (1836) 7 C & P 303. In that case, the defendant appeared to be, on arraignment, deaf, dumb and also of 'non-sane mind'. Three separate issues were put to the jury: whether the defendant was mute of malice or by the visitation of God; whether he was able to plead; and whether he was sane or not. On the last issue, the jury was directed to enquire whether the defendant was of sufficient intellect to comprehend the course of proceedings of the trial, so as to make a proper defence, to challenge a juror to whom he might wish to object, and to understand the details of the evidence. The judge directed that if there was no certain mode of communicating to the defendant the details of the evidence so that he could clearly understand them and be able properly to make his defence to the charge against him, the jury ought to find that he was not of sane mind. That test has been subsequently approved in a number of authorities.

10.2.3 In *R* v. *M (John)* [2003] EWCA Crim 3452, the Court of Appeal considered (and approved) the trial judge's directions to the jury (this being prior to the DVCVA 2004) as to how they should approach the question of whether the defendant was fit to plead. These directions were that, in order to be fit to stand trial at all, a defendant must be capable of doing six things. It was sufficient for the defence to persuade the jury on the balance of probabilities that any one of those six things were beyond the defendant's capabilities. The 'six things' he had to be capable of were as follows:

- understanding the charges;
- deciding whether to plead guilty or not;
- exercising his right to challenge jurors;
- instructing solicitors and counsel;

- following the course of proceedings;
- giving evidence in his own defence.

10.2.4 A number of other points have arisen from the consideration of the *Pritchard* criteria in subsequent authorities.

(i) An accused may be unfit to plead even though he is not insane within the meaning of the *M'Naghten* Rules: *Governor of Stafford Prison ex p. Emery* [1909] 2 KB 81.

(ii) The fact that a court may think that a defendant is incapable of acting in his own interests is insufficient by itself for a conclusion to be reached that he is unfit to plead: see *R* v. *Robertson* [1968] 1 WLR 1767, in which a defendant who suffered a form of persecution mania directed against freemasons and the unions in the USA, but was otherwise able to give a lucid account of the matters upon which he faced trial, was properly found to be fit to plead, the medical concerns being limited to potential irrational objections to jurors.

(iii) A high degree of abnormality does not necessarily mean that a defendant is incapable of following a trial, giving evidence or instructing counsel: *R* v. *Berry* (1978) 66 Cr App R 156.

(iv) In *R* v. *Moyle* [2008] EWCA Crim 3059, the Court of Appeal observed that whilst each case depends upon its own facts, delusions as to the court's powers of sentence, or as to the objectivity of the court, or as to the evil influences which are thought to be present in the proceedings, do not necessarily require a finding that a person is unable to give instructions and to understand the proceedings. In that case, the court rejected submissions (supported by psychiatric evidence) that the defendant had been unfit to plead at the time of his trial. In so doing, the court had regard to the fact that the defendant had been represented at trial by leading and junior counsel and a solicitor, who had found no reason to query the defendant's fitness to plead. The trial had been conducted by an experienced judge, who had allowed it to proceed; and the defendant's evidence at trial gave rise to no doubts about his ability to participate in proceedings. In the event, the psychiatric evidence on appeal enabled the court to quash the conviction for murder and substitute a conviction for manslaughter on the ground of diminished responsibility.

Procedure in unfit to plead cases (CPIA 1964, s.4)

10.2.5 The issue as to whether a defendant is fit to plead is now determined by a judge alone, rather than by a jury, as was the case prior to the amendment of CP(I)A 1964 by DVCVA 2004. The written or oral evidence of two or more registered medical practitioners, at least one of whom is s.12 approved, is required before a court can make a finding of unfitness (CP(I)A 1964, s.4(6)). A judge is entitled to reject such evidence, although he must keep the issue under review (*R* v. *M* [2006] EWCA Crim 2391).

10.2.6 There is no requirement that such evidence should be given live, and, in practice, if the issue of fitness is not contested by the Crown, there should be no need for such evidence to be called. Clearly, if the issue is to be contested, live evidence will have to be given, so that it can be tested by each side.

10.2.7 If the issue of fitness to plead is raised by the defence, the burden of proof rests upon the defence to establish on a balance of probabilities that the accused is unfit (*Robertson*, see **10.2.4**). If the Crown raises the issue, it bears the burden of proof beyond reasonable doubt (see *R* v. *Podola* [1960]1 QB 325).

10.2.8 In practice, whether or not the Crown has alerted the court and the defence to a potential issue as to a defendant's fitness to plead, it will be the defence who, in the process of trial preparation, will have undertaken the task of obtaining the necessary medical evidence in order to establish whether or not the defendant is 'under a disability', i.e. unfit to plead (see CP(I)A 1964, s.4(1)). Section 4(4) of CP(I)A 1964 requires the issue of fitness to be determined 'as soon as it arises' – which in practice means as a preliminary issue, and quite separately from any evidence being called as to the facts alleged. However, under s.4(2), the court can postpone consideration of unfitness until any time up to the opening of the defence case, if of the opinion that having regard to the nature of the supposed disability, postponement is expedient and in the interests of the accused.

10.2.9 Postponement of the issue of unfitness has in the past been approved as a useful tactic where there is a reasonable prospect of the Crown's case being successfully challenged so that the defence will not be called upon: see *R* v. *Webb* [1969] 2 QB 278; *R* v. *Burles* [1970] 2 QB 278. However, with the present emphasis on the early identification of trial issues it may be that a court would have to be persuaded that this was a proper approach, and clearly careful consideration would have to be given to the timetabling of the case (a point made in *Norman*, see **10.2.16**). If a defendant who has been found unfit to plead and to have done the act becomes fit to plead before final disposal of the case, the proper course is for the court to hold a second hearing on the issue of fitness to plead. If then the defendant is found to be fit, the need to proceed under CP(I)A 1964, ss.4(A) and 5 would be obviated: *R (on the application of Hasani)* v. *Crown Court at Blackfriars* [2006] 1 Cr App R 27, DC.

10.2.10 In *R* v. *B & Others* [2008] EWCA Crim 1996 the Court of Appeal considered the question (which arose on appeal from a preliminary hearing) of whether to try a defendant who was unfit to plead together with those defendants who were fit. The case involved allegations of serious sexual abuse against 10 people over a period of 40 years from 1968 to 2007. The court held that it was possible to try all defendants together, the jury only having to decide in respect of the unfit defendant whether the *actus reus* was proven. That would equally be the case where a defendant became unfit during a multi-handed trial; in those circumstances, the jury could switch to the fact-finding exercise in respect of that defendant. This decision raises all sorts of questions from a practical viewpoint, not least how a 'cut throat' trial could be conducted in those circumstances. If the advocate finds himself representing an unfit defendant in a multi-handed trial as above, clearly the court's powers of severance would need to be kept under continual review.

The act/omission hearing

10.2.11 If a determination is made that a defendant is unfit, the procedure set out in CP(I)A 1964, s.4A must be followed. A jury will be sworn, and that jury must decide whether the defendant 'did the act or made the omission charged against him as the offence'. If satisfied that he did, they must find accordingly; if not so satisfied, they must acquit. At this stage, the burden of proof to the criminal standard applies. Furthermore, the same rules of evidence apply to a trial of the facts as to a conventional criminal trial: *R* v. *Chal* [2007] EWCA Crim 2647.

10.2.12 However, the jury trying whether the defendant did the act or made the omission do not consider the mental element of the offence being tried: *R* v. *Antoine* [2001] 1 AC 340. In that case, in which the defendant was charged with murder, the House of Lords held that the defence of diminished responsibility could not be raised. In using the word 'act' rather than 'offence' in CP(I)A 1964, Parliament had made it clear that the jury was not to consider the mental elements of the offence. However if there was objective evidence upon which mistake, accident, or self-defence was raised, then the jury should not find that the defendant 'did the act' unless they were satisfied beyond reasonable doubt on all the evidence that the prosecution had negatived that defence. *R (on the application of Grant)* v. *DPP* [2001] EWCA Crim 2611 similarly held that provocation could not be raised at the s.4A hearing, since it inevitably required examination of the defendant's state of mind, rather than whether he 'did the act charged'.

10.2.13 The separation of the elements of an offence into *actus reus* and *mens rea* is not necessarily straightforward. In particular, in certain statutory provisions the question of whether a defendant's 'intention' is part of the *actus reus* or the *mens rea* can cause difficulties: see *R (on the application of Young)* v. *Central Criminal Court* [2002] EWHC 548 (Admin), a case concerning the concealment of material facts contrary to the Financial Services Act 1986, s.47(1), in which the requisite intention was held to be part of the *actus reus*, whereas dishonesty and the defendant's 'purpose' were part of the *mens rea*.

Defence evidence in the act/omission hearing

10.2.14 It was said in *R* v. *Antoine* (**10.2.12** above) that following a finding that a defendant is under a disability, the judge and counsel should always give careful consideration as to whether it is right that the defendant should be called to give evidence in the act/omission hearing. In practice, it is difficult to envisage circumstances in which it would be appropriate to do so. That does not preclude the calling by the defence of other evidence on the defendant's behalf: indeed, CP(I)A 1964, s.4A(2)(b) anticipates such circumstances. That subsection refers to evidence 'adduced by a person appointed by the court under this section to put the case for the defence'.

10.2.15 Conducting an act/omission hearing where the advocate has few or no instructions from the defendant is obviously very different from conducting a 'normal' trial, where the advocate will have specific instructions from his client. It may be that there is other evidence that can be called to undermine the Crown's case; it may be that there is none. In some cases it will be proper to test the evidence called by the Crown; in others it may be that it is proper to ask no questions at all. It is impossible to lay down any general guidance as each case will depend on its facts and be a matter of individual judgement for the advocate.

10.2.16 The advocate's role in these circumstances was considered in *R* v. *Norman* [2008] EWCA Crim 1810, in which the Court of Appeal noted that the advocate who deals with this stage of the proceedings 'may not necessarily be the same person who has represented the defendant to date, as it is the responsibility of the court to be satisfied that the person appointed is the right person for this difficult task'. It is clear from this case that any advocate contemplating undertaking both stages of the fitness to plead procedure should be ready to satisfy the court if necessary that he is sufficiently experienced in the conduct of such matters.

Disposals under CP(I)A 1964

10.2.17 If the defendant is found to be both unfit to plead, and to have done the act/made the omission charged (or is found not guilty by reason of insanity, see below at **10.3**), the court must make one of the following orders pursuant to CP(I)A 1964, s.5:

- a hospital order (with or without a restriction order);
- a supervision order; or
- an absolute discharge.

10.2.18 Such a defendant is a 'relevant offender' for the purposes of the notification requirements under s.80 of the Sexual Offences Act 2003 (i.e. the 'Sex Offenders Register') where the finding is in respect of an offence listed in Sched. 3 to the Sexual Offences Act.

10.2.19 The Crown Court can also proceed to disposal under CP(I)A 1964, s.5 where a defendant is found to have 'done the act' in respect of a summary only matter included on an indictment by virtue of the Criminal Justice Act 1988, s.40, where that summary offence is the only count on the indictment in respect of which the defendant was convicted: *R (on the application of Koncar)* v. *Southwark Crown Court* [1988] 1 Cr App R 321, DC.

10.2.20 It should be noted that the Rehabilitation of Offenders Act 1974, s.1(4)(b) applies not just to those convicted of an offence, but also to 'any finding (other than a finding linked with a finding of insanity) in any criminal proceedings that a person has committed an offence or has done the act or made the omission charged'.

Hospital orders

10.2.21 If a defendant is found to have done the act/made the omission charged on an indictment for murder, or is found to be not guilty by reason of insanity on such an indictment, a s.41 restriction order must be imposed, provided the conditions for making a hospital order are met. If conditions are not met, the court's options are limited to a supervision order or an absolute discharge.

10.2.22 If the court wishes to make an order for admission to hospital, it must apply the provisions of s.37 of the Act, including the requirements for medical evidence. Under CP(I)A 1964, s.5A(4) the court is able to require a hospital to admit that defendant, whereas there is no such power in respect of those convicted of an offence. This reflects the fact that the court has the option of a criminal justice disposal following conviction, but has no such option following a finding of unfitness or insanity. The interim orders under ss.35, 36 and 38 of the Act (see **Chapters 9** and **11**) are available to the court prior to final disposal of the matter: CP(I)A 1964, s.5A(2).

10.2.23 A defendant who has been made the subject of a hospital order with a restriction order under the provisions of CP(I)A 1964, s.5(2) faces the possibility that, should he become fit to plead, he may be remitted for trial. Section 5A(4) of CP(I)A 1964 provides that, in such circumstances, the Secretary of State may, if satisfied after consultation with the responsible clinician that the defendant can be properly tried, remit the defendant for trial, either to the court of trial or to a prison. On the person's arrival at court or prison, the hospital order and restriction order cease to have effect. This provision applies only to those defendants who are still subject to the restriction order, including patients on leave of absence from hospital, but not those who have been conditionally discharged and not recalled to hospital. It should be noted that the RC is in any event under a duty to produce written reports to the Secretary of State at regular intervals in respect of the progress of any patient who is the subject of a restriction order (whether made under these provisions, or following conviction).

Supervision orders

10.2.24 The provisions in relation to supervision orders are to be found in Sched. 1A to CP(I)A 1964 (see **Appendix 2**). Before making a supervision order, the court has to be satisfied that having regard to all the circumstances of the case, the making of a supervision order is the most suitable means of dealing with the defendant.

10.2.25 A supervision order made under the CP(I)A provisions must be for a specified period of not more than two years. Supervision is provided either by social services or by the Probation Service. The defendant can be required to submit during the whole or part of the order to medical treatment as directed, although the court cannot impose such a requirement without the written or oral evidence of two registered medical practitioners.

10.2.26 Paragraph 4 of Sched. 1A contains provision for the supervision and treatment of defendants who require treatment for either a mental or a physical disorder. In the case of mental disorder, one of the doctors providing medical evidence must be s.12 approved; the court must be satisfied that the defendant's mental condition is such as requires and may be susceptible to treatment, but is not such as to warrant the making of a hospital order within the meaning of the Act. In the case of physical disorder, the court must be satisfied that because of his medical condition, other than his mental condition, the defendant is likely to pose a risk to himself or others, and the condition may be susceptible to treatment.

10.2.27 Paragraph 8 of Sched. 1A contains provisions enabling a court to make a residence requirement. The court must consider the 'home surroundings' of the defendant before imposing such a requirement.

10.2.28 Supervision orders made under CP(I)A 1964 can be revoked or amended (see Part 3 of the Schedule) but cannot be 'breached'; that is, there is no power to revoke and re-sentence. This is because supervision orders are made pursuant to a finding of the act/omission, rather than upon conviction.

10.2.29 It follows from the above that supervision orders will be made in circumstances where the offence in question is more than trivial, but medical evidence does not support the making of a hospital order. This might be the case where a defendant is suffering from mental impairment/learning disability of a degree which has left him unfit to plead, but for which hospital treatment is neither suitable nor available.

Absolute discharge

10.2.30 Where the court is of the view that an order for absolute discharge (CP(I)A 1964, s.5A(6)) would be 'most suitable in all the circumstances of the case', such an order can be made. This is likely only to be the case where the offence was trivial, and the defendant requires neither hospital treatment nor supervision and treatment in the community.

10.3 INSANITY

10.3.1 Insanity trials are relatively rare. Prior to CP(IUP)A 1991, following a finding of not guilty by reason of insanity the court had no option but to order the defendant to be admitted to such hospital as specified by the Secretary of State. The court now has the same choice of disposals as on a finding of unfit to plead where the act/omission is proved (see **10.2.17**).

10.3.2 The defence of insanity is based on the absence of *mens rea*. The mental condition recognised by the law as insanity for this purpose is not the same as insanity or mental illness recognised by medical science. Many of the authorities in which insanity has been considered are concerned with the defence of automatism (see **10.4**).

The legal test of insanity

10.3.3 The defence of insanity is still governed by the *M'Naghten* Rules (*M'Naghten's Case* (1843) 10 CL & F 200). The rules have long been treated as authoritative, and were confirmed to be so by the House of Lords in *R* v. *Sullivan* [1984] AC 156 (see **10.3.6**). The relevant passage from *M'Naghten* is as follows:

> Every man is presumed to be sane, and to possess a sufficient degree of reason to be responsible for his crimes, until the contrary be proved to their satisfaction; and that to establish a defence on the ground of insanity, it must be clearly proved that at the time of committing of the act the party accused was labouring under such a defect of reason, from disease of the mind, as not to know the nature and quality of the act he was doing; or, if he did know it, that he did not know that it was wrong.

10.3.4 The material time is 'at the time of committing the act', as opposed to the defendant's mental state at the time he comes to trial. It is entirely possible for a defendant to be able to advance insanity as a defence at trial, whilst being fit to plead at the point of that trial. For instance, a defendant who suffers from a treatable mental illness, and who, following arrest, has received treatment so as to enable him to recover sufficiently to be able to plead to the indictment, give instructions and follow proceedings, may still advance the insanity defence, if at the time of the commission of the offence he can bring himself within the *M'Naghten* Rules.

10.3.5 'Such a defect of reasoning' means that a defendant's power of reasoning must be impaired. A mere failure to use the power of reasoning would not fall within the *M'Naghten* Rules. Thus in *R* v. *Clarke* [1972] 1 All ER 219, the defendant, charged with shoplifting, was entitled to have the simple defence of lack of *mens rea* considered by the jury rather than insanity, the position being that she was suffering not from a defect of reason but 'at most, a mere absent minded failure to use the powers of reasoning she undoubtedly still possessed'.

10.3.6 'Disease of the mind' is a legal question for the judge to decide, in accordance with the test set out by Lord Diplock in *Sullivan* [1984] AC 156, although medical evidence will be required under CP(IUP)A 1991:

> The nomenclature adopted by the medical profession may change from time to time ... But the meaning of the expression 'disease of the mind' as the cause of a 'defect of reason' remains unchanged for the purpose of the *M'Naghten* Rules ... 'mind' in the *M'Naghten* Rules is used in the ordinary sense of the mental faculties of reason, memory and understanding. If the effect of a disease is to impair these faculties so severely as to have either of the consequences referred to in the latter part of the rules, it matters not whether the etiology of the impairment is organic, as in epilepsy, or functional, or whether the impairment itself is permanent or transient or intermittent, provided that it subsisted at the time of the commission of the act.

10.3.7 The phrase 'as not to know the nature and quality of the act he was doing' refers to the physical rather than the moral quality of the act: see *R* v. *Sullivan* (**10.3.6**), in which it was said that: 'addressed to an audience of jurors in the 1980s it might more aptly be expressed as "he did not know what he was doing".'

10.3.8 The phrase 'that he did not know that it was wrong' has the meaning of *legally* wrong rather than *morally* wrong (*R* v. *Windle* [1952] 2 QB 826). Windle thought it was morally right to kill his suicidal wife and yet he knew it was legally wrong. He was properly found not to be insane. More recently, in *R* v. *Johnson* [2007] EWCA Crim 1978, the defendant, a paranoid schizophrenic, had stabbed his victim with a knife. He knew his actions were against the law but he did not consider them to be morally wrong. The court again held that 'wrong' meant contrary to law and 'did not have a vague meaning that might vary according to the opinion of different persons whether a particular act might or might not be justified'.

Procedure and the special verdict of insanity

10.3.9 Section 2(1) of the Trial of Lunatics Act 1883 as amended by CP(I)A 1964, s.1 provides for the 'special verdict':

> Where in any indictment or information any act or omission is charged against any person as an offence, and it is given in evidence on the trial of such person for that offence that he was insane, so as not to be responsible, according to law, for his action at the time when the act was done or omission made, then, if it appears to the jury before whom such person is tried that he did the act or made the omission charged, but was insane as aforesaid at the time when he did or made the same, the jury shall return a special verdict that the accused is not guilty by reason of insanity

A 'special verdict' must be returned by a jury, after trial. The Crown has no power to accept such a verdict, even if medical evidence is not contested: see *R* v. *Crown Court at Maidstone ex p Harrow LBC* [2000] 1 Cr App R 117, DC.

10.3.10 Before the jury can return a 'special verdict', the prosecution must first prove (the burden of proof to the criminal standard applies) that the defendant did the act or made the omission charged. If they fail to do so, the defendant is entitled to an outright acquittal, whether or not he was insane at the time of the alleged offence. The meaning of 'act or omission' in the context of insanity was considered by the Court of Appeal in *Attorney General's Reference (No. 3 of 1998)* [1999] 2 Cr App R 214, CA. The court held that, in determining whether the defendant 'did the act or made the omission charged' for the purposes of the Trial of Lunatics Act 1883, s.2(1) as amended, the prosecution was only required to prove the ingredients which comprise the *actus reus* of the offence, a decision confirmed as correct by the House of Lords in *R* v. *Antoine* (see **10.2.12** above).

10.3.11 Expert evidence is a prerequisite of an acquittal on the ground of insanity. Section 1(1) of CPIUP 1991 stipulates that the 'special verdict' shall not be returned except on the evidence of two registered medical practitioners at least one of whom is a s.12 'duly approved' doctor.

10.3.12 Insanity can be raised by either prosecution or defence, or by the court. If the defendant raises insanity, the burden of proof falls upon the defendant, on the balance of probabilities. If insanity is raised by the Crown, the proof is to the normal standard, i.e. beyond reasonable doubt (*Woolmington* v. *DPP* [1935] AC 462).

10.3.13 *R* v. *Casey* (1948) 32 C App R 91 gives guidance on trial procedure where the defence of insanity is relied upon. The court held that it is for the defence to call any witness whose evidence is directed to that issue; the prosecution's duty is limited to supplying the defence with a copy of any report or statement of any prison medical officer who can give evidence on that issue and to making such a person available as a witness for the defence. Although this case was decided in 1947 it is still cited in the current edition of *Archbold*.

10.3.14 The Crown is entitled to call evidence in rebuttal, and, on an indictment for murder, may also raise the issue of diminished responsibility (see further at **10.5**).

Disposals

10.3.15 The choice of disposals is the same as on a finding of unfit to plead (see **10.2.17** above).

10.4 AUTOMATISM

10.4.1 If the evidence raises issues of both insanity and automatism, it is necessary for the court to distinguish clearly between them as a matter of law (*R* v. *Sullivan* [1984] AC 156). Where the immediate cause of the alleged automatism could be internal or external the court must leave the defence of insanity (that is 'insane' automatism) and the defence of non-insane automatism to the jury, directing it to consider which was the immediate cause.

10.4.2 The defence of automatism can only be raised if there was a total lack of voluntary control during the commission of the offence. The cause must be external, e.g. lack of consciousness due to a blow to the head (*Bratty* v. *Attorney General for Northern Ireland* [1963] AC 386) or reflex actions when startled by a sudden loud noise (*Hill* v. *Baxter* [1958] 1 QB 277). It may be self-induced if not caused by drink or drugs and the defendant had no reason to be reckless as to the outcome of his actions. Automatism can be a defence to cases of 'specific intent' (*DPP* v. *Majewski* [1977] AC 443).

10.4.3 In crimes requiring only basic intent, the key element will be whether the defendant was reckless. For example, in the cases of *R* v. *Cunningham* [1957] 2 QB 396 and *R* v. *Quick* [1973] QB 910 the court had to consider whether a defendant knew or was reckless that failure to eat after an insulin injection could make him liable to uncontrollable conduct. In the case of *R* v. *Bailey* [1983] 1 WLR 760 the Court of Appeal held that:

> self-induced automatism, other than due to intoxication due to alcohol or drugs, may provide a defence to crimes of basic intent. The question in each case will be whether the prosecution has provided the necessary element of recklessness. In cases of assault, if the accused knows that his action or inaction are likely to make him aggressive, unpredictable or uncontrolled with the result that he may cause some injury to others and he persists in the action or takes no remedial action when he knows it is required, it will be open to the jury to find that he was reckless.

Thus a diabetic falling into a state of hypoglycaemia is not necessarily at fault in failing to take food after an insulin injection as it is not inevitably common knowledge, even among diabetics, that this will lead to aggressive conduct. In *R* v. *C* [2007] EWCA Crim 1862 the court held that if the defendant wished to raise the defence of automatism following a hypoglycaemic attack when driving, he would have to show both that he was unable to control the car and that the attack was unforeseen. He would have to provide an evidential basis for asserting that he could not reasonably have avoided the attack by advance testing and that there had been no advance warnings during the course of his driving. These cases can be contrasted with the case of a person having an epileptic seizure leading to an uncontrollable action. In the latter case the defence would be under insanity as epilepsy is a 'disease of the mind'.

10.4.4 The burden of proof lies upon the prosecution once there is sufficient evidence on the issue of automatism to be left to the jury to prove the absence of automatism beyond reasonable doubt.

10.5 DIMINISHED RESPONSIBILITY

10.5.1 Diminished responsibility is a defence which is only available on an indictment for murder. The defence is not available on a charge of attempted murder (*R* v. *Campbell* [1997] Crim LR 495), nor following a finding of unfitness to plead on an indictment alleging murder: see *Antoine*, above at **10.2.12**. If successful, it reduces murder to manslaughter. A defendant cannot be charged with manslaughter by reason of diminished responsibility. However, it can be 'perfectly proper, where medical evidence is plainly to this effect ... to accept a plea on that ground, and avoid a trial for murder' (*R* v. *Cox* [1968] 1 WLR 308).

The legal test

10.5.2 Section 2 of the Homicide Act 1957 states that:

> (1) Where a person kills or is party to the killing of another, he shall not be convicted of murder if he was suffering from such abnormality of mind (whether arising from a condition of arrested or retarded development of mind or any inherent causes or induced by disease or injury) as substantially impaired his mental responsibility for his acts or omissions in doing or being a party to the killing.
> (2) On a charge of murder, it shall be for the defence to prove that the person charged is by virtue of this section not liable to be convicted of murder.
> (3) A person who but for this section would be liable, whether as principal or as accessory, to be convicted of murder shall be liable instead to be convicted of manslaughter.
> (4) The fact that one party to a killing is by virtue of this section not liable to be convicted of murder shall not affect the question whether the killing amounted to murder in the case of any other party to it.

10.5.3 As will be apparent from s.2(2), the burden of proof lies with the defence, and is discharged by establishing the contention on the balance of probabilities: *R* v. *Dunbar* (1958) 41 Cr App R 182.

10.5.4 'Abnormality of mind' has been said to be:

> a state of mind so different from that of ordinary human beings that the reasonable man would term it abnormal ... wide enough to cover the mind's activities in all its aspects, not only the perception of physical acts and matters and the ability to form a rational judgment whether an act is right or wrong, but also the ability to exercise willpower to control physical acts in accordance with that rational judgment. The expression 'mental responsibility for his acts' points to a consideration of the extent to which the accused's mind is answerable for his physical acts which must include a consideration of the extent of his ability to exercise will power to control his physical acts. (per Lord Parker CJ in *R* v. *Byrne* (1960) 44 Cr App R 246)

It is held that abnormality of mind is a matter for the jury. Medical evidence is obviously important, but the jury must take into account all the evidence, including the acts and statements of the defendant, and his demeanor. However, the etiology of the abnormality of mind (that is, whether it arose from a condition of arrested or retarded development of mind or any inherent cause, or was induced by disease or injury) is a matter to be determined on expert evidence.

10.5.5 For the defence of diminished responsibility to succeed, the jury must be satisfied on the balance of probabilities that the defendant's abnormality was such as 'substantially' impaired his mental responsibility for his acts in doing or being a party to the killing. This is a question of degree, and, again, a matter for the jury. The following jury direction has been approved:

> substantial does not mean total, that is to say the mental responsibility need not be totally impaired, so to speak destroyed altogether. At the other end of the scale substantial does not mean trivial or minimal. It is something in between and Parliament has left it to you (the jury) to say on the evidence: was the mental responsibility impaired, and, if so, was it substantially impaired (*R* v. *Lloyd* [1967] 1 QB 175).

10.5.6 It is scientifically impossible to distinguish between the 'abnormal' defendant who *did not* resist an impulse and such a defendant who *could not* do so. The jury must approach the issue in a broad, common-sense manner. It may be appropriate to direct the jury that such abnormality as 'substantially impairs his mental responsibility' involves a mental state which in popular language (that is, not that of the *M'Naghten* Rules) the jury would regard as amounting to partial or borderline insanity. However it is clear from subsequent authorities that in some cases it will not be appropriate. For example, in *R* v. *Seers* (1984) 79 Cr App R 261, where the defendant suffered from chronic reactive depression, which the doctors giving evidence had agreed was nowhere near the borderline of insanity, such a direction was inappropriate.

10.5.7 Inability to exercise willpower due to abnormality of mind from one of the causes is sufficient; difficulty in controlling physical acts, depending on degree of difficulty, may be.

10.5.8 A study conducted on diminished responsibility pleas between 1997 and 2001 found that the most frequent primary diagnosis used in connection with the plea was depression (28.7 per cent), followed by schizophrenia (23.6 per cent), personality disorder (12.7 per cent) and other psychosis (12.7 per cent). Diminished responsibility has been successfully advanced in (*inter alia*) the following circumstances:

(i) Alcohol dependency syndrome (*R* v. *Wood* [2008] 2 Cr App R 34). However, diminished responsibility cannot be relied upon where a defendant was solely under the influence of drink and drugs on the occasion of the alleged offence (*R* v. *Gittens* [1984] QB 698; *R* v. *Dietschmann* [2003] 1 AC 1209, HL).
(ii) Post-natal depression and pre-menstrual tension (*R* v. *Reynolds* [1988] Crim LR 679, CA).
(iii) Battered women's syndrome (*R* v. *Hobson* [1998] 1 Cr App R 31, CA).

Procedure

10.5.9 Although there is no statutory requirement as to the calling of medical evidence in support of a diminished responsibility defence, in practice, such evidence is essential if the defence is to succeed, as the onus is on the defendant: *R* v. *Byrne* (**10.5.4** above). It should not be assumed that, even where the medical evidence is uncontradicted, but the jury nonetheless returns a guilty verdict of murder, such a conviction will be quashed on appeal. The Court of Appeal has considered a number of appeals in which juries have rejected medical evidence supporting a diminished responsibility defence. In *R* v. *Matheson* [1958] 1 WLR 474, it was said that where there are no facts or circumstances to give the jury a proper basis to disagree with the medical evidence, a conviction for murder is liable to be quashed and a conviction for manslaughter substituted. In *R* v. *Bailey* (1978) 66 Cr App R 31, CCA the court held that a jury should not 'perversely' reject medical evidence. In contrast, in *Walton* v. *R* [1978] AC 788 where the medical evidence in support of the defence was uncontradicted, such evidence was said to be a matter for the jury and accordingly the murder conviction was safe. Where medical experts differ, it is a matter for jury alone (*R* v. *Jennion* [1962] 1 All ER 689). What is clear from these authorities is that evidence of the conduct of the defendant before, at the time of, and after the killing is a relevant consideration in the success or otherwise of such appeals, as it inevitably is at trial.

10.5.10 The success or otherwise of a defence of diminished responsibility will also turn upon the extent to which the defence is able to establish the truth of the facts upon which the defence is based: *R* v. *Ahmed Din* (1962) 46 Cr App R 269, CCA. In that case, the defendant stabbed to death a man with whom he believed his wife had been having an affair. His diminished responsibility defence (paranoia) was supported by medical evidence and by the Crown. He was convicted of murder. On appeal, criticism was made both of the Crown, for not properly scrutinising the factual and medical evidence with care in order to see whether or not the defendant's belief was delusional and the defence, for a failure to prove facts upon which the doctors would have been able to rely upon as evidence, for instance by calling the wife to give evidence.

10.5.11 The same point was made in *R* v. *Bradshaw* (1986) 82 Cr App R 79. The court observed that in a proper case, where the defendant had fully recovered (as he had in this case), he would be able to provide relevant evidence himself in support of the factual basis of his defence. The court also said that, where there is no evidence in support of the defence other than the defendant's hearsay statements to a doctor, a judge would be entitled to direct the jury that there was 'but a flimsy foundation' to the defendant's case.

10.5.12 It follows that in preparing a defence of diminished responsibility, the solicitor must ensure that the medical reports deal not just with whether the s.2 criteria are made out, but the conduct of the defendant before, during and after the killing in the context of his abnormality of mind (see **6.5.1 (ix)**). The defence will need to seek support for the defendant's case, not simply in the usual way of obtaining supporting evidence as to the facts of the offence (if appropriate), but by obtaining as complete and independent a history as is possible to substantiate his abnormality of mind.

Defence evidence

10.5.13 It was held in *R* v. *Bathurst* [1968] 2 QB 99 that only rarely would it be appropriate for the defendant himself to be called in a trial where the defence of diminished responsibility is advanced. In a series of cases which pre-date CJPOA 1994, s.35 (including *Bathurst*), the Court of Appeal observed that it would be improper for the judge to comment on the failure of the defendant advancing a diminished responsibility defence to give evidence in all but the rarest cases (for instance where the defendant has recovered fully from any abnormality by the time of the trial). The observation is made in the current edition of *Archbold* that, in considering whether a direction under s.35 would be appropriate, it would appear probable that (save in those exceptional cases) judges will continue to direct juries that it would be improper to draw any adverse inference in respect of the defendant from his failure to give evidence.

Evidence for the Crown on insanity or diminished responsibility

10.5.14 Where in a murder trial a defendant advances the defence of either insanity or diminished responsibility, the Crown may adduce evidence to prove the other contention (i.e. insanity if diminished responsibility is advanced, and vice versa). The standard of proof in such circumstances is beyond reasonable doubt and the court can give directions as to the stage of the proceedings at which the prosecution may advance such evidence (CP(I)A 1964, s.6). Section 39 of the Coroners and Justice Act 2009 amends s.6 of CP(I)A 1964 by substituting in (6)(b) 'mental functioning' for 'mind'.

Disposals

10.5.15 Provided that the psychiatric reports recommend and justify a hospital order this is the likely disposal: *R* v. *Chambers* [1983] Crim LR 688, CA. The Criminal Justice Act (CJA) 2003 'dangerousness provisions' apply to a manslaughter conviction.

10.5.16 Sentencing in manslaughter cases has most recently been further considered by the Court of Appeal in *R* v. *Wood* [2009] EWCA Crim 651. The court noted that the mere fact that a case is one of manslaughter on the grounds of diminished responsibility does not preclude a sentence of imprisonment for life; however, in reality that sentence will be rare and will usually be reserved for particularly grave cases where the defendant's responsibility for his actions, although diminished, remains high. Secondly it held that the assessment of the seriousness of an offence of manslaughter on the grounds of diminished responsibility should not be focused exclusively on the defendant's culpability without considering the harm consequent on his actions. Thirdly, whilst there is no express link between the guidance given in Sched.

21 to CJA 2003 (determination of the minimum terms in relation to mandatory life sentence for murder) and the principles to be applied in diminished responsibility cases, when assessing the seriousness of such an offence with a view to fixing the minimum custodial term, there is no logical reason why, subject to the specific element of reduced culpability inherent in the defence, the guidance should be ignored. A vast disproportion between sentences for murder and sentences for manslaughter bordering on murder would be inimical to the administration of justice and thus actual sentences imposed in cases decided before the 2003 Act came into force should be treated with the utmost caution.

10.6 PROVOCATION

10.6.1 Provocation is a defence which is only available on an indictment for murder. The defence is not available on a charge of attempted murder (*R* v. *Campbell* [1997] Crim LR 495), nor following a finding of unfitness to plead on an indictment alleging murder: see *R* v. *Antoine* (**10.2.12** above). If successful, it reduces murder to manslaughter.

The legal test

10.6.2 This is set out at the Homicide Act 1957, s.3 as follows:

> Where on a charge of murder there is evidence on which the jury can find the person charged was provoked (whether by things done or by things said or by both together) to lose his self-control, the question whether the provocation was enough to make a reasonable man do as he did shall be left to be determined by the jury; and in determining that question the jury shall take into account everything both done and said according to the effect which, in their opinion, it would have on a reasonable man.

10.6.3 The burden of proof lies upon the prosecution, once there is sufficient evidence on the issue of provocation to be left to the jury, to prove the absence of provocation beyond reasonable doubt: *R* v. *McPherson* (1957) 41 Cr App R 213, CCA.

10.6.4 In *Attorney General's Reference (Nos. 74, 95 and 118 of 2002) (Suratan and others)* [2003] 2 Cr App R (S) 42, the Court of Appeal set out a number of assumptions that a judge must make in favour of a defendant found not guilty of murder but guilty of manslaughter by reason of provocation. These assumptions provide a useful summary of the elements of the offence and the basis upon which a manslaughter verdict can properly be returned:

- First, that the offender had, at the time of the killing, lost self-control; mere loss of temper or jealous rage is not sufficient.
- Second, that the offender was caused to lose self-control by things said or done, normally by the person killed.

- Third, that the offender's loss of control was reasonable in all the circumstances, even bearing in mind that people are expected to exercise reasonable control over their emotions and that, as society advances, it ought to call for a higher measure of self-control.
- Fourth that the circumstances were such as to make the loss of self-control sufficiently excusable to reduce the gravity of the offence from murder to manslaughter.

10.6.5 Where a jury is considering the first ingredient of provocation, that is, whether the defendant was provoked into losing his self-control, all evidence which is probative is admissible. This includes evidence of any mental or other abnormality making it more or less likely that the defendant lost his self-control. On this issue, psychiatric evidence may be relevant (see **6.5.1 (ix)**).

10.6.6 The potential difficulty for the mentally disordered defendant lies with the third, and objective test; that is, whether the provocation was enough to make a reasonable man do as he did. Prior to the leading Privy Council decision in *Attorney General for Jersey* v. *Holley* [2005] AC 580 there had been a conflict in the authorities as to how a jury should approach the question of the objective standard of self-control required. It is now clear from this case that even a defendant suffering from serious mental abnormality has to be judged by the standard of a person having ordinary powers of self-control. It was held in *Holley* that a 'reasonable man' meant a person of ordinary powers of self-control (*R* v. *Camplin* [1978] AC 705). That meant there was a risk under the statute of an individual defendant being temperamentally unable to achieve that standard. If the defendant suffered from abnormality of mind the defence of diminished responsibility was available under the Homicide Act 1957, s.2. The jury could take into account the defendant's characteristics when considering the gravity of the provocation. Therefore the statutory reasonable man had the powers of self-control to be expected of an ordinary person of like sex and age and in other respects shared such of the defendant's characteristics as the jury thought would affect the gravity of the provocation. The standard of self-control was uniform and objective and was not to be judged by the self-control which the defendant was able to exercise in the view of the jury. A more flexible test was inconsistent with the statute. If a defendant was taunted on account of his intoxication, that might be a relevant matter for a jury to take into account when assessing the gravity of the taunt to the defendant. But the defendant's intoxicated state was not a matter to be taken into account by the jury when considering whether the defendant exercised ordinary self-control.

10.6.7 The Privy Council made the point in particular that the Homicide Act 1957, s.2 is:

> apt to embrace some cases where it is inappropriate to apply to the defendant the standard of self-control of an ordinary person. Section 3, with its objective standard, is to be read with this in mind. The statutory provision regarding

diminished responsibility in section 2 represents the legislature's view on how cases of mental abnormality are to be accommodated in the law of homicide.

Consideration of the interrelation of the two defences is given in *Holley* (**10.6.6**) in the analysis of the proper approach to those cases of women who are more prone to lose their self-control because they are suffering from post-natal depression, battered woman's syndrome, or a personality disorder. It was said that evidence of the woman's condition may be relevant on two issues: whether she lost her self-control, and the gravity of the provocation for her. The jury will then decide whether in their opinion, having regard to the actual provocation and their view of its gravity for the defendant, a woman of her age having ordinary powers of self-control might have done what the defendant did. More importantly, in each of these three cases the defendant will in principle have available to her the defence of diminished responsibility. The potential availability of this defence in these cases underlines the importance of not viewing the defence of provocation in isolation from the defence of diminished responsibility. The two defences must be read together to obtain an overall, balanced view of the law in this field.

10.6.8 The history of the two perhaps best known appeals in this category are illustrative of the complexities that can arise in practice where defences of either or both diminished responsibility and provocation can arise:

(i) In *R* v. *Ahluwalia* (1993) 96 Cr App R 133, provocation only was relied upon at trial. The defendant was convicted. The Court of Appeal rejected an appeal on the basis of the judge's direction on provocation, but quashed the conviction and directed a re-trial on the basis of fresh evidence supporting a defence of diminished responsibility (a plea to which the Crown then accepted).

(ii) In *R* v. *Thornton (No. 2)* [1996] 2 Cr App R 108, CA diminished responsibility was relied upon by the defence at trial; provocation was also left to the jury by the judge (who, on the basis of the authorities, was obliged to do so). The defendant was convicted of murder, and her first appeal against conviction rejected. Her second appeal was allowed on the basis of fresh evidence demonstrating that she was suffering from a personality disorder and battered woman's syndrome at the material time; both were relevant matters for consideration by the jury.

Disposals

10.6.9 Reference should be had to the Sentencing Guidelines Council's Guideline of November 2005. The foreword to the Guideline makes it clear that the guideline is for use where the conviction for manslaughter is founded on provocation alone. There will be additional, different and more complicated matters to be taken into account where the other main partial defence, diminished responsibility, is a factor.

10.7 DURESS

10.7.1 Duress is a defence to all charges other than murder. It is therefore available in both summary proceedings and at trial on indictment, and is included here because, like the defence of provocation, the defence of duress contains both subjective and objective elements. It will be noted however that the 'sober person of reasonable firmness sharing the defendant's characteristics' (see below) is by no means identical to the 'statutory reasonable man' under the Homicide Act 1957, s.3. A mentally disordered offender may be vulnerable to pressure from other more sophisticated offenders. In those circumstances, the availability of a defence of duress may fall to be considered.

The legal test

10.7.2 The established test for duress derives from the cases of *DPP* v. *Lynch* (NI) [1975] AC 653, HL; *R* v. *Howe* [1987] AC 417, HL; and *R* v. *Graham* (1982) 74 Cr App R 235. Was a threat of physical harm to the person (including possibly of imprisonment) made, which was of such gravity that it might well have caused a sober person of reasonable firmness sharing the defendant's characteristics and placed in the same situation to act in the same way as the defendant acted?

10.7.3 In *R* v. *Bowen* [1996] 2 Cr App R 157, CA, the Court of Appeal considered the relevant characteristics to which the court should have regard. It was said that the mere fact that the accused was more timid than the ordinary person is irrelevant. It would be relevant that the accused belonged to a category of persons less able to resist pressure than people not within that category; obvious examples were youth, pregnancy, physical disability, recognised mental illness or a psychiatric condition, such as post-traumatic stress disorder leading to learned helplessness. A low intelligence quotient, short of mental impairment or defectiveness, was irrelevant, since it did not make a person less able to withstand threats than an ordinary person. Characteristics due to self-imposed abuse were also irrelevant. Psychiatric evidence might be admissible to show that the accused was suffering from mental illness or impairment or such a recognised psychiatric condition, provided that persons generally suffering from such a condition might be more susceptible to pressure and threats, and thus to assist the jury in deciding whether a reasonable person suffering from such condition might have been compelled to act as the defendant did.

10.7.4 Asperger's Syndrome has been held to be a mental illness or psychiatric condition of a kind relevant to the issue of duress and is a characteristic to which the court may have regard: *R* v. *Rogers* [1999] 9 Archbold News 1, CA.

10.8 INFANTICIDE

10.8.1 The offence of infanticide is found at s.1 of the Infanticide Act 1938 and as such pre-dates the Homicide Act 1957. Unlike cases of manslaughter by diminished responsibility, the offence of infanticide can be charged from the outset and can also be returned as alternative verdict to murder.

Legal test

10.8.2 The elements of the offence are as follows:

- a woman's wilful act or omission
- causes death of her child age under 12 months
- at the time when the balance of her mind was disturbed by reason of her not having fully recovered from the effect of giving birth to her child or by reason of the effects of lactation consequent upon the birth of the child.

10.8.3 If the above can be satisfied then, 'notwithstanding that the circumstances were such that but for this Act the offence would have amounted to murder, she shall be guilty of felony, to wit of infanticide, and may for such offence be dealt with and punished as if she had been guilty of the offence of manslaughter of the child.' In order to satisfy the third criterion it will obviously be necessary to instruct a psychiatrist to advise on her 'balance of mind'.

Disposals

10.8.4 Although the offence carries a sentence of life imprisonment, a custodial sentence is unlikely. In *R* v. *Sainsbury* (1989) 11 Cr App R(S) 533 a 12-month sentence was quashed on appeal. The court was informed that of 59 cases of infanticide before the courts between 1979 and 1988 none resulted in a custodial sentence (excluding a s.37 hospital order which is available).

10.9 CORONERS AND JUSTICE ACT 2009

10.9.1 The Coroners and Justice Act 2009 (see **Appendix 11**) received Royal Assent on 12 November 2009. It amends current legislation in relation to the defences of diminished responsibility, provocation and the law on infanticide. At the time of writing, no date has been fixed for these provisions to come into force.

10.9.2 In respect of diminished responsibility, the Homicide Act 1957, s.2(1) is substituted by a new test in which the main change is that the person who kills or is a party to the killing of another is not to be convicted of murder if he was suffering from an abnormality of mental functioning which arose from a recognised medical condition. This condition must substantially impair his ability to understand the nature of his conduct, to form a rational judgement or to exercise self-control and it provides an explanation for the defendant's acts and omissions in doing or being a party to the killing (s.52).

10.9.3 The Act abolishes the current defence of provocation and replaces it with the 'partial defence to murder: loss of control' (s.54). The purpose of the reforms have been described by the Justice Secretary Jack Straw as being 'to ensure that those who kill out of anger face up to their crimes and the distress they have caused the families of their victims; the existing partial defence of provocation is too generous to those who kill in anger and poorly tailored to killings in response to fear'.

10.9.4 The law on infanticide is amended so that if the elements of the offence are made out as at **10.8.2** then '*if* the circumstances were such that but for this Act the offence would have amounted to murder *or manslaughter*, she shall be guilty of felony, to wit infanticide, and may for such offence be dealt with and punished as if she had been guilty of the offence of manslaughter of the child' (s.57).

CHAPTER 11

Sentencing

11.1 GENERAL CONSIDERATIONS

11.1.1 In a relatively minor case involving a mentally disordered offender, a court may be persuaded to proceed to sentence in the absence of a pre-sentence report (PSR) or psychiatric report, particularly where the offence is not serious, the defendant has been remanded in custody for a significant period of time and the court is satisfied that he either does not need treatment at present or will accept it voluntarily. In those circumstances, to avoid a further adjournment for reports, the advocate may wish to submit that the court could and should deal with the case by means of an absolute or conditional discharge or fine.

11.1.2 However, in the vast majority of cases involving the sentencing of a mentally disordered offender, the court will require an up-to-date PSR and psychiatric report prior to sentence so as to assist with the question of disposal. In the case of a disposal under the Act, psychiatric reports are a statutory requirement. For a community order/suspended sentence with a mental health treatment requirement, a PSR and a psychiatric report will be necessary. Furthermore, where a court is considering custody, CJA 2003, s.157 provides that the court must obtain and consider a medical report on any defendant who is, or appears to be, mentally disordered.

11.1.3 Where a court is considering making a hospital order with a restriction order under s.37/s.41of the Act, the psychiatric report should contain a proper risk assessment upon which the court can base its findings. Similarly, when a court is considering invoking the CJA dangerousness provisions where a defendant is potentially 'dangerous' by virtue of his mental disorder, such a report should also be obtained. There may be other situations in which the court or a solicitor may seek a risk assessment from a mental health professional, in practice a psychologist or psychiatrist. It is important to understand the fundamental difficulties inherent in this process. The court is interested in the individual defendant and whether he will, or will not, re-offend or pose a risk to the public. However, social science research into risk of violence or other anti-social behaviour depends upon studying large groups of individuals in order to identify factors relevant to the risk of violence. Using group data regarding risk to predict risk at an individual level is not a straightforward process.

11.1.4 When a psychiatrist is asked to assess risk it should be noted that research has demonstrated that an unstructured clinical assessment of risk is no better than chance at predicting future violence. In practice, therefore, most psychiatrists employ some form of structured risk assessment, commonly known as 'structured professional judgement'. This combines static or actuarial risk factors and dynamic risk factors. Actuarial factors are unchangeable factors in the defendant's history such as any previous offences of violence, which cannot change but which taken as a whole 'anchor' the individual in a particular risk group. These are usually defined as low, medium or high risk. There are many dynamic risk factors including response to treatment if mentally ill, the presence of an active drug or alcohol problem and homelessness. These are amenable to change and addressing them is likely to lower the risk. The psychiatrist should be encouraged to provide reasons for his opinion, including outlining the risk factors and how they could be addressed, rather than simply finding that an individual is in a low, medium or high risk group.

11.1.5 More generally, the advocate will need to be in a position to assist the court as to any further reports that will be needed, and from whom these should be obtained. If a possible outcome is either a hospital order or a community order with a condition of treatment, a report should be sought from the appropriate catchment area hospital psychiatrist. If a psychiatric report has already been obtained on a defendant who is not in need of hospital admission but who might be a candidate for a community order with a condition of treatment, if the report is supportive of this course of action, it should be served on the Probation Service.

11.1.6 It will be helpful in any event to share any information on the defendant's mental disorder with the relevant authorities. The point was made by the Bradley Report that in many cases, a defendant put over for a PSR may well have mental health problems or a learning disability about which the Probation Service will have no information. Unless the defendant is forthcoming (if he is indeed able to be so), where there are no liaison or diversion services available, it can fall to probation staff untrained in mental health or learning disability to recognise the potential signs of a mental health problem or learning disability. One of the recommendations in the report is that all probation staff, including those based in courts, should receive mental health and learning disability awareness training.

11.2 CUSTODY

11.2.1 It has been recognised for some time that prison is likely to have a detrimental effect on the mental health of a mentally disordered offender. Home Office Circular 66/90 (see **Appendix 4**) Provision for Mentally Disordered Offenders states:

> It is the government's policy to divert mentally disordered persons from the criminal justice system in cases where the public interest does not require their prosecution. Where prosecution is necessary it is important to find non-penal

> disposals wherever appropriate and the police, courts, and probation service are asked to work together with their local health and social services to make effective use of the provisions of the Mental Health Act 1983 and the services which exist to help the mentally disordered.

This is confirmed by the Bradley Report which observed that 'custody can exacerbate mental ill health, heighten vulnerability and increase the risk of self-harm and suicide'.

11.2.2 Whilst few would argue with these assessments of the impact of custody on mentally disordered offenders, avoiding a custodial disposal for such a defendant is by no means a straightforward matter. Sentencing is often a complex exercise involving the weighing up of different and competing factors, of which a defendant's mental disorder is only one element. The court is bound to have regard to CJA 2003, s.142(1) (the 'five purposes of sentencing'), the relevant guideline authorities and the Sentencing Guidelines Council (SGC) sentencing guidelines. A departure from sentencing guidelines requires justification. Considerations as to deterrence and public protection will often override personal mitigating factors, such as a defendant's mental disorder.

11.2.3 Specific provision is made for the sentencing of a mentally disordered offender in CJA 2003 and in a number of the SGC guidelines which are set out below.

Medical report

11.2.4 Section 157 of CJA 2003 requires the court to obtain and consider a medical report on any defendant who is, or appears to be, mentally disordered before imposing a custodial sentence. However, such a report may be dispensed with if the court considers that it is not necessary. Section 157(3) further provides that before passing a custodial sentence (other than one fixed by law) on an offender who is or appears to be mentally disordered the court must consider:

(i) any information before it which relates to his mental condition (whether given in a medical report, pre-sentence report or otherwise); and
(ii) the likely effect of such a sentence on that condition and on any treatment which may be available for it.

11.2.5 This provision applies in summary proceedings and in the Crown Court. A custodial sentence imposed without the court obtaining the above report is not invalidated by the failure, although on appeal (if any) the appellate court is required to obtain and consider such a report (s.157(4)). 'Medical report' means a report by a s.12 approved doctor, and 'mentally disordered' means suffering from a mental disorder within the meaning of the Mental Health Act 1983.

Flexibility when sentencing

11.2.6 Some recognition of the need for flexibility in determining the appropriate disposal when sentencing mentally disordered defendants is to be found in CJA 2003, s.166(1) and (5). The section provides 'savings for powers to mitigate sentences and deal appropriately with mentally disordered offenders'. This effectively allows a court to depart from the requirement to focus on the aggravating factors of an offence, where it is appropriate to do so when dealing with a mentally disordered offender.

Sentencing Guidelines Council guidelines

11.2.7 'Mental illness or disability' is identified as a mitigating factor (a 'factor indicating significantly lower culpability') in the SGC guideline 'Overarching Principles: Seriousness' 2008 (para. 1.25) This guideline applies to sentencing in all offences and is therefore of considerable importance when determining sentence in the case of any mentally disordered offenders. It should be noted however that caution is required when considering mitigation in the case of a mentally disordered potentially 'dangerous offender': see further below.

11.2.8 In certain of the SGC guidelines relating to sentencing in cases of manslaughter by reason of provocation, assaults on children, child cruelty, ASBO cases and attempted murder, mental disorder is specifically identified as a mitigating factor. Below are the most relevant guidelines:

(a) **Overarching Principles: Assaults on Children and Cruelty to a Child** (March 2008)
Mental illness/depression is identified as a relevant area of personal mitigation; and 'indifference or apathy resulting from low intelligence ... immaturity or social deprivation resulting in an inability to cope with the pressures of caring for children [and] psychiatric illness' are potential issues relevant to a defendant's culpability (p.9).

(b) **Attempted Murder** (July 2009)
This identifies as a specific mitigating factor the fact that the offender suffered from an mental disorder or mental disability which lowered his degree of culpability (p.7).

(c) **Manslaughter by Reason of Provocation** (November 2005)
A court is advised that in assessing the nature, degree and duration of provocation it may consider 'any mental condition which may affect the offender's perception of what amounts to provocation' (p.4).

(d) **Breach of an Anti-Social Behaviour Order** (January 2009)
'Offender mitigation' is said to be particularly relevant to an ASBO breach, 'as compliance with the order depends on the ability to understand its terms and make rational decisions in relation to these'.

Sentence may therefore be mitigated where a defendant has a 'lower level of understanding due to mental health issues or learning difficulties' (p.5).

(e) **Overarching Principles: Sentencing Youths** (November 2009)
This guideline makes specific reference to the need by a court, when considering the welfare of a child or young person under CYPA 1933, s.44, to ensure that it is alert to the high incidence of mental health issues, learning difficulties or learning disabilities among young people in the criminal justice system. It must also be aware of the impact of a young defendant's speech or language difficulties upon his communication and understanding and the vulnerability of young people to self-harm, particularly in a custodial setting. All these factors are to be regarded as of importance when balancing the relevant sentencing considerations.

11.3 SENTENCING IN MURDER, ARSON AND SEXUAL OFFENCES CASES

11.3.1 Although there is no statutory requirement to obtain such a report in a case of arson, it was held in *R* v. *Calladine* (1975) *The Times*, 3 December, CA that it is unwise to sentence in such a case without a psychiatric report.

11.3.2 When sentencing for a sexual offence, the SGC Guideline to the Sexual Offences Act 2003 states that a PSR should normally be prepared, 'as this may contain important information about the sexually deviant tendencies of an offender and an assessment of the likelihood of re-offending; a psychiatric report may also be appropriate' (para. 1.23).

11.4 ORDERS UNDER THE MENTAL HEALTH ACT 1983 (AS AMENDED)

11.4.1 All the sections of the Act discussed below are set out in full detail at **Appendix 1**.

Interim hospital order: magistrates' court, youth court and Crown Court

11.4.2 A defendant who is suffering from mental disorder, and who has been remanded in custody prior to conviction, may well be a suitable candidate for a hospital order under s.37 of the Act, whether with or without a restriction order under s.41. However, such a defendant may have been seen only relatively briefly in custody during that remand period by a doctor (whether the visiting prison psychiatrist and/or a doctor instructed on behalf of the defence). In those circumstances it can be difficult for the court to assess whether or not a hospital order would be an appropriate disposal. In circumstances such as these, where inpatient assessment and treatment is required prior to final disposal, the court is empowered by s.38 of the Act to make an interim hospital order for a period of up to 12 months.

11.4.3 The purpose of a s.38 order is 'so that the offender's response in hospital can be evaluated without any irrevocable commitment on either side to this method of dealing with the offender if it should prove unsuitable' (Home Office Circular 71/1984). It is available both in summary proceedings and in the Crown Court, where a defendant has been convicted of an imprisonable offence (other than murder). The court must be satisfied on the written or oral evidence of two registered medical practitioners that the defendant is suffering from a mental disorder, and that there is reason to suppose that it may be appropriate to make a hospital order.

11.4.4 The order should initially be for a period not exceeding 12 weeks. It can be renewed thereafter for further periods of 28 days, subject to a maximum overall period of 12 months. Renewals of the order can take place in the absence of the defendant, provided he is represented. The court can also make a hospital order where a defendant is subject to an interim hospital order in that defendant's absence provided he is represented. In practice, it is only in unusual cases that renewals are for longer than a total of six months' duration. It is good practice for the solicitor to keep in contact with the treating team at the hospital to ensure that letters are sent to the Crown Court on time where there is a request for renewal of the order.

11.4.5 In summary proceedings, the court has no power to make an interim hospital order under s.38 in the case of a defendant found to have 'done the act or made the omission' under the PCC(S)A 2000, s.11(1) procedure, as such a defendant has not been 'convicted' by the court. However, such an order is available to the Crown Court following a finding that the defendant had done the act or made the omission in CP(I)A 1964 proceedings in the Crown Court and is also available where a defendant has been found not guilty by reason of insanity: CP(I)A 1964, s.5A(2)(d) (see **Chapter 10**).

11.4.6 A defendant who is made the subject of an order under s.38 has no right to apply to the Mental Health Review Tribunal nor can he be discharged, granted leave of absence or transferred to another hospital (see **Chapter 1**).

Hospital order: magistrates' court, youth court and Crown Court

11.4.7 An order under s.37 of the Act is an order for compulsory hospital treatment for a minimum of six months, and is the principal means of ensuring that a mentally disordered offender receives treatment rather than punishment. A hospital order is available to the court both in summary proceedings and in the Crown Court, where a defendant has been convicted of an imprisonable offence (other than murder), and the court is satisfied on the written or oral evidence of two registered medical practitioners that the defendant is suffering from mental disorder of a nature or degree which justifies his detention in hospital for appropriate medical treatment which is available for him. The court must be of the opinion, having regard to all the circumstances, including the nature of the offence and the character and antecedents of the offender, and to the other available methods of dealing with him, that the most suitable means of disposing of the case is by an order under the section.

11.4.8 It is important to note that, for the purposes of this section, the defendant's mental disorder as at the time of the offence is not at issue. The court has to be satisfied that the defendant is suffering from mental disorder of an appropriate degree as at the date of disposal. The Court of Appeal has remarked that the wording of the section is such that a hospital order may be made even though the mental disorder suffered by the defendant has developed since the date of the offence: *R* v. *Smith* [2001] EWCA Crim 743. The defendant's consent is not required for the making of a hospital order (*R* v. *Gunnee* [1972] Crim LR 261).

11.4.9 The court cannot make a hospital order unless a hospital bed is available within 28 days of the making of the order (s.37(4)). If the court makes the order and the defendant is not admitted to the hospital named in the order within the 28-day period starting from the date of the order, the order ceases to have effect and ceases therefore to provide authority for conveyanace to hospital and detention in that hospital after the expiry of the 28 days: *R (on the application of DB)* v. *Nottingham Healthcare NHS Trust* [2008] EWCA Civ 1354. It is good practice for the solicitor to liaise with the admitting hospital so as to be in a position to tell the court whether or not a bed is available.

11.4.10 A hospital order can be made even where there is no causal link between a defendant's mental disorder and the offence committed. The gravity of the offence is of concern to the court only in so far as the offence is an indication of the need for treatment in special conditions. A hospital order can properly be made in respect of a defendant guilty of a minor (albeit imprisonable) offence, but who is in need of treatment.

11.4.11 It should be noted that murder is the only offence for which a hospital order is not an available disposal. For those offences which in other circumstances would attract a mandatory minimum sentence (e.g. firearms offences under the Firearms Act 1968, s.51(A), third 'class A' drug trafficking offences and third domestic burglary offences under PCC(S)A 2000, s.110(2) and s.111(2), and certain offences under the Violent Crime Reduction Act 2006, ss.28 and 29, of using someone to mind a weapon) the power to make a hospital order is specifically preserved by s.37(1A). However, in a serious case, it should not be assumed that the court will inevitably follow a recommendation for a hospital order. The Court of Appeal has upheld the imposition of substantial prison sentences in two fairly recent cases, in both of which reports were available to the court recommending hospital orders and the s.37(2) requirements were met in full:

(a) In *R* v. *Nafei* [2005] 2 Cr App R (S) 24, the defendant was sentenced to 12 years' imprisonment following his plea to the importation of 30 kgs (15.38 kgs at 100 per cent) of cocaine. He had a long history of psychiatric illness and was suffering from schizophrenia at the time of sentence. The Court of Appeal upheld the sentence, noting that there was no causal connection between the offending and the defendant's mental illness, and emphasised that in such cases 'personal factors' were of less importance than other sentencing principles of policy and deterrence. The court also remarked that medical treatment was available in prison, and in hospital if necessary by way of the s.47/s.49 transfer procedure (see **Chapter 1**).

(b) In *R* v. *Khelifi* [2006] 2 Cr App R (S) 100 the defendant had pleaded guilty to a conspiracy to defraud, accepting responsibility for a loss of £155,000. He had been suffering from paranoid schizophrenia since 1994. He was sentenced to five years' imprisonment. The Court of Appeal reduced his sentence to three and a half years' imprisonment to take into account the impact of custody upon his mental health, but otherwise applied the principle in *Nafei*, noting that whilst the welfare of the offender is important, that has to be assessed in the light of the seriousness of the offence, and, in a case such as this, where co-defendants are to receive substantial terms of imprisonment, it is not wrong in principle to take into account parity of sentencing.

11.5 HOSPITAL ORDERS WITHOUT CONVICTION

Magistrates' court, youth court and Crown Court

11.5.1 Where an unsentenced defendant has been transferred to hospital under the provisions of s.48 of the Act, the court has the power under s.51(5) of the Act to make a hospital order (in the Crown Court with or without a restriction order attached), in the defendant's absence and without convicting him. The written or oral evidence of two medical practitioners is required before such an order can be made (one of whom must be s.12 approved) and the court must be 'of the opinion, after considering any depositions, or other documents required to be sent to the proper officer of the court, that it is proper to make such an order'.

11.5.2 In *R (on the application of Kenneally)* v. *Snaresbrook Crown Court* [2001] EWHC Admin 968 the court held that 'to pass sentence, even a sentence one of the objects of which is to the assist the defendant, without first convicting him is a drastic step, one that should be taken only in exceptional circumstances'. The power to make a hospital order under s.51(5) can only be exercised where it is 'impractical or inappropriate' to bring a defendant before the court. It was made clear that 'inappropriate' had to be construed restrictively. Whilst it did not mean physically impossible, a high degree of disablement or relevant disorder had to be present. It could not be used routinely to avoid a potentially troublesome trial as it was a short cut with significant long-term implications.

11.6 RESTRICTION ORDER

Crown Court

11.6.1 A restriction order under s.41 of the Act is not a 'stand-alone' order or a separate means of disposal. It is an order which is attached to a hospital order under s.37, affecting fundamentally the circumstances in which a defendant is detained.

11.6.2 The Crown Court may make a restriction order in addition to a hospital order if it appears to the court having regard to:

(a) the nature of the offence; and
(b) the antecedents of the offender; and
(c) the risk of his committing further offences if set at large,

that a restriction order is necessary for the protection of the public from serious harm. At least one of the registered medical practitioners whose evidence has been taken into account must give oral evidence to the court. It is desirable that the doctor giving oral evidence is on the staff of the admitting hospital: *R* v. *Blackwood* (1974) Cr App R 170. A restriction order could previously be made for a determinate period (although this was seldom done). As a result of amendment of the 1983 Act by the Mental Health Act 2007, the order now must be made without limit of time.

11.6.3 The court must assess not only the seriousness of the risk that a defendant will re-offend, but the risk that if he does so, the public will suffer serious harm: *R* v. *Birch* (1989) 11 Cr App R (S) 202, in which the following principles are set out:

- harm need not be limited to personal injury;
- it would be sufficient if a category of persons, or even a single individual were at risk;
- the seriousness of the offence cannot necessarily be equated with the probability that a restriction order will be made and is only one of the factors to be taken into account;
- the responsibility for assessing the risk lies with the court, which is not bound to follow the advice of medical witnesses;
- a restriction order should not be imposed therefore to mark the gravity of the case, nor as a means of punishment.

11.6.4 It follows that a court may make a restriction order even though medical witnesses recommend that no restriction order should be made (*Birch*, **11.6.3** above), although the power and discretion to impose such an order in these circumstances should only be exercised after careful consideration and with some caution (*R* v. *Roberts* [2003] EWCA Crim 858). If medical opinion is rejected, reasons must be given (*R* v. *Hurst* [2007] EWCA Crim 3436, a case in which a restriction order was quashed where there was insufficient evidence to justify the making of the order, and the judge had departed from the medical recommendations that a restriction order was not necessary).

11.6.5 Risk assessment is discussed at **11.1.3–11.1.5** above. It should not be assumed that a defendant who has no history of serious violence will not be made subject to a restriction order if, on the medical evidence, he is said to have the potential for causing serious harm in the future. Moreover, in *R* v. *Golding* [2006] EWCA Crim 1965 the Court of Appeal upheld the imposition of a restriction order on an appellant who had multiple convictions for burglary but had never acted violently. It found that the 'serious harm' criterion was satisfied because the appellant's psychosis was not controlled and his predilection for drugs could well lead him to act violently if confronted by a householder.

11.6.6 The Crown Court has jurisdiction to make a restriction order where there has been a conviction or plea in that court to a 'summary' offence triable only in the Crown Court by virtue of CJA 1988, s.40 (*R* v. *Avbunudje* [1999] 2 Cr App R (S) 189). See **9.3** for the court's powers to impose a restriction order following a committal for sentence under s.43(1) of the Act.

Preparing for a s.41 hearing

11.6.7 In any case where a restriction order may be made, the advocate will need to be ready to explore the need for such an order with the doctor giving oral evidence at the disposal hearing. If a judge has formed a clear provisional view that a restriction order is appropriate, the parties should be informed so that they can deal with it (*R* v. *Goode* [2002] EWCA Crim 1698).

11.6.8 All the material in the case must be scrutinised carefully, with regard in particular being given to the following:

- The nature of offence itself, including the defendant's attitude to it (if this can be ascertained).
- The defendant's antecedents; if there is nothing in the antecedents to indicate that serious harm has been caused in the past this is not conclusive, but is helpful.
- The fact that a judge conducting a risk assessment is likely (and entitled) to have regard to matters referred to in medical reports which may not have resulted in conviction, such as violence in a hospital setting or in prison whilst on remand; instructions will need to be taken on these matters and consideration given to the reliability/relevance of such material.
- The nature of the defendant's mental disorder.
- The current degree of the disorder.
- The relationship between the mental disorder and offending.
- The defendant's insight into his mental disorder.
- The defendant's conduct and compliance with medication (if relevant) during the period of remand/hospital admission prior to sentence.
- Treatment/treatability of the disorder – what is available and proposed and is the doctor able to estimate the length of time needed for such

treatment (regard may be had to any previous admissions under section or otherwise and speed of response to treatment).

- On the basis that the risk of committing further offences is reduced by hospital treatment, does such treatment need to be given under the auspices of a restriction order?
- Has the defendant shown that he can cooperate with mental health services (including taking medication) in the community? A s.41 order may be less likely in a borderline case where the court could have some confidence that a s.37 could be followed with a CTO if needed, with a reasonable prospect of success.

11.6.9 Ultimately, the deciding factor for the court is likely to be the stark differences in the release provisions and the very much greater degree of public protection where a restriction order is imposed (see further below).

11.7 HOSPITAL AND LIMITATION DIRECTION

Crown Court

11.7.1 Section 45A of the Act empowers the Crown Court, when imposing a prison sentence on a mentally disordered offender convicted of an offence other than murder, to give a direction for immediate admission to and detention in a specified hospital (a 'hospital direction') together with a direction that he be subject to the special restrictions set out in s.41 (a 'limitation direction'). The requirements as to medical evidence (including the need for oral evidence) and as to bed availability prior to the order being made are identical to those required for the making of a restriction order under s.41. A hospital and limitation direction cannot be made unless the court first considers making a hospital order.

11.7.2 The section enables the defendant's RC to transfer the patient to prison at any time before his release date if no further treatment is necessary or is unlikely to be beneficial. The powers granted by this section were previously only available (prior to amendment of the Act) to those defendants whose mental disorder was classified as psychopathic disorder – this is no longer the case.

11.7.3 Section 45A was inserted into the Act by the Crime (Sentences) Act 1997. It is a 'public protection' provision, and as such, is most likely to be used where the sentence of imprisonment imposed in conjunction with the hospital and limitation direction is an indeterminate one (i.e. a life sentence or IPP/DPP under the CJA dangerousness provisions; see **11.14**).

11.7.4 The power has rarely been used in practice but now that its application is no longer limited to those suffering from psychopathic disorder, it may be used more widely. The House of Lords in *R* v. *Drew* [2003] UKHL 25 and the Court of Appeal in *R* v. *IA* (see below at **11.9.1**) expressed the view that widening the ambit of s.45A (as the 2007 Act has now done) would provide a solution to the difficulties and dilemmas faced by a court when making a choice between imposing a hospital order with a restriction order or a discretionary life sentence (see further below at **11.9**).

11.7.5 A defendant who is made subject to a hospital and limitation direction can apply to the Mental Health Tribunal (MHT) on the same basis as a defendant made subject to a restriction order. However, if successful before the MHT, he will not be released, but will be transferred to prison to complete his sentence (see **Chapter 1**).

11.8 CHOICE OF HOSPITAL/LEVEL OF SECURITY

11.8.1 Where an order under s.41 or s.45A of the Act is made, the court has the power to direct that the defendant be detained in hospital at a level of security the court deems necessary to ensure protection of the public. Section 47 of the Crime (Sentences) Act 1997 provides that the court can name a hospital unit when directing admission of a restricted patient to hospital under a hospital order or a hospital and limitation direction.

11.8.2 The court may wish to specify a level of security if it is of the view that the defendant presents a risk of serious harm to others, or where there is a risk of escape, or where his hospital admission is attached to a life or indeterminate sentence under the terms of a hospital and limitation direction. If the court does not have adequate knowledge of the levels of security available in the hospital to which it wishes to order admission, s.39 of the Act enables that information to be obtained. Although an RC who would be responsible for the patient's care should be able to advise the court on the appropriate level of security, such a decision is in the discretion of the sentencing judge.

11.9 RESTRICTION ORDERS AND DISCRETIONARY LIFE SENTENCE

11.9.1 In *R* v. *IA* [2006] 1 Cr App R (S) 91, the Court of Appeal reviewed a number of authorities on the approach that a court should adopt when faced with a choice between a discretionary life sentence and a hospital and restriction order under s.37/s.41 of the Act. The appellant had been sentenced to life imprisonment in respect of a series of sex offences against young boys, including rape. He was 18 and suffered from mental impairment, learning disability and autism. Reports had been available to the judge recommending the imposition of a hospital order with a restriction order. The judge had declined to impose such an order, remarking that a life sentence had been necessary for the long-term security of young boys, but expressing the hope that the appellant could be treated in a medium secure hospital on a transfer under s.47 of the Act. The Court of Appeal considered at some length the difficulties which had arisen in practice for the appellant in obtaining the medical treatment he required. The court also considered the different release regimes under a discretionary life sentence and a restriction order, noting that the MHT will not necessarily afford significantly less protection to the public than the Parole Board. Confirming that the court still has the discretion to impose a custodial sentence where the conditions for a s.37/s.41 order are met, on the facts of this case, the life sentence was quashed and a s.37/s.41 order made in its place.

11.9.2 In the subsequent case of *R* v. *Simpson* [2007] EWCA Crim 2666, the Court of Appeal again quashed a sentence of life imprisonment imposed under CJA 2003, s.225 (see further below) and substituted a s.37/s.41 order. Commenting upon the decision, DA Thomas QC said that the 'general effect of the decision is that the new legislative framework (i.e. the 2003 Act) has not changed the general approach of the court, which is that a sentence of life imprisonment should not normally be imposed on an offender who is eligible for a hospital order and for whom a suitable establishment is available' ([2008] Crim LR 236).

11.9.3 Now that cases such as these can be dealt with under the provisions of s.45A of the Act the dilemma facing the sentencing court in these two cases (and in those cases which are considered within the decisions) may be largely academic.

11.10 HOSPITAL ORDERS AND RESTRICTION ORDERS IN PRACTICE

11.10.1 The effect of a s.37 hospital order was described by the Court of Appeal in the case of *R* v. *Birch* (**11.6.3** above):

> Once the offender is admitted to hospital pursuant to a hospital order ... without restriction on discharge, his position is almost exactly the same as if he were a civil patient. In effect he passes out of the penal system and into the hospital regime. Neither the Court nor the Secretary of State has any say in his disposal.

The defendant becomes a patient, to be managed at the discretion of his RC, by whom he can be granted leave, transferred to another hospital, and discharged at any time that the criteria for his detention are no longer made out (see **Chapter 1**). Once discharged, whether by the MHT or by the RC (or hospital managers), the unrestricted hospital order is terminated absolutely.

11.10.2 In a s.37/s.41 case, decisions on liberty (including the grant of leave) are no longer the preserve of clinical discretion. A restriction order has to be made of indefinite duration and does not require regular renewal to prevent it from lapsing. It remains in force indefinitely until it is discharged in one of the following circumstances:

- by the RC with the agreement of the Secretary of State (s.23);
- by the Secretary of State (s.42); or
- by the MHT (s.73 or s.75).

11.10.3 The RC is required to obtain the Secretary of State's agreement to certain decisions (in practice, the Mental Health Unit at the Ministry of Justice undertakes this role). Section 41(3)(c) of the Act provides that the agreement of the Secretary of State is required before the patient can be given leave in the community, transferred to a different hospital or discharged into the community. A defendant who is made subject to a restriction order is entitled to apply to the MHT (see **Chapter 1**).

11.10.4 It follows that it is impossible to advise a defendant who is made the subject of a restriction order how long he will remain in hospital. As was said in *Birch* (**11.6.3** above):

> A patient who has been subject to a restriction order is likely to be detained in hospital for much longer than one who is not, and will have fewer opportunities for leave of absence.

11.10.5 When the defendant/patient is discharged into the community, he almost invariably will be 'conditionally discharged' subject to conditions such as supervision, residence and medical treatment. His social and psychiatric supervisors have to keep the Secretary of State informed of his progress and behaviour in the community. He can be recalled to hospital by the Secretary of State at any time if it is thought to be necessary for the protection of the public, and provided there is current medical evidence of mental disorder. The conditionally discharged patient remains liable to detention in hospital, and consequently to recall, unless and until the Secretary of State lifts his restrictions under s.42(1), or until the Tribunal orders absolute discharge from his restrictions under s.75 of the Act.

11.11 GUARDIANSHIP

Magistrates' court, youth court and Crown Court

11.11.1 In an appropriate case, the court can make a guardianship order under s.37 of the Act for a defendant aged 16 years or over. Such an order may be suitable in the case of a mentally disordered defendant who does not require hospital treatment. In practice, guardianship is more likely to be suitable for an adult whose mental disorder is learning disability and/or mental impairment, as opposed to mental illness.

11.11.2 The purpose of guardianship is primarily to ensure that a defendant receives care and protection rather than medical treatment, although the guardian does have the power to require the defendant to attend at specified times for medical treatment. In addition, the guardian has the power to require the defendant to live at a specific place, to attend specific places at specified times for occupation, education or training and to require the defendant to give access at his place of residence to any doctor, approved social worker, or other person specified by the guardian.

11.11.3 The requirement for medical evidence is the same as for the making of a s.37 hospital order. In addition, the consent of the potential guardian is required.

The guardian may be either a local social services authority or someone else approved by that authority (a 'private guardian'), but is normally the former. The defendant's consent is not required. Where the proposed guardian is the local authority, the court's judgement about the suitability of making a guardianship order must be subordinate to the willingness of the local authority to accept the guardianship. The authority has a wide discretion as to the factors it is able properly to take into account, which must be exercised having regard to every material consideration relevant to its ability to manage a defendant under guardianship, its own policy on guardianship and the relevant chapter of the Act's Code of Practice: see *R (on the application of Bukowicki* v. *Northamptonshire County Council)* [2007] EWHC 310 (Admin).

11.12 COMMUNITY ORDER/MENTAL HEALTH TREATMENT REQUIREMENT

11.12.1 Where a defendant does not require inpatient care, or has been treated in hospital since the commission of the offence so that his mental state has improved to a point where care in the community is appropriate, the court may wish to consider making a community order with a mental health treatment requirement (CJA 2003, s.177/s.207). Such a disposal may be appropriate in a case where the custody threshold has been passed (as well as those cases in which it has not), but where the defendant's culpability is substantially mitigated by his mental state at the time of the commission of the offence, and where the public interest is served by ensuring he continues to receive treatment for his mental disorder. It is usually not suitable for a defendant who is unlikely to comply with treatment or who has a very chaotic lifestyle.

11.12.2 Advocates will be familiar with the power of the magistrates' court or Crown Court under CJA 2003, s.177 to make a community order following a defendant's guilty plea or conviction after trial and the need, when making the order, for the inclusion of at least one of the requirements specified in s.177(1)(a)–(l). Of these, the mental health treatment requirement (s.177(1)(h)) is of the most obvious relevance. A condition for treatment can only be attached to the order if the court receives a written or oral report from an approved mental health specialist that the mental condition of the defendant is such as requires and may be susceptible to treatment but his condition is not such as to merit either a hospital or a guardianship order.

11.12.3 The court must be satisfied that arrangements have been made or can be made for the treatment specified in the order. Treatment must be one of the following:

- as a resident patient in an independent hospital or care home within the meaning of the Care Standards Act 2000 or a hospital within the meaning of the Act, but not in hospital premises where high security psychiatric services within the meaning of the Act are provided;

- as a non-resident patient at such institution or place as may be specified in the order;
- by or under the direction of such registered medical practitioner or chartered psychologist as may be so specified.

11.12.4 The court cannot attach the treatment requirement to a community order unless satisfied that arrangements have been made for the provision of the treatment specified in the requirement. The court must also be satisfied that the defendant has expressed his willingness to comply with such an order. If he has not, the order cannot be made. Once the order is in force, the defendant (with his consent) may be treated at an institution or place other than that specified in the order, if the medical practitioner/chartered psychologist is of the view such treatment is more suitable or more convenient. This can include inpatient treatment at an institution which could not have been specified as part of the original order (CJA 2003, s.208). Both the requirement and the community order itself can be for a maximum of three years.

Youths

11.12.5 At present, a similar requirement can be attached to a community rehabilitation order (a sentence still in existence in respect of defendants aged 16 and 17). This disposal is to be replaced in late 2009 by a youth rehabilitation order under the Criminal Justice and Immigration Act 2008, which will apply to all young persons under the age of 18. Under s.1(1)(k) of and Sched. 1 to the Act the court will be able to attach a mental health treatment requirement to the order.

11.12.6 It should be noted that all the above community orders are available to the court only following *conviction*. A community order is not available as a disposal in summary proceedings following a finding under s.37(3) or PCC(S)A 2000, s.11. Nor is such an order available in the Crown Court following a finding of unfitness to plead, where the defendant is also found to have done the act or made the omission charged; nor is it available where a defendant is not guilty by reason of insanity. In such cases, where supervision and/or treatment in the community is appropriate, CP(I)A 1964 provides a separate regime of community treatment and supervision (supervision orders) – see **Chapter 10**.

11.13 SUSPENDED SENTENCES

Magistrates' court and Crown Court

11.13.1 The court is empowered by CJA 2003, s.189 when passing a prison sentence (or a sentence of detention in a young offender institution (DYOI) in respect of a defendant aged 18–21) of at least 14 days but not more than 12 months (at least 14 days and no more than six months in the magistrates' court) to suspend that sentence, and to order that the defendant comply with one or more of the requirements in s.190(1) during a period specified as the supervision period (which may or may not be the same as the operational period of the suspended sentence). The supervision period and the operational period must each be a period of not less than six months and not more than two years beginning with the date of the order, and the former must not end later than the latter.

11.13.2 Section 190 lists the requirements which can be imposed under the terms of a suspended sentence order. These are identical to the s.177 community order requirements (see above). This means that in the case of a mentally disordered offender, a mental health treatment requirement of up to two years can be coupled with a suspended sentence, provided the operational period of the suspended sentence is no shorter than the length of the requirement. This is obviously a useful sentencing tool, in a case where (for whatever reason) the offence has to be marked by a term of custody but where there is a need for treatment, such treatment is available, and the term of the custodial sentence falls properly within the 14 days to 12 months sentencing bracket. It follows that the maximum period for which the defendant can be made subject to a mental health treatment requirement under this provision is two years. In an appropriate case there may well be a good argument that the public interest (as well as the defendant's interests) would be better served by a three-year community order with a treatment requirement for the full term, such disposal providing a greater degree of public protection.

11.14 DANGEROUS OFFENDERS

11.14.1 The Criminal Justice Act 2003 introduced new sentences for offenders before the Crown Court who commit certain offences and are deemed to be dangerous (CJA 2003, ss.224–236). These provisions were the subject of a significant number of appeals and have been substantially amended by the Criminal Justice and Immigration Act 2008.

11.14.2 The full provisions are not set out here and the advocate should refer to the relevant chapter in *Archbold* or *Blackstone's*. In addition, the Sentencing Guidelines Council (SGC) 'Guide for Sentencers and Practitioners' is of great assistance in setting out clearly the statutory framework of the revised dangerousness provisions, and providing a summary of the relevant Court of Appeal guidance regarding the application of those requirements. Further helpful discussion of the effect of the revised regime is to be found in *Attorney General's Reference (No. 55 of 2008) sub nom. R* v. *C* [2009] Crim LR 221, in which the principles involved in making a dangerousness assessment which were identified and explained in *R* v. *Johnson and others* [2007] 1 Cr App R(S) 112 were said to be unchanged.

11.14.3 Where the conditions for a finding of 'dangerousness' are met (that is, where the court is of the opinion that there is a significant risk to members of the public of serious harm occasioned by the commission by him of further specified offences) the court is not precluded from making a hospital order under s.37 of the Act. This is provided that the conditions for making such an order are made out, and the court is of the opinion that such a disposal is the most suitable in the circumstances (s.37 as amended by CJA 2003, Sched. 32, para.38(b) and *R* v. *Lang* [2005] EWCA Crim 2864 at **11.14.8**). In such circumstances, a hospital order could be imposed with or without a restriction order under s.41, although it is difficult to contemplate a set of facts upon which a finding of dangerousness has been made and a s.41 restriction order would not be considered necessary. See **11.9** for consideration of the proper approach of the sentencing court when faced with a choice between indeterminate imprisonment and disposal under the Act.

11.14.4 The court may however be faced with sentencing a 'dangerous' mentally disordered offender whose mental disorder is not treatable (or for whom no treatment is available), who is, in part at least, dangerous by virtue of his mental disorder. Such a defendant therefore cannot be dealt with by means of a disposal under the Act. By way of example, three of the appellants in *Johnson and others* (**11.14.2** above) suffered from mental disorder; none met the criteria for a sentence under the Act. One (Hamilton), convicted of an armed robbery and an attempted robbery, had a very low IQ, with tests suggesting moderate learning disability. Another (Lawton), who had pleaded guilty to arson with intent and criminal damage, suffered from mental impairment which affected his judgement and reasoning, in combination with extremely heavy drinking. A third (Jones) had been convicted of affray and attempted murder, and was assessed as suffering from an unstable personality disorder. This case was decided under the original CJA provisions and for each of these appellants, the statutory assumption, which is no longer a part of the sentencing framework, was found not to be displaced. However, the nature of the mental disorder in these cases is perhaps not untypical of the range of psychiatric difficulties presented to a sentencing court as 'untreatable' within the terms of the Act.

11.14.5 As the above case illustrates, there can be a fine line between mental disorder as mitigating factor and mental disorder as an aggravating factor, for sentencing purposes. The point was made in *Johnson and others* (**11.14.2** above) that the characteristics of an offender such as inadequacy, suggestibility or vulnerability may serve to mitigate his culpability; but they may also serve to produce or reinforce the conclusion that he is dangerous.

11.14.6 More recently in *R* v. *C* (**11.14.2** above), the Court of Appeal considered the inter-relation between CJA 2003, s.143 and sentencing in 'dangerousness' cases. Under s.143, the sentencing court must address the offender's 'culpability in committing the offence and any harm which the offence has caused, was intended to cause, or might foreseeably have caused'. In contrast, in the assessment of dangerousness, the issue remains the risk to the public, not simply what the offender desired or intended. The court held that a reckless offender, or an offender with little or no insight into the consequences of his actions, may represent a significant risk to the public.

11.14.7 It may be the case that a mentally disordered defendant who falls outside the Act, perhaps with learning disability, severe mental impairment, or a personality disorder would be assessed as having 'little or no insight into the consequences of his actions'. It cannot however be assumed that a defendant suffering from mental disorder of any description will be 'dangerous' or more dangerous by virtue of his mental disorder. A careful risk assessment will be necessary in each case.

11.14.8 It was contemplated in *R* v. *Lang* [2005] EWCA Crim 2864 that, in the vast majority of cases, a PSR would be sufficient to assist the court with a determination of dangerousness. However, it was also said that 'in the small number of cases where the circumstances of the current offence or the history of the offender suggests mental abnormality, a medical report should usually be obtained before any sentence is passed which is based on significant risk of serious harm'.

11.14.9 As in s.41 cases, the assessment of dangerousness is for the court, which is not bound by the conclusions reached in the reports; although if the sentencing judge is contemplating differing from the assessment, both advocates should be given the opportunity of addressing the point (*Lang*, **11.14.8** above). Unlike in s.41 cases, there is no requirement for live evidence before a finding of dangerousness, even where such a finding is based on psychiatric evidence. Where there were conflicting psychiatric reports, and the judge indicated it was unnecessary to hear evidence from the psychiatrists, the Court of Appeal held in *R* v. *Strachan* [2007] EWCA Crim 1571 that the defendant was entitled to expect that the evidence of the defence psychiatrist would be accepted.

11.14.10 When preparing a plea in mitigation in a sentence to which the dangerousness provisions apply, the advocate should place the defendant's mental disorder in the context of the other factors to be born in mind when assessing significant risk. These other factors identified in *Lang* (**11.14.8** above) are:

- the nature and circumstances of the current offence;
- the offender's history of offending (including kind of offence, its circumstances, sentence passed, whether offending demonstrates any pattern);
- social and economic factors in relation to the offender (including accommodation, employability, education, associates, relationships and drug and alcohol abuse) and the offender's thinking/attitude towards offending and supervision and his emotional state.

11.14.11 Given that the courts now have a discretion as to whether or not to impose a sentence under the dangerousness provisions, even where the criteria are met, there should be much greater scope than hitherto to argue against the imposition of imprisonment or detention for public protection (IPP/DPP), in circumstances where previously such a disposal was inevitable. It was made absolutely plain in *R* v. *C* (above) that, where the necessary criteria are established for the imposition of a sentence of imprisonment for public protection 'the court is entitled to and should have in mind all the alternative and cumulative methods of providing the necessary public protection against the risk posed by the individual offender'. It confirmed that:

> the primary question is the nature and extent of the risk posed by the individual offender, and the most appropriate method of addressing that risk and providing public protection. If what we have described as the overall sentencing package provides appropriate protection, imprisonment for public protection should not be imposed.

It follows that any risk assessment of a potentially dangerous mentally disordered offender should specifically address not just the statutory criteria for dangerousness, but also the question of what, if any, treatment may be available in the community as part of an 'overall sentencing package', if necessary within the terms of an extended sentence.

11.14.12 In *R* v. *Kehoe* [2008] EWCA Crim 819, the Court of Appeal made it clear that a life sentence under the dangerousness provisions should be reserved for those cases where the culpability of the offender was particularly high or the offence was particularly grave. In that case, the appellant had pleaded guilty to manslaughter on the grounds of diminished responsibility. She had suffered considerable abuse during her childhood which had distorted her psychological development and at the time of the killing she had been suffering from an abnormality of mind as a result of her personality disorder and alcohol dependence. The case was summarised by the court as 'the un-premeditated killing of one drunk by another'. The life sentence imposed under the CJA provisions was quashed, and replaced by IPP.

APPENDIX 1

Mental Health Act 1983 (as amended), extracts

PART II COMPULSORY ADMISSION TO HOSPITAL AND GUARDIANSHIP

Procedure for hospital admission

2 Admission for assessment

(1) A patient may be admitted to a hospital and detained there for the period allowed by sub-section (4) below in pursuance of an application (in this Act referred to as 'an application for admission for assessment') made in accordance with subsections (2) and (3) below.

(2) An application for admission for assessment may be made in respect of a patient on the grounds that –

- (a) he is suffering from mental disorder of a nature or degree which warrants the detention of the patient in a hospital for assessment (or for assessment followed by medical treatment) for at least a limited period; and
- (b) he ought to be so detained in the interests of his own health or safety or with a view to the protection of other persons.

(3) An application for admission for assessment shall be founded on the written recommendations in the prescribed form of two registered medical practitioners, including in each case a statement that in the opinion of the practitioner the conditions set out in subsection (2) above are complied with.

(4) Subject to the provisions of section 29(4) below, a patient admitted to hospital in pursuance of an application for admission for assessment may be detained for a period not exceeding 28 days beginning with the day on which he is admitted, but shall not be detained after the expiration of that period unless before it has expired he has become liable to be detained by virtue of a subsequent application, order or direction under the following provisions of this Act.

3 Admission for treatment

(1) A patient may be admitted to a hospital and detained there for the period allowed by the following provisions of this Act in pursuance of an application (in this Act referred to as 'an application for admission for treatment') made in accordance with this section.

(2) An application for admission for treatment may be made in respect of a patient on the grounds that –

(a) he is suffering from mental disorder of a nature or degree which makes it appropriate for him to receive medical treatment in a hospital; and
(b) ...
(c) it is necessary for the health or safety of the patient or for the protection of other persons that he should receive such treatment and it cannot be provided unless he is detained under this section; and
(d) appropriate medical treatment is available for him.

(3) An application for admission for treatment shall be founded on the written recommendations in the prescribed form of two registered medical practitioners, including in each case a statement that in the opinion of the practitioner the conditions set out in subsection (2) above are complied with; and each such recommendation shall include –

(a) such particulars as may be prescribed of the grounds for that opinion so far as it relates to the conditions set out in paragraphs (a) and [(d)] of that subsection; and
(b) a statement of the reasons for that opinion so far as it relates to the conditions set out in paragraph (c) of that subsection, specifying whether other methods of dealing with the patient are available and, if so, why they are not appropriate.

(4) In this Act, references to appropriate medical treatment, in relation to a person suffering from mental disorder, are references to medical treatment which is appropriate in his case, taking into account the nature and degree of the mental disorder and all other circumstances of his case.

4 Admission for assessment in cases of emergency

(1) In any case of urgent necessity, an application for admission for assessment may be made in respect of a patient in accordance with the following provisions of this section, and any application so made is in this Act referred to as 'an emergency application'.

(2) An emergency application may be made either by an approved mental health professional or by the nearest relative of the patient; and every such application shall include a statement that it is of urgent necessity for the patient to be admitted and detained under section 2 above, and that compliance with the provisions of this Part of this Act relating to applications under that section would involve undesirable delay.

(3) An emergency application shall be sufficient in the first instance if founded on one of the medical recommendations required by section 2 above, given, if practicable, by a practitioner who has previous acquaintance with the patient and otherwise complying with the requirements of section 12 below so far as applicable to a single recommendation, and verifying the statement referred to in subsection (2) above.

(4) An emergency application shall cease to have effect on the expiration of a period of 72 hours from the time when the patient is admitted to the hospital unless –

(a) the second medical recommendation required by section 2 above is given and received by the managers within that period; and
(b) that recommendation and the recommendation referred to in subsection (3) above together comply with all the requirements of section 12 below (other than the requirement as to the time of signature of the second recommendation).

(5) In relation to an emergency application, section 11 below shall have effect as if in subsection (5) of that section for the words 'the period of 14 days ending with the date of the application' there were substituted the words 'the previous 24 hours'.

5 Application in respect of patient already in hospital

(1) An application for the admission of a patient to a hospital may be made under this Part of this Act notwithstanding that the patient is already an in-patient in that hospital or, in the case of an application for admission for treatment, that the patient is for the time being liable to be detained in the hospital in pursuance of an application for admission for assessment; and where an application is so made the patient shall be treated for the purposes of this Part of this Act as if he had been admitted to the hospital at the time when that application was received by the managers.

(2) If, in the case of a patient who is an in-patient in a hospital, it appears to the registered medical practitioner or approved clinician in charge of the treatment of the patient that an application ought to be made under this Part of this Act for the admission of the patient to hospital, he may furnish to the managers a report in writing to that effect; and in any such case the patient may be detained in the hospital for a period of 72 hours from the time when the report is so furnished.

(3) The registered medical practitioner or approved clinician in charge of the treatment of a patient in a hospital may nominate one (but not more than one) person to act for him under sub-section (2) above in his absence.

(3A) For the purposes of subsection (3) above –

- (a) the registered medical practitioner may nominate another registered medical practitioner, or an approved clinician, on the staff of the hospital; and
- (b) the approved clinician may nominate another approved clinician, or a registered medical practitioner, on the staff of the hospital.

(4) If, in the case of a patient who is receiving treatment for mental disorder as an in-patient in a hospital, it appears to a nurse of the prescribed class –

- (a) that the patient is suffering from mental disorder to such a degree that it is necessary for his health or safety or for the protection of others for him to be immediately restrained from leaving the hospital; and
- (b) that it is not practicable to secure the immediate attendance of a practitioner or clinician for the purpose of furnishing a report under subsection (2) above,

the nurse may record that fact in writing; and in that event the patient may be detained in the hospital for a period of six hours from the time when that fact is so recorded or until the earlier arrival at the place where the patient is detained of a practitioner or clinician having power to furnish a report under that subsection.

(5) A record made under subsection (4) above shall be delivered by the nurse (or by a person authorised by the nurse in that behalf) to the managers of the hospital as soon as possible after it is made; and where a record is made under that subsection the period mentioned in subsection (2) above shall begin at the time when it is made.

(6) The reference in subsection (1) above to an in-patient does not include an in-patient who is liable to be detained in pursuance of an application under this Part of this Act or a community patient and the references in subsections (2) and (4) above do not include an in-patient who is liable to be detained in a hospital under this Part of this Act or a community patient.

(7) In subsection (4) above 'prescribed' means prescribed by an order made by the Secretary of State.

Guardianship

7 Application for guardianship

(1) A patient who has attained the age of 16 years may be received into guardianship, for the period allowed by the following provisions of this Act, in pursuance of an application (in this Act referred to as 'a guardianship application') made in accordance with this section.

(2) A guardianship application may be made in respect of a patient on the grounds that –

(a) he is suffering from mental disorder . . . of a nature or degree which warrants his reception into guardianship under this section; and
(b) it is necessary in the interests of the welfare of the patient or for the protection of other persons that the patient should be so received.

(3) A guardianship application shall be founded on the written recommendations in the prescribed form of two registered medical practitioners, including in each case a statement that in the opinion of the practitioner the conditions set out in subsection (2) above are complied with; and each such recommendation shall include –

(a) such particulars as may be prescribed of the grounds for that opinion so far as it relates to the conditions set out in paragraph (a) of that subsection; and
(b) a statement of the reasons for that opinion so far as it relates to the conditions set out in paragraph (b) of that subsection.

(4) A guardianship application shall state the age of the patient or, if his exact age is not known to the applicant, shall state (if it be the fact) that the patient is believed to have attained the age of 16 years.

(5) The person named as guardian in a guardianship application may be either a local social services authority or any other person (including the applicant himself); but a guardianship application in which a person other than a local social services authority is named as guardian shall be of no effect unless it is accepted on behalf of that person by the local social services authority for the area in which he resides, and shall be accompanied by a statement in writing by that person that he is willing to act as guardian.

8 Effect of guardianship application, etc

(1) Where a guardianship application, duly made under the provisions of this Part of this Act and forwarded to the local social services authority within the period allowed by subsection (2) below is accepted by that authority, the application shall, subject to regulations made by the Secretary of State, confer on the authority or person named in the application as guardian, to the exclusion of any other person –

(a) the power to require the patient to reside at a place specified by the authority or person named as guardian;

(b) the power to require the patient to attend at places and times so specified for the purpose of medical treatment, occupation, education or training;
(c) the power to require access to the patient to be given, at any place where the patient is residing, to any registered medical practitioner, approved mental health professional or other person so specified.

(2) The period within which a guardianship application is required for the purposes of this section to be forwarded to the local social services authority is the period of 14 days beginning with the date on which the patient was last examined by a registered medical practitioner before giving a medical recommendation for the purposes of the application.

(3) A guardianship application which appears to be duly made and to be founded on the necessary medical recommendations may be acted upon without further proof of the signature or qualification of the person by whom the application or any such medical recommendation is made or given, or of any matter of fact or opinion stated in the application.

(4) If within the period of 14 days beginning with the day on which a guardianship application has been accepted by the local social services authority the application, or any medical recommendation given for the purposes of the application, is found to be in any respect incorrect or defective, the application or recommendation may, within that period and with the consent of that authority, be amended by the person by whom it was signed; and upon such amendment being made the application or recommendation shall have effect and shall be deemed to have had effect as if it had been originally made as so amended.

(5) Where a patient is received into guardianship in pursuance of a guardianship application, any previous application under this Part of this Act by virtue of which he was subject to guardianship or liable to be detained in a hospital shall cease to have effect.

17A Community treatment orders

(1) The responsible clinician may by order in writing discharge a detained patient from hospital subject to his being liable to recall in accordance with section 17E below.

(2) A detained patient is a patient who is liable to be detained in a hospital in pursuance of an application for admission for treatment.

(3) An order under subsection (1) above is referred to in this Act as a 'community treatment order'.

(4) The responsible clinician may not make a community treatment order unless –

(a) in his opinion, the relevant criteria are met; and
(b) an approved mental health professional states in writing –

(i) that he agrees with that opinion; and
(ii) that it is appropriate to make the order.

(5) The relevant criteria are –

(a) the patient is suffering from mental disorder of a nature or degree which makes it appropriate for him to receive medical treatment;
(b) it is necessary for his health or safety or for the protection of other persons that he should receive such treatment;

(c) subject to his being liable to be recalled as mentioned in paragraph (d) below, such treatment can be provided without his continuing to be detained in a hospital;
(d) it is necessary that the responsible clinician should be able to exercise the power under section 17E(1) below to recall the patient to hospital; and
(e) appropriate medical treatment is available for him.

(6) In determining whether the criterion in subsection (5)(d) above is met, the responsible clinician shall, in particular, consider, having regard to the patient's history of mental disorder and any other relevant factors, what risk there would be of a deterioration of the patient's condition if he were not detained in a hospital (as a result, for example, of his refusing or neglecting to receive the medical treatment he requires for his mental disorder).

(7) In this Act –

'community patient' means a patient in respect of whom a community treatment order is in force;

'the community treatment order', in relation to such a patient, means the community treatment order in force in respect of him; and

'the responsible hospital', in relation to such a patient, means the hospital in which he was liable to be detained immediately before the community treatment order was made, subject to section 19A below.

17B Conditions

(1) A community treatment order shall specify conditions to which the patient is to be subject while the order remains in force.

(2) But, subject to subsection (3) below, the order may specify conditions only if the responsible clinician, with the agreement of the approved mental health professional mentioned in section 17A(4)(b) above, thinks them necessary or appropriate for one or more of the following purposes –

(a) ensuring that the patient receives medical treatment;
(b) preventing risk of harm to the patient's health or safety;
(c) protecting other persons.

(3) The order shall specify –

(a) a condition that the patient make himself available for examination under section 20A below; and
(b) a condition that, if it is proposed to give a certificate under Part 4A of this Act in his case, he make himself available for examination so as to enable the certificate to be given.

(4) The responsible clinician may from time to time by order in writing vary the conditions specified in a community treatment order.

(5) He may also suspend any conditions specified in a community treatment order.

(6) If a community patient fails to comply with a condition specified in the community treatment order by virtue of subsection (2) above, that fact may be taken into account for the purposes of exercising the power of recall under section 17E(1) below.

(7) But nothing in this section restricts the exercise of that power to cases where there is such a failure.

PART III PATIENTS CONCERNED IN CRIMINAL PROCEEDINGS OR UNDER SENTENCE

Remands to hospital

35 Remand to hospital for report on accused's mental condition

(1) Subject to the provisions of this section, the Crown Court or a magistrates' court may remand an accused person to a hospital specified by the court for a report on his mental condition.

(2) For the purposes of this section an accused person is –

(a) in relation to the Crown Court, any person who is awaiting trial before the court for an offence punishable with imprisonment or who has been arraigned before the court for such an offence and has not yet been sentenced or otherwise dealt with for the offence on which he has been arraigned;
(b) in relation to a magistrates' court, any person who has been convicted by the court of an offence punishable on summary conviction with imprisonment and any person charged with such an offence if the court is satisfied that he did the act or made the omission charged or he has consented to the exercise by the court of the powers conferred by this section.

(3) Subject to subsection (4) below, the powers conferred by this section may be exercised if –

(a) the court is satisfied, on the written or oral evidence of a registered medical practitioner, that there is reason to suspect that the accused person is suffering from mental disorder; and
(b) the court is of the opinion that it would be impracticable for a report on his mental condition to be made if he were remanded on bail;

but those powers shall not be exercised by the Crown Court in respect of a person who has been convicted before the court if the sentence for the offence of which he has been convicted is fixed by law.

(4) The court shall not remand an accused person to a hospital under this section unless satisfied, on the written or oral evidence of the approved clinician who would be responsible for making the report or of some other person representing the managers of the hospital, that arrangements have been made for his admission to that hospital and for his admission to it within the period of seven days beginning with the date of the remand; and if the court is so satisfied it may, pending his admission, give directions for his conveyance to and detention in a place of safety.

(5) Where a court has remanded an accused person under this section it may further remand him if it appears to the court, on the written or oral evidence of the approved clinician responsible for making the report, that a further remand is necessary for completing the assessment of the accused person's mental condition.

(6) The power of further remanding an accused person under this section may be exercised by the court without his being brought before the court if he is represented by counsel or a solicitor and his counsel or solicitor is given an opportunity of being heard.

(7) An accused person shall not be remanded or further remanded under this section for more than 28 days at a time or for more than 12 weeks in all; and the court may at any time terminate the remand if it appears to the court that it is appropriate to do so.

(8) An accused person remanded to hospital under this section shall be entitled to obtain at his own expense an independent report on his mental condition from a registered medical practitioner or approved clinician chosen by him and to apply to the court on the basis of it for his remand to be terminated under subsection (7) above.

(9) Where an accused person is remanded under this section –

(a) a constable or any other person directed to do so by the court shall convey the accused person to the hospital specified by the court within the period mentioned in subsection (4) above; and
(b) the managers of the hospital shall admit him within that period and thereafter detain him in accordance with the provisions of this section.

(10) If an accused person absconds from a hospital to which he has been remanded under this section, or while being conveyed to or from that hospital, he may be arrested without warrant by any constable and shall, after being arrested, be brought as soon as practicable before the court that remanded him; and the court may thereupon terminate the remand and deal with him in any way in which it could have dealt with him if he had not been remanded under this section.

36 Remand of accused person to hospital for treatment

(1) Subject to the provisions of this section, the Crown Court may, instead of remanding an accused person in custody, remand him to a hospital specified by the court if satisfied, on the written or oral evidence of two registered medical practitioners, that –

(a) he is suffering from mental disorder of a nature or degree which makes it appropriate for him to be detained in a hospital for medical treatment; and
(b) appropriate medical treatment is available for him.

(2) For the purposes of this section an accused person is any person who is in custody awaiting trial before the Crown Court for an offence punishable with imprisonment (other than an offence the sentence for which is fixed by law) or who at any time before sentence is in custody in the course of a trial before that court for such an offence.

(3) The court shall not remand an accused person under this section to a hospital unless it is satisfied, on the written or oral evidence of the approved clinician who would have overall responsibility for his case or of some other person representing the managers of the hospital, that arrangements have been made for his admission to that hospital and for his admission to it within the period of seven days beginning with the date of the remand; and if the court is so satisfied it may, pending his admission, give directions for his conveyance to and detention in a place of safety.

(4) Where a court has remanded an accused person under this section it may further remand him if it appears to the court, on the written or oral evidence of the responsible clinician, that a further remand is warranted.

(5) The power of further remanding an accused person under this section may be exercised by the court without his being brought before the court if he is represented by counsel or a solicitor and his counsel or solicitor is given an opportunity of being heard.

(6) An accused person shall not be remanded or further remanded under this section for more than 28 days at a time or for more than 12 weeks in all; and the court may at any time terminate the remand if it appears to the court that it is appropriate to do so.

(7) An accused person remanded to hospital under this section shall be entitled to obtain at his own expense an independent report on his mental condition from a registered medical practitioner or approved clinician chosen by him and to apply to the court on the basis of it for his remand to be terminated under subsection (6) above.

(8) Subsections (9) and (10) of section 35 above shall have effect in relation to a remand under this section as they have effect in relation to a remand under that section.

Hospital and guardianship orders

37 Powers of courts to order hospital admission or guardianship

(1) Where a person is convicted before the Crown Court of an offence punishable with imprisonment other than an offence the sentence for which is fixed by law . . ., or is convicted by a magistrates' court of an offence punishable on summary conviction with imprisonment, and the conditions mentioned in subsection (2) below are satisfied, the court may by order authorise his admission to and detention in such hospital as may be specified in the order or, as the case may be, place him under the guardianship of a local social services authority or of such other person approved by a local social services authority as may be so specified.

(1A) In the case of an offence the sentence for which would otherwise fall to be imposed –

- (a) under section 51A(2) of the Firearms Act 1968,
- (b) under section 110(2) or 111(2) of the Powers of Criminal Courts (Sentencing) Act 2000, . . .
- (c) under section 225(2) or 226(2) of the Criminal Justice Act 2003, or
- (d) under section 29(4) or (6) of the Violent Crime Reduction Act 2006 (minimum sentences in certain cases of using someone to mind a weapon),

nothing in those provisions shall prevent a court from making an order under subsection (1) above for the admission of the offender to a hospital.

(1B) References in subsection (1A) above to a sentence falling to be imposed under any of the provisions mentioned in that subsection are to be read in accordance with section 305(4) of the Criminal Justice Act 2003.

(2) The conditions referred to in subsection (1) above are that –

- (a) the court is satisfied, on the written or oral evidence of two registered medical practitioners, that the offender is suffering from mental disorder and that either –

(i) the mental disorder from which the offender is suffering is of a nature or degree which makes it appropriate for him to be detained in a hospital for medical treatment and appropriate medical treatment is available for him; or

(ii) in the case of an offender who has attained the age of 16 years, the mental disorder is of a nature or degree which warrants his reception into guardianship under this Act; and

(b) the court is of the opinion, having regard to all the circumstances including the nature of the offence and the character and antecedents of the offender, and to the other available methods of dealing with him, that the most suitable method of disposing of the case is by means of an order under this section.

(3) Where a person is charged before a magistrates' court with any act or omission as an offence and the court would have power, on convicting him of that offence, to make an order under subsection (1) above in his case . . ., then, if the court is satisfied that the accused did the act or made the omission charged, the court may, if it thinks fit, make such an order without convicting him.

(4) An order for the admission of an offender to a hospital (in this Act referred to as 'a hospital order') shall not be made under this section unless the court is satisfied on the written or oral evidence of the approved clinician who would have overall responsibility for his case or of some other person representing the managers of the hospital that arrangements have been made for his admission to that hospital . . ., and for his admission to it within the period of 28 days beginning with the date of the making of such an order; and the court may, pending his admission within that period, give such directions as it thinks fit for his conveyance to and detention in a place of safety.

(5) If within the said period of 28 days it appears to the Secretary of State that by reason of an emergency or other special circumstances it is not practicable for the patient to be received into the hospital specified in the order, he may give directions for the admission of the patient to such other hospital as appears to be appropriate instead of the hospital so specified; and where such directions are given –

(a) the Secretary of State shall cause the person having the custody of the patient to be informed, and

(b) the hospital order shall have effect as if the hospital specified in the directions were substituted for the hospital specified in the order.

(6) An order placing an offender under the guardianship of a local social services authority or of any other person (in this Act referred to as 'a guardianship order') shall not be made under this section unless the court is satisfied that that authority or person is willing to receive the offender into guardianship.

(7) . . .

(8) Where an order is made under this section, the court shall not –

(a) pass sentence of imprisonment or impose a fine or make a community order (within the meaning of Part 12 of the Criminal Justice Act 2003) or a youth rehabilitation order (within the meaning of Part 1 of the Criminal Justice and Immigration Act 2008) in respect of the offence,

(b) if the order under this section is a hospital order, make a referral order (within the meaning of the Powers of Criminal Courts (Sentencing) Act 2000) in respect of the offence, or
(c) make in respect of the offender a supervision order (within the meaning of that Act) or an order under section 150 of that Act (binding over of parent or guardian),

but the court may make any other order which it has power to make apart from this section; and for the purposes of this subsection 'sentence of imprisonment' includes any sentence or order for detention.

38 Interim hospital orders

(1) Where a person is convicted before the Crown Court of an offence punishable with imprisonment (other than an offence the sentence for which is fixed by law) or is convicted by a magistrates' court of an offence punishable on summary conviction with imprisonment and the court before or by which he is convicted is satisfied, on the written or oral evidence of two registered medical practitioners –

(a) that the offender is suffering from mental disorder; and
(b) that there is reason to suppose that the mental disorder from which the offender is suffering is such that it may be appropriate for a hospital order to be made in his case,

the court may, before making a hospital order or dealing with him in some other way, make an order (in this Act referred to as 'an interim hospital order') authorising his admission to such hospital as may be specified in the order and his detention there in accordance with this section.

(2) In the case of an offender who is subject to an interim hospital order the court may make a hospital order without his being brought before the court if he is represented by counsel or a solicitor and his counsel or solicitor is given an opportunity of being heard.

(3) At least one of the registered medical practitioners whose evidence is taken into account under subsection (1) above shall be employed at the hospital which is to be specified in the order.

(4) An interim hospital order shall not be made for the admission of an offender to a hospital unless the court is satisfied, on the written or oral evidence of the approved clinician who would have overall responsibility for his case or of some other person representing the managers of the hospital, that arrangements have been made for his admission to that hospital and for his admission to it within the period of 28 days beginning with the date of the order; and if the court is so satisfied the court may, pending his admission, give directions for his conveyance to and detention in a place of safety.

(5) An interim hospital order –

(a) shall be in force for such period, not exceeding 12 weeks, as the court may specify when making the order; but
(b) may be renewed for further periods of not more than 28 days at a time if it appears to the court, on the written or oral evidence of the responsible clinician, that the continuation of the order is warranted;

but no such order shall continue in force for more than twelve months in all and the court shall terminate the order if it makes a hospital order in respect of the offender or decides after considering the written or oral evidence of the responsible clinician to deal with the offender in some other way.

(6) The power of renewing an interim hospital order may be exercised without the offender being brought before the court if he is represented by counsel or a solicitor and his counsel or solicitor is given an opportunity of being heard.

(7) If an offender absconds from a hospital in which he is detained in pursuance of an interim hospital order, or while being conveyed to or from such a hospital, he may be arrested without warrant by a constable and shall, after being arrested, be brought as soon as practicable before the court that made the order; and the court may thereupon terminate the order and deal with him in any way in which it could have dealt with him if no such order had been made.

39 Information as to hospitals

(1) Where a court is minded to make a hospital order or interim hospital order in respect of any person it may request –

(a) the Primary Care Trust or Local Health Board for the area in which that person resides or last resided; or
(b) the National Assembly for Wales or any other Primary Care Trust or Local Health Board that appears to the court to be appropriate,

to furnish the court with such information as that Primary Care Trust or Local Health Board or National Assembly for Wales have or can reasonably obtain with respect to the hospital or hospitals (if any) in their area or elsewhere at which arrangements could be made for the admission of that person in pursuance of the order, and that Primary Care Trust or Local Health Board or National Assembly for Wales shall comply with any such request.

(1A) In relation to a person who has not attained the age of 18 years, subsection (1) above shall have effect as if the reference to the making of a hospital order included a reference to a remand under section 35 or 36 above or the making of an order under section 44 below.

(1B) Where the person concerned has not attained the age of 18 years, the information which may be requested under subsection (1) above includes, in particular, information about the availability of accommodation or facilities designed so as to be specially suitable for patients who have not attained the age of 18 years.

(2) ...

39A Information to facilitate guardianship orders

Where a court is minded to make a guardianship order in respect of any offender, it may request the local social services authority for the area in which the offender resides or last resided, or any other local social services authority that appears to the court to be appropriate –

(a) to inform the court whether it or any other person approved by it is willing to receive the offender into guardianship; and

(b) if so, to give such information as it reasonably can about how it or the other person could be expected to exercise in relation to the offender the powers conferred by section 40(2) below;

and that authority shall comply with any such request.

40 Effect of hospital orders, guardianship orders and interim hospital orders

(1) A hospital order shall be sufficient authority –

(a) for a constable, an approved mental health professional or any other person directed to do so by the court to convey the patient to the hospital specified in the order within a period of 28 days; and
(b) for the managers of the hospital to admit him at any time within that period and thereafter detain him in accordance with the provisions of this Act.

(2) A guardianship order shall confer on the authority or person named in the order as guardian the same powers as a guardianship application made and accepted under Part II of this Act.

(3) Where an interim hospital order is made in respect of an offender –

(a) a constable or any other person directed to do so by the court shall convey the offender to the hospital specified in the order within the period mentioned in section 38(4) above; and
(b) the managers of the hospital shall admit him within that period and thereafter detain him in accordance with the provisions of section 38 above.

(4) A patient who is admitted to a hospital in pursuance of a hospital order, or placed under guardianship by a guardianship order, shall, subject to the provisions of this subsection, be treated for the purposes of the provisions of this Act mentioned in Part I of Schedule 1 to this Act as if he had been so admitted or placed on the date of the order in pursuance of an application for admission for treatment or a guardianship application, as the case may be, duly made under Part II of this Act, but subject to any modifications of those provisions specified in that Part of that Schedule.

(5) Where a patient is admitted to a hospital in pursuance of a hospital order, or placed under guardianship by a guardianship order, any previous application, hospital order or guardianship order by virtue of which he was liable to be detained in a hospital or subject to guardianship shall cease to have effect; but if the first-mentioned order, or the conviction on which it was made, is quashed on appeal, this subsection shall not apply and section 22 above shall have effect as if during any period for which the patient was liable to be detained or subject to guardianship under the order, he had been detained in custody as mentioned in that section.

(6) Where –

(a) a patient admitted to a hospital in pursuance of a hospital order is absent without leave;
(b) a warrant to arrest him has been issued under section 72 of the Criminal Justice Act 1967; and
(c) he is held pursuant to the warrant in any country or territory other than the United Kingdom, any of the Channel Islands and the Isle of Man,

he shall be treated as having been taken into custody under section 18 above on first being so held.

Restriction orders

41 Power of higher courts to restrict discharge from hospital

(1) Where a hospital order is made in respect of an offender by the Crown Court, and it appears to the court, having regard to the nature of the offence, the antecedents of the offender and the risk of his committing further offences if set at large, that it is necessary for the protection of the public from serious harm so to do, the court may, subject to the provisions of this section, further order that the offender shall be subject to the special restrictions set out in this section. . .; and an order under this section shall be known as 'a restriction order'.

(2) A restriction order shall not be made in the case of any person unless at least one of the registered medical practitioners whose evidence is taken into account by the court under section 37(2)(a) above has given evidence orally before the court.

(3) The special restrictions applicable to a patient in respect of whom a restriction order is in force are as follows –

- (a) none of the provisions of Part II of this Act relating to the duration, renewal and expiration of authority for the detention of patients shall apply, and the patient shall continue to be liable to be detained by virtue of the relevant hospital order until he is duly discharged under the said Part II or absolutely discharged under section 42, 73, 74 or 75 below;
- (aa) none of the provisions of Part II of this Act relating to community treatment orders and community patients shall apply;
- (b) no application shall be made to the appropriate tribunal in respect of a patient under section 66 or 69(1) below;
- (c) the following powers shall be exercisable only with the consent of the Secretary of State, namely –
  - (i) power to grant leave of absence to the patient under section 17 above;
  - (ii) power to transfer the patient in pursuance of regulations under section 19 above or in pursuance of subsection (3) of that section; and
  - (iii) power to order the discharge of the patient under section 23 above;

  and if leave of absence is granted under the said section 17 power to recall the patient under that section shall vest in the Secretary of State as well as the responsible clinician; and

- (d) the power of the Secretary of State to recall the patient under the said section 17 and power to take the patient into custody and return him under section 18 above may be exercised at any time;

and in relation to any such patient section 40(4) above shall have effect as if it referred to Part II of Schedule 1 to this Act instead of Part I of that Schedule.

(4) A hospital order shall not cease to have effect under section 40(5) above if a restriction order in respect of the patient is in force at the material time.

(5) Where a restriction order in respect of a patient ceases to have effect while the relevant hospital order continues in force, the provisions of section 40 above and Part I of Schedule 1 to this Act shall apply to the patient as if he had been admitted to the hospital in pursuance of a hospital order (without a restriction order) made on the date on which the restriction order ceased to have effect.

(6) While a person is subject to a restriction order the responsible clinician shall at such intervals (not exceeding one year) as the Secretary of State may direct examine and report to the Secretary of State on that person; and every report shall contain such particulars as the Secretary of State may require.

42 Powers of Secretary of State in respect of patients subject to restriction orders

(1) If the Secretary of State is satisfied that in the case of any patient a restriction order is no longer required for the protection of the public from serious harm, he may direct that the patient cease to be subject to the special restrictions set out in section 41(3) above; and where the Secretary of State so directs, the restriction order shall cease to have effect, and section 41(5) above shall apply accordingly.

(2) At any time while a restriction order is in force in respect of a patient, the Secretary of State may, if he thinks fit, by warrant discharge the patient from hospital, either absolutely or subject to conditions; and where a person is absolutely discharged under this subsection, he shall thereupon cease to be liable to be detained by virtue of the relevant hospital order, and the restriction order shall cease to have effect accordingly.

(3) The Secretary of State may at any time during the continuance in force of a restriction order in respect of a patient who has been conditionally discharged under subsection (2) above by warrant recall the patient to such hospital as may be specified in the warrant.

(4) Where a patient is recalled as mentioned in subsection (3) above –

- (a) if the hospital specified in the warrant is not the hospital from which the patient was conditionally discharged, the hospital order and the restriction order shall have effect as if the hospital specified in the warrant were substituted for the hospital specified in the hospital order;
- (b) in any case, the patient shall be treated for the purposes of section 18 above as if he had absented himself without leave from the hospital specified in the warrant. . . .

(5) If a restriction order in respect of a patient ceases to have effect after the patient has been conditionally discharged under this section, the patient shall, unless previously recalled under sub-section (3) above, be deemed to be absolutely discharged on the date when the order ceases to have effect, and shall cease to be liable to be detained by virtue of the relevant hospital order accordingly.

(6) The Secretary of State may, if satisfied that the attendance at any place in Great Britain of a patient who is subject to a restriction order is desirable in the interests of justice or for the purposes of any public inquiry, direct him to be taken to that place; and where a patient is directed under this subsection to be taken to any place he shall, unless the Secretary of State otherwise

directs, be kept in custody while being so taken, while at that place and while being taken back to the hospital in which he is liable to be detained.

43 Power of magistrates' courts to commit for restriction order

(1) If in the case of a person of or over the age of 14 years who is convicted by a magistrates' court of an offence punishable on summary conviction with imprisonment –

(a) the conditions which under section 37(1) above are required to be satisfied for the making of a hospital order are satisfied in respect of the offender; but
(b) it appears to the court, having regard to the nature of the offence, the antecedents of the offender and the risk of his committing further offences if set at large, that if a hospital order is made a restriction order should also be made,

the court may, instead of making a hospital order or dealing with him in any other manner, commit him in custody to the Crown Court to be dealt with in respect of the offence.

(2) Where an offender is committed to the Crown Court under this section, the Crown Court shall inquire into the circumstances of the case and may –

(a) if that court would have power so to do under the foregoing provisions of this Part of this Act upon the conviction of the offender before that court of such an offence as is described in section 37(1) above, make a hospital order in his case, with or without a restriction order;
(b) if the court does not make such an order, deal with the offender in any other manner in which the magistrates' court might have dealt with him.

(3) The Crown Court shall have the same power to make orders under sections 35, 36 and 38 above in the case of a person committed to the court under this section as the Crown Court has under those sections in the case of an accused person within the meaning of section 35 or 36 above or of a person convicted before that court as mentioned in section 38 above.

(4) The power of a magistrates' court under section 3 of the Powers of Criminal Courts (Sentencing) Act 2000 (which enables such a court to commit an offender to the Crown Court where the court is of the opinion that greater punishment should be inflicted for the offence than the court has power to inflict) shall also be exercisable by a magistrates' court where it is of the opinion that greater punishment should be inflicted as aforesaid on the offender unless a hospital order is made in his case with a restriction order.

(4) The powers of a magistrates' court under section 3 or 3B of the Powers of Criminal Courts (Sentencing) Act 2000 (which enable such a court to commit an offender to the Crown Court where the court is of the opinion, or it appears to the court, as mentioned in the section in question) shall also be exercisable by a magistrates' court where it is of that opinion (or it so appears to it) unless a hospital order is made in the offender's case with a restriction order.

(5) The power of the Crown Court to make a hospital order, with or without a restriction order, in the case of a person convicted before that court of an offence may, in the same circumstances and subject to the same conditions, be exercised by such a court in the case of a person committed to the court under section 5 of the Vagrancy Act 1824 (which provides for the committal to the Crown Court of persons who are incorrigible rogues within the meaning of that section).

44 Committal to hospital under s 43

(1) Where an offender is committed under section 43(1) above and the magistrates' court by which he is committed is satisfied on written or oral evidence that arrangements have been made for the admission of the offender to a hospital in the event of an order being made under this section, the court may, instead of committing him in custody, by order direct him to be admitted to that hospital, specifying it, and to be detained there until the case is disposed of by the Crown Court, and may give such directions as it thinks fit for his production from the hospital to attend the Crown Court by which his case is to be dealt with.

(2) The evidence required by subsection (1) above shall be given by the approved clinician who would have overall responsibility for the offender's case or by some other person representing the managers of the hospital in question.

(3) The power to give directions under section 37(4) above, section 37(5) above and section 40(1) above shall apply in relation to an order under this section as they apply in relation to a hospital order, but as if references to the period of 28 days mentioned in section 40(1) above were omitted; and subject as aforesaid an order under this section shall, until the offender's case is disposed of by the Crown Court, have the same effect as a hospital order together with a restriction order . . ..

45 Appeals from magistrates' courts

(1) Where on the trial of an information charging a person with an offence a magistrates' court makes a hospital order or guardianship order in respect of him without convicting him, he shall have the same right of appeal against the order as if it had been made on his conviction; and on any such appeal the Crown Court shall have the same powers as if the appeal had been against both conviction and sentence.

(2) An appeal by a child or young person with respect to whom any such order has been made, whether the appeal is against the order or against the finding upon which the order was made, may be brought by him or by his parent or guardian on his behalf.

Hospital and limitation directions

45A Power of higher courts to direct hospital admission

(1) This section applies where, in the case of a person convicted before the Crown Court of an offence the sentence for which is not fixed by law –

(a) the conditions mentioned in subsection (2) below are fulfilled; and
(b) . . ., the court considers making a hospital order in respect of him before deciding to impose a sentence of imprisonment ('the relevant sentence') in respect of the offence.

(2) The conditions referred to in subsection (1) above are that the court is satisfied, on the written or oral evidence of two registered medical practitioners –

(a) that the offender is suffering from mental disorder;

(b) that the mental disorder from which the offender is suffering is of a nature or degree which makes it appropriate for him to be detained in a hospital for medical treatment; and
(c) that appropriate medical treatment is available for him.

(3) The court may give both of the following directions, namely –

(a) a direction that, instead of being removed to and detained in a prison, the offender be removed to and detained in such hospital as may be specified in the direction (in this Act referred to as a 'hospital direction'); and
(b) a direction that the offender be subject to the special restrictions set out in section 41 above (in this Act referred to as a 'limitation direction').

(4) A hospital direction and a limitation direction shall not be given in relation to an offender unless at least one of the medical practitioners whose evidence is taken into account by the court under subsection (2) above has given evidence orally before the court.

(5) A hospital direction and a limitation direction shall not be given in relation to an offender unless the court is satisfied on the written or oral evidence of the approved clinician who would have overall responsibility for his case, or of some other person representing the managers of the hospital that arrangements have been made –

(a) for his admission to that hospital; and
(b) for his admission to it within the period of 28 days beginning with the day of the giving of such directions;

and the court may, pending his admission within that period, give such directions as it thinks fit for his conveyance to and detention in a place of safety.

(6) If within the said period of 28 days it appears to the Secretary of State that by reason of an emergency or other special circumstances it is not practicable for the patient to be received into the hospital specified in the hospital direction, he may give instructions for the admission of the patient to such other hospital as appears to be appropriate instead of the hospital so specified.

(7) Where such instructions are given –

(a) the Secretary of State shall cause the person having the custody of the patient to be informed, and
(b) the hospital direction shall have effect as if the hospital specified in the instructions were substituted for the hospital specified in the hospital direction.

(8) Section 38(1) and (5) and section 39 above shall have effect as if any reference to the making of a hospital order included a reference to the giving of a hospital direction and a limitation direction.

(9) A hospital direction and a limitation direction given in relation to an offender shall have effect not only as regards the relevant sentence but also (so far as applicable) as regards any other sentence of imprisonment imposed on the same or a previous occasion.

(10) ...

(11) ...

45B Effect of hospital and limitation directions

(1) A hospital direction and a limitation direction shall be sufficient authority –

(a) for a constable or any other person directed to do so by the court to convey the patient to the hospital specified in the hospital direction within a period of 28 days; and
(b) for the managers of the hospital to admit him at any time within that period and thereafter detain him in accordance with the provisions of this Act.

(2) With respect to any person –

(a) a hospital direction shall have effect as a transfer direction; and
(b) a limitation direction shall have effect as a restriction direction.

(3) While a person is subject to a hospital direction and a limitation direction the responsible clinician shall at such intervals (not exceeding one year) as the Secretary of State may direct examine and report to the Secretary of State on that person; and every report shall contain such particulars as the Secretary of State may require.

46 . . .

Transfer to hospital of prisoners, etc

47 Removal to hospital of persons serving sentences of imprisonment, etc

(1) If in the case of a person serving a sentence of imprisonment the Secretary of State is satisfied, by reports from at least two registered medical practitioners –

(a) that the said person is suffering from mental disorder; and
(b) that the mental disorder from which that person is suffering is of a nature or degree which makes it appropriate for him to be detained in a hospital for medical treatment; and
(c) that appropriate medical treatment is available for him;

the Secretary of State may, if he is of the opinion having regard to the public interest and all the circumstances that it is expedient so to do, by warrant direct that that person be removed to and detained in such hospital . . . as may be specified in the direction; and a direction under this section shall be known as 'a transfer direction'.

(2) A transfer direction shall cease to have effect at the expiration of the period of 14 days beginning with the date on which it is given unless within that period the person with respect to whom it was given has been received into the hospital specified in the direction.

(3) A transfer direction with respect to any person shall have the same effect as a hospital order made in his case.

(4) . . .

(5) References in this Part of this Act to a person serving a sentence of imprisonment include references –

(a) to a person detained in pursuance of any sentence or order for detention made by a court in criminal proceedings or service disciplinary proceedings (other than an order [made in consequence of a finding of insanity or unfitness to stand trial or a sentence of service detention within the meaning of the Armed Forces Act 2006);
(b) to a person committed to custody under section 115(3) of the Magistrates' Courts Act 1980 (which relates to persons who fail to comply with an order to enter into recognisances to keep the peace or be of good behaviour); and
(c) to a person committed by a court to a prison or other institution to which the Prison Act 1952 applies in default of payment of any sum adjudged to be paid on his conviction.

(6) In subsection (5)(a) 'service disciplinary proceedings' means proceedings in respect of a service offence within the meaning of the Armed Forces Act 2006.

48 Removal to hospital of other prisoners

(1) If in the case of a person to whom this section applies the Secretary of State is satisfied by the same reports as are required for the purposes of section 47 above that –

(a) that person is suffering from mental disorder of a nature or degree which makes it appropriate for him to be detained in a hospital for medical treatment; and
(b) he is in urgent need of such treatment; and
(c) appropriate medical treatment is available for him;

the Secretary of State shall have the same power of giving a transfer direction in respect of him under that section as if he were serving a sentence of imprisonment.

(2) This section applies to the following persons, that is to say –

(a) persons detained in a prison or remand centre, not being persons serving a sentence of imprisonment or persons falling within the following paragraphs of this subsection;
(b) persons remanded in custody by a magistrates' court;
(c) civil prisoners, that is to say, persons committed by a court to prison for a limited term . . ., who are not persons falling to be dealt with under section 47 above;
(d) persons detained under the Immigration Act 1971 or under section 62 of the Nationality, Immigration and Asylum Act 2002 (detention by Secretary of State).

(3) Subsections (2) and (3) of section 47 above shall apply for the purposes of this section and of any transfer direction given by virtue of this section as they apply for the purposes of that section and of any transfer direction under that section.

49 Restriction on discharge of prisoners removed to hospital

(1) Where a transfer direction is given in respect of any person, the Secretary of State, if he thinks fit, may by warrant further direct that that person shall be subject to the special restrictions set out in section 41 above; and where the Secretary of State gives a transfer direction in respect of any such person as is described in paragraph (a) or (b) of section 48(2) above, he shall also give a direction under this section applying those restrictions to him.

(2) A direction under this section shall have the same effect as a restriction order made under section 41 above and shall be known as 'a restriction direction'.

(3) While a person is subject to a restriction direction the responsible clinician shall at such intervals (not exceeding one year) as the Secretary of State may direct examine and report to the Secretary of State on that person; and every report shall contain such particulars as the Secretary of State may require.

50 Further provisions as to prisoners under sentence

(1) Where a transfer direction and a restriction direction have been given in respect of a person serving a sentence of imprisonment and before his release date the Secretary of State is notified by the responsible clinician, any other approved clinician or the appropriate tribunal that that person no longer requires treatment in hospital for mental disorder or that no effective treatment for his disorder can be given in the hospital to which he has been removed, the Secretary of State may –

(a) by warrant direct that he be remitted to any prison or other institution in which he might have been detained if he had not been removed to hospital, there to be dealt with as if he had not been so removed; or
(b) exercise any power of releasing him on licence or discharging him under supervision which could have been exercisable if he had been remitted to such a prison or institution as aforesaid,

and on his arrival in the prison or other institution or, as the case may be, his release or discharge as aforesaid, the transfer direction and the restriction direction shall cease to have effect.

(2) A restriction direction in the case of a person serving a sentence of imprisonment shall cease to have effect, if it has not previously done so, on his release date.

(3) In this section, references to a person's release date are to the day (if any) on which he would be entitled to be released (whether unconditionally or on licence) from any prison or other institution in which he might have been detained if the transfer direction had not been given; and in determining that day there shall be disregarded –

(a) any powers that would be exercisable by the Parole Board if he were detained in such a prison or other institution, and
(b) any practice of the Secretary of State in relation to the early release under discretionary powers of persons detained in such a prison or other institution.

(4) For the purposes of section 49(2) of the Prison Act 1952 (which provides for discounting from the sentences of certain prisoners periods while they are unlawfully at large) a patient who, having been transferred in pursuance of a transfer direction from any such institution as is referred to in that section, is at large in circumstances in which he is liable to be taken into custody under any provision of this Act, shall be treated as unlawfully at large and absent from that institution.

(5) The preceding provisions of this section shall have effect as if –

(a) the reference in subsection (1) to a transfer direction and a restriction direction having been given in respect of a person serving a sentence of imprisonment included a reference to a hospital direction and a limitation direction having been given in respect of a person sentenced to imprisonment;
(b) the reference in subsection (2) to a restriction direction included a reference to a limitation direction; and

(c) references in subsections (3) and (4) to a transfer direction included references to a hospital direction.

51 Further provisions as to detained persons

(1) This section has effect where a transfer direction has been given in respect of any such person as is described in paragraph (a) of section 48(2) above and that person is in this section referred to as 'the detainee'.

(2) The transfer direction shall cease to have effect when the detainee's case is disposed of by the court having jurisdiction to try or otherwise deal with him, but without prejudice to any power of that court to make a hospital order or other order under this Part of this Act in his case.

(3) If the Secretary of State is notified by the responsible clinician, any other approved clinician or the appropriate tribunal at any time before the detainee's case is disposed of by that court –

(a) that the detainee no longer requires treatment in hospital for mental disorder; or
(b) that no effective treatment for his disorder can be given at the hospital to which he has been removed,

the Secretary of State may by warrant direct that he be remitted to any place where he might have been detained if he had not been removed to hospital, there to be dealt with as if he had not been so removed, and on his arrival at the place to which he is so remitted the transfer direction shall cease to have effect.

(4) If (no direction having been given under subsection (3) above) the court having jurisdiction to try or otherwise deal with the detainee is satisfied on the written or oral evidence of the responsible clinician –

(a) that the detainee no longer requires treatment in hospital for mental disorder; or
(b) that no effective treatment for his disorder can be given at the hospital to which he has been removed,

the court may order him to be remitted to any such place as is mentioned in subsection (3) above or, subject to section 25 of the Criminal Justice and Public Order Act 1994, released on bail and on his arrival at that place or, as the case may be, his release on bail the transfer direction shall cease to have effect.

(5) If (no direction or order having been given or made under subsection (3) or (4) above) it appears to the court having jurisdiction to try or otherwise deal with the detainee –

(a) that it is impracticable or inappropriate to bring the detainee before the court; and
(b) that the conditions set out in subsection (6) below are satisfied,

the court may make a hospital order (with or without a restriction order) in his case in his absence and, in the case of a person awaiting trial, without convicting him.

(6) A hospital order may be made in respect of a person under subsection (5) above if the court –

(a) is satisfied, on the written or oral evidence of at least two registered medical practitioners, that –

- (i) the detainee is suffering from mental disorder of a nature or degree which makes it appropriate for the patient to be detained in a hospital for medical treatment; and
- (ii) appropriate medical treatment is available for him; and

(b) is of the opinion, after considering any depositions or other documents required to be sent to the proper officer of the court, that it is proper to make such an order.

(7) Where a person committed to the Crown Court to be dealt with under section 43 above is admitted to a hospital in pursuance of an order under section 44 above, subsections (5) and (6) above shall apply as if he were a person subject to a transfer direction.

52 Further provisions as to persons remanded by magistrates' courts

(1) This section has effect where a transfer direction has been given in respect of any such person as is described in paragraph (b) of section 48(2) above; and that person is in this section referred to as 'the accused'.

(2) Subject to subsection (5) below, the transfer direction shall cease to have effect on the expiration of the period of remand unless the accused is sent in custody to the Crown Court for trial or to be otherwise dealt with.

(3) Subject to subsection (4) below, the power of further remanding the accused under section 128 of the Magistrates' Courts Act 1980 may be exercised by the court without his being brought before the court; and if the court further remands the accused in custody (whether or not he is brought before the court) the period of remand shall, for the purposes of this section, be deemed not to have expired.

(4) The court shall not under subsection (3) above further remand the accused in his absence unless he has appeared before the court within the previous six months.

(5) If the magistrates' court is satisfied, on the written or oral evidence of the responsible clinician –

- (a) that the accused no longer requires treatment in hospital for mental disorder; or
- (b) that no effective treatment for his disorder can be given in the hospital to which he has been removed,

the court may direct that the transfer direction shall cease to have effect notwithstanding that the period of remand has not expired or that the accused is sent to the Crown Court as mentioned in subsection (2) above.

(6) If the accused is sent to the Crown Court as mentioned in subsection (2) above and the transfer direction has not ceased to have effect under subsection (5) above, section 51 above shall apply as if the transfer direction given in his case were a direction given in respect of a person falling within that section.

(7) The magistrates' court may, in the absence of the accused, send him to the Crown Court for trial under section 51 or 51A of the Crime and Disorder Act 1998 if –

- (a) the court is satisfied, on the written or oral evidence of the responsible clinician, that the accused is unfit to take part in the proceedings; and
- (b) . . ., the accused is represented by counsel or a solicitor.

53 Further provisions as to civil prisoners and persons detained under the Immigration Acts

(1) Subject to subsection (2) below, a transfer direction given in respect of any such person as is described in paragraph (c) or (d) of section 48(2) above shall cease to have effect on the expiration of the period during which he would, but for his removal to hospital, be liable to be detained in the place from which he was removed.

(2) Where a transfer direction and a restriction direction have been given in respect of any such person as is mentioned in subsection (1) above, then, if the Secretary of State is notified by the responsible clinician, any other approved clinician or the appropriate tribunal at any time before the expiration of the period there mentioned –

- (a) that that person no longer requires treatment in hospital for mental disorder; or
- (b) that no effective treatment for his disorder can be given in the hospital to which he has been removed,

the Secretary of State may by warrant direct that he be remitted to any place where he might have been detained if he had not been removed to hospital, and on his arrival at the place to which he is so remitted the transfer direction and the restriction direction shall cease to have effect.

Supplemental

54 Requirements as to medical evidence

(1) The registered medical practitioner whose evidence is taken into account under section 35(3)(a) above and at least one of the registered medical practitioners whose evidence is taken into account under sections 36(1), 37(2)(a), 38(1), 45A(2) and 51(6)(a) above and whose reports are taken into account under sections 47(1) and 48(1) above shall be a practitioner approved for the purposes of section 12 above by the Secretary of State as having special experience in the diagnosis or treatment of mental disorder.

(2) For the purposes of any provision of this Part of this Act under which a court may act on the written evidence of any person, a report in writing purporting to be signed by that person may, subject to the provisions of this section, be received in evidence without proof of the following –

- (a) the signature of the person; or
- (b) his having the requisite qualifications or approval or authority or being of the requisite description to give the report.

(2A) But the court may require the signatory of any such report to be called to give oral evidence.

(3) Where, in pursuance of a direction of the court, any such report is tendered in evidence otherwise than by or on behalf of the person who is the subject of the report, then –

- (a) if that person is represented by counsel or a solicitor, a copy of the report shall be given to his counsel or solicitor;

(b) if that person is not so represented, the substance of the report shall be disclosed to him or, where he is a child or young person, to his parent or guardian if present in court; and

(c) except where the report relates only to arrangements for his admission to a hospital, that person may require the signatory of the report to be called to give oral evidence, and evidence to rebut the evidence contained in the report may be called by or on behalf of that person.

54A Reduction of period for making hospital orders

(1) The Secretary of State may by order reduce the length of the periods mentioned in sections 37(4) and (5) and 38(4) above.

(2) An order under subsection (1) above may make such consequential amendments of sections 40(1) and 44(3) above as appear to the Secretary of State to be necessary or expedient.

55 Interpretation of Part III

(1) In this Part of this Act –

'child' and 'young person' have the same meaning as in the Children and Young Persons Act 1933;

'civil prisoner' has the meaning given to it by section 48(2)(c) above;

'guardian', in relation to a child or young person, has the same meaning as in the Children and Young Persons Act 1933;

'place of safety', in relation to a person who is not a child or young person, means any police station, prison or remand centre, or any hospital the managers of which are willing temporarily to receive him, and in relation to a child or young person has the same meaning as in the Children and Young Persons Act 1933;

'responsible clinician', in relation to a person liable to be detained in a hospital within the meaning of Part 2 of this Act, means the approved clinician with overall responsibility for the patient's case.

(2) Any reference in this Part of this Act to an offence punishable on summary conviction with imprisonment shall be construed without regard to any prohibition or restriction imposed by or under any enactment relating to the imprisonment of young offenders.

(3) . . .

(4) Any reference to a hospital order, a guardianship order or a restriction order in section 40(2), (4) or (5), section 41(3) to (5), or section 42 above or section 69(1) below shall be construed as including a reference to any order or direction under this Part of this Act having the same effect as the first-mentioned order; and the exceptions and modifications set out in Schedule 1 to this Act in respect of the provisions of this Act described in that Schedule accordingly include those which are consequential on the provisions of this subsection.

(5) Section 34(2) above shall apply for the purposes of this Part of this Act as it applies for the purposes of Part II of this Act.

(6) References in this Part of this Act to persons serving a sentence of imprisonment shall be construed in accordance with section 47(5) above.

(7) Section 99 of the Children and Young Persons Act 1933 (which relates to the presumption and determination of age) shall apply for the purposes of this Part of this Act as it applies for the purposes of that Act.

APPENDIX 2

Criminal Procedure (Insanity) Act 1964 (as amended), extracts

4 Finding of unfitness to plead

(1) This section applies where on the trial of a person the question arises (at the instance of the defence or otherwise) whether the accused is under a disability, that is to say, under any disability such that apart from this Act it would constitute a bar to his being tried.

(2) If, having regard to the nature of the supposed disability, the court are of opinion that it is expedient to do so and in the interests of the accused, they may postpone consideration of the question of fitness to be tried until any time up to the opening of the case for the defence.

(3) If, before the question of fitness to be tried falls to be determined, the jury return a verdict of acquittal on the count or each of the counts on which the accused is being tried, that question shall not be determined.

(4) Subject to subsections (2) and (3) above, the question of fitness to be tried shall be determined as soon as it arises.

(5) The question of fitness to be tried shall be determined by the court without a jury.

(6) The court shall not make a determination under subsection (5) above except on the written or oral evidence of two or more registered medical practitioners at least one of whom is duly approved.

4A Finding that the accused did the act or made the omission charged against him

(1) This section applies where in accordance with section 4(5) above it is determined by a court that the accused is under a disability.

(2) The trial shall not proceed or further proceed but it shall be determined by a jury –

(a) on the evidence (if any) already given in the trial; and
(b) on such evidence as may be adduced or further adduced by the prosecution, or adduced by a person appointed by the court under this section to put the case for the defence,

whether they are satisfied, as respects the count or each of the counts on which the accused was to be or was being tried, that he did the act or made the omission charged against him as the offence.

(3) If as respects that count or any of those counts the jury are satisfied as mentioned in subsection (2) above, they shall make a finding that the accused did the act or made the omission charged against him.

(4) If as respects that count or any of those counts the jury are not so satisfied, they shall return a verdict of acquittal as if on the count in question the trial had proceeded to a conclusion.

(5) Where the question of disability was determined after arraignment of the accused, the determination under subsection (2) is to be made by the jury by whom he was being tried.

5 Powers to deal with persons not guilty by reason of insanity or unfit to plead etc

(1) This section applies where –

- (a) a special verdict is returned that the accused is not guilty by reason of insanity; or
- (b) findings have been made that the accused is under a disability and that he did the act or made the omission charged against him.

(2) The court shall make in respect of the accused –

- (a) a hospital order (with or without a restriction order);
- (b) a supervision order; or
- (c) an order for his absolute discharge.

(3) Where –

- (a) the offence to which the special verdict or the findings relate is an offence the sentence for which is fixed by law, and
- (b) the court have power to make a hospital order,

the court shall make a hospital order with a restriction order (whether or not they would have power to make a restriction order apart from this subsection).

(4) In this section –

'hospital order' has the meaning given in section 37 of the Mental Health Act 1983;

'restriction order' has the meaning given to it by section 41 of that Act;

'supervision order' has the meaning given in Part 1 of Schedule 1A to this Act.

5A Orders made under or by virtue of section 5

(1) In relation to the making of an order by virtue of subsection (2)(a) of section 5 above, section 37 (hospital orders etc) of the Mental Health Act 1983 ('the 1983 Act') shall have effect as if –

- (a) the reference in subsection (1) to a person being convicted before the Crown Court included a reference to the case where section 5 above applies;
- (b) the words after 'punishable with imprisonment' and before 'or is convicted' were omitted; and
- (c) for subsections (4) and (5) there were substituted –

> '(4) Where an order is made under this section requiring a person to be admitted to a hospital ("a hospital order"), it shall be the duty of the managers of the hospital specified in the order to admit him in accordance with it.'

(2) In relation to a case where section 5 above applies but the court have not yet made one of the disposals mentioned in subsection (2) of that section –

(a) section 35 of the 1983 Act (remand to hospital for report on accused's mental condition) shall have effect with the omission of the words after paragraph (b) in subsection (3);
(b) section 36 of that Act (remand of accused person to hospital for treatment) shall have effect with the omission of the words '(other than an offence the sentence for which is fixed by law)' in subsection (2);
(c) references in sections 35 and 36 of that Act to an accused person shall be construed as including a person in whose case this subsection applies; and
(d) section 38 of that Act (interim hospital orders) shall have effect as if –

(i) the reference in subsection (1) to a person being convicted before the Crown Court included a reference to the case where section 5 above applies; and
(ii) the words '(other than an offence the sentence for which is fixed by law)' in that subsection were omitted.

(3) In relation to the making of any order under the 1983 Act by virtue of this Act, references in the 1983 Act to an offender shall be construed as including references to a person in whose case section 5 above applies, and references to an offence shall be construed accordingly.

(4) Where –

(a) a person is detained in pursuance of a hospital order which the court had power to make by virtue of section 5(1)(b) above, and
(b) the court also made a restriction order, and that order has not ceased to have effect,

the Secretary of State, if satisfied after consultation with the responsible clinician that the person can properly be tried, may remit the person for trial, either to the court of trial or to a prison.

On the person's arrival at the court or prison, the hospital order and the restriction order shall cease to have effect.

(5) Schedule 1A to this Act (supervision orders) has effect with respect to the making of supervision orders under subsection (2)(b) of section 5 above, and with respect to the revocation and amendment of such orders.

(6) In relation to the making of an order under subsection (2)(c) of section 5 above, section 12(1) of the Powers of Criminal Courts (Sentencing) Act 2000 (absolute and conditional discharge) shall have effect as if –

(a) the reference to a person being convicted by or before a court of such an offence as is there mentioned included a reference to the case where section 5 above applies; and
(b) the reference to the court being of opinion that it is inexpedient to inflict punishment included a reference to it thinking that an order for absolute discharge would be most suitable in all the circumstances of the case.]

SCHEDULE 1A SUPERVISION ORDERS

PART 1 PRELIMINARY

1 (1) In this Schedule 'supervision order' means an order which requires the person in respect of whom it is made ('the supervised person') to be under the supervision of a social worker, an officer of a local probation board or an officer of a provider of probation services ('the supervising officer') for a period specified in the order of not more than two years.

(2) A supervision order may, in accordance with paragraph 4 or 5 below, require the supervised person to submit, during the whole of that period or such part of it as may be specified in the order, to treatment by or under the direction of a registered medical practitioner.

(3) The Secretary of State may by order direct that sub-paragraph (1) above shall be amended by substituting, for the period for the time being specified there, such period as may be specified in the order.

(4) An order under sub-paragraph (3) above may make in paragraph 11(2) below any amendment which the Secretary of State thinks necessary in consequence of any substitution made by the order.

(5) The power of the Secretary of State to make orders under sub-paragraph (3) above shall be exercisable by statutory instrument which shall be subject to annulment in pursuance of a resolution of either House of Parliament.

PART 2 MAKING AND EFFECT OF ORDERS

Circumstances in which orders may be made

2 (1) The court shall not make a supervision order unless it is satisfied that, having regard to all the circumstances of the case, the making of such an order is the most suitable means of dealing with the accused or appellant.

(2) The court shall not make a supervision order unless it is also satisfied –

(a) that the supervising officer intended to be specified in the order is willing to undertake the supervision; and

(b) that arrangements have been made for the treatment intended to be specified in the order.

Making of orders and general requirements

3 (1) A supervision order shall either –

(a) specify the local social services authority area in which the supervised person resides or will reside, and require him to be under the supervision of a social worker of the local social services authority for that area; or

(b) specify the local justice area in which that person resides or will reside, and require him to be under the supervision of an officer of a local probation board appointed for or assigned to that area, or (as the case may be) an officer of a provider of probation services acting in that area.

(2) Before making such an order, the court shall explain to the supervised person in ordinary language –

(a) the effect of the order (including any requirements proposed to be included in the order in accordance with paragraph 4, 5 or 8 below); and
(b) that a magistrates' court has power under paragraphs 9 to 11 below to review the order on the application either of the supervised person or of the supervising officer.

(3) After making such an order, the court shall forthwith give copies of the order to an officer of a local probation board assigned to the court or an officer of a provider of probation services acting at the court, and he shall give a copy –

(a) to the supervised person; and
(b) to the supervising officer.

(4) After making such an order, the court shall also send to the designated officer for the local justice area in which the supervised person resides or will reside ('the local justice area concerned') –

(a) a copy of the order; and
(b) such documents and information relating to the case as it considers likely to be of assistance to a court acting for that area in the exercise of its functions in relation to the order.

(5) Where such an order is made, the supervised person shall keep in touch with the supervising officer in accordance with such instructions as he may from time to time be given by that officer and shall notify him of any change of address.

Requirements as to medical treatment

4 (1) A supervision order may, if the court is satisfied as mentioned in sub-paragraph (2) below, include a requirement that the supervised person shall submit, during the whole of the period specified in the order or during such part of that period as may be so specified, to treatment by or under the direction of a registered medical practitioner with a view to the improvement of his mental condition.

(2) The court may impose such a requirement only if satisfied on the written or oral evidence of two or more registered medical practitioners, at least one of whom is duly registered, that the mental condition of the supervised person –

(a) is such as requires and may be susceptible to treatment; but
(b) is not such as to warrant the making of a hospital order within the meaning of the Mental Health Act 1983.

(3) The treatment required under this paragraph by any such order shall be such one of the following kinds of treatment as may be specified in the order, that is to say –

(a) treatment as a non-resident patient at such institution or place as may be specified in the order; and
(b) treatment by or under the direction of such registered medical practitioner as may be so specified;

but the nature of the treatment shall not be specified in the order except as mentioned in paragraph (a) or (b) above.

5 (1) This paragraph applies where the court is satisfied on the written or oral evidence of two or more registered medical practitioners that –

(a) because of his medical condition, other than his mental condition, the supervised person is likely to pose a risk to himself or others; and
(b) the condition may be susceptible to treatment.

(2) The supervision order may (whether or not it includes a requirement under paragraph 4 above) include a requirement that the supervised person shall submit, during the whole of the period specified in the order or during such part of that period as may be so specified, to treatment by or under the direction of a registered medical practitioner with a view to the improvement of the condition.

(3) The treatment required under this paragraph by any such order shall be such one of the following kinds of treatment as may be specified in the order, that is to say –

(a) treatment as a non-resident patient at such institution or place as may be specified in the order; and
(b) treatment by or under the direction of such registered medical practitioner as may be so specified;

but the nature of the treatment shall not be specified in the order except as mentioned in paragraph (a) or (b) above.

6 (1) Where the medical practitioner by whom or under whose direction the supervised person is being treated in pursuance of a requirement under paragraph 4 or 5 above is of the opinion that part of the treatment can be better or more conveniently given in or at an institution or place which –

(a) is not specified in the order, and
(b) is one in or at which the treatment of the supervised person will be given by or under the direction of a registered medical practitioner,

he may, with the consent of the supervised person, make arrangements for him to be treated accordingly.

(2) Such arrangements may provide for the supervised person to receive part of his treatment as a resident patient in an institution or place of any description.

(3) Where any such arrangements are made for the treatment of a supervised person –

(a) the medical practitioner by whom the arrangements are made shall give notice in writing to the supervising officer, specifying the institution or place in or at which the treatment is to be carried out; and
(b) the treatment provided for by the arrangements shall be deemed to be treatment to which he is required to submit in pursuance of the supervision order.

7 While the supervised person is under treatment as a resident patient in pursuance of arrangements under paragraph 6 above, the supervising officer shall carry out the supervision to such extent only as may be necessary for the purpose of the revocation or amendment of the order.

Requirements as to residence

8 (1) Subject to sub-paragraph (2) below, a supervision order may include requirements as to the residence of the supervised person.

(2) Before making such an order containing any such requirement, the court shall consider the home surroundings of the supervised person.

APPENDIX 3

PACE Codes of Practice (2008), Code C, Annex E

ANNEX E – SUMMARY OF PROVISIONS RELATING TO MENTALLY DISORDERED AND OTHERWISE MENTALLY VULNERABLE PEOPLE

1. If an officer has any suspicion, or is told in good faith, that a person of any age may be mentally disordered or otherwise mentally vulnerable, or mentally incapable of understanding the significance of questions or their replies that person shall be treated as mentally disordered or otherwise mentally vulnerable for the purposes of this Code. *See paragraph 1.4*

2. In the case of a person who is mentally disordered or otherwise mentally vulnerable, 'the appropriate adult' means:

- (a) a relative, guardian or other person responsible for their care or custody;
- (b) someone experienced in dealing with mentally disordered or mentally vulnerable people but who is not a police officer or employed by the police;
- (c) failing these, some other responsible adult aged 18 or over who is not a police officer or employed by the police.

See paragraph 1.7(b) and Note 1D

3. If the custody officer authorises the detention of a person who is mentally vulnerable or appears to be suffering from a mental disorder, the custody officer must as soon as practicable inform the appropriate adult of the grounds for detention and the person's whereabouts, and ask the adult to come to the police station to see them. If the appropriate adult:

- is already at the station when information is given as in paragraphs 3.1 to 3.5 the information must be given in their presence
- is not at the station when the provisions of paragraph 3.1 to 3.5 are complied with these provisions must be complied with again in their presence once they arrive.

See paragraphs 3.15 to 3.17

4. If the appropriate adult, having been informed of the right to legal advice, considers legal advice should be taken, the provisions of section 6 apply as if the mentally disordered or otherwise mentally vulnerable person had requested access to legal advice. *See paragraph 3.19 and Note E1.*

5. The custody officer must make sure a person receives appropriate clinical attention as soon as reasonably practicable if the person appears to be suffering from a mental disorder or in urgent cases immediately call the nearest health care professional or an ambulance. It is not intended

these provisions delay the transfer of a detainee to a place of safety under the Mental Health Act 1983, section 136 if that is applicable. If an assessment under that Act is to take place at a police station, the custody officer must consider whether an appropriate health care professional should be called to conduct an initial clinical check on the detainee. *See paragraph 9.5 and 9.6*

6. It is imperative a mentally disordered or otherwise mentally vulnerable person detained under the Mental Health Act 1983, section 136 be assessed as soon as possible. If that assessment is to take place at the police station, an approved social worker and registered medical practitioner shall be called to the station as soon as possible in order to interview and examine the detainee. Once the detainee has been interviewed, examined and suitable arrangements been made for their treatment or care, they can no longer be detained under section 136. A detainee should be immediately discharged from detention if a registered medical practitioner having examined them, concludes they are not mentally disordered within the meaning of the Act. *See paragraph 3.16*

7. If a mentally disordered or otherwise mentally vulnerable person is cautioned in the absence of the appropriate adult, the caution must be repeated in the appropriate adult's presence. *See paragraph 10.12*

8. A mentally disordered or otherwise mentally vulnerable person must not be interviewed or asked to provide or sign a written statement in the absence of the appropriate adult unless the provisions of paragraphs 11.1 or 11.18 to 11.20 apply. Questioning in these circumstances may not continue in the absence of the appropriate adult once sufficient information to avert the risk has been obtained. A record shall be made of the grounds for any decision to begin an interview in these circumstances. *See paragraphs 11.1, 11.15 and 11.18 to 11.20*

9. If the appropriate adult is present at an interview, they shall be informed they are not expected to act simply as an observer and the purposes of their presence are to:

- advise the interviewee
- observe whether or not the interview is being conducted properly and fairly
- facilitate communication with the interviewee

See paragraph 11.17

10. If the detention of a mentally disordered or otherwise mentally vulnerable person is reviewed by a review officer or a superintendent, the appropriate adult must, if available at the time, be given an opportunity to make representations to the officer about the need for continuing detention. *See paragraph 15.3*

11. If the custody officer charges a mentally disordered or otherwise mentally vulnerable person with an offence or takes such other action as is appropriate when there is sufficient evidence for a prosecution this must be done in the presence of the appropriate adult. The written notice embodying any charge must be given to the appropriate adult. *See paragraphs 16.1 to 16.4A*

12. An intimate or strip search of a mentally disordered or otherwise mentally vulnerable person may take place only in the presence of the appropriate adult of the same sex, unless the detainee specifically requests the presence of a particular adult of the opposite sex. A strip search may take place in the absence of an appropriate adult only in cases of urgency when there is a risk of serious harm to the detainee or others. *See Annex A, paragraphs 5 and 11(c)*

13. Particular care must be taken when deciding whether to use any form of approved restraints on a mentally disordered or otherwise mentally vulnerable person in a locked cell. *See paragraph 8.2*

NOTES FOR GUIDANCE

E1 The purpose of the provision at paragraph 3.19 is to protect the rights of a mentally disordered or otherwise mentally vulnerable detained person who does not understand the significance of what is said to them. If the detained person wants to exercise the right to legal advice, the appropriate action should be taken and not delayed until the appropriate adult arrives. A mentally disordered or otherwise mentally vulnerable detained person should always be given an opportunity, when an appropriate adult is called to the police station, to consult privately with a solicitor in the absence of the appropriate adult if they want.

E2 Although people who are mentally disordered or otherwise mentally vulnerable are often capable of providing reliable evidence, they may, without knowing or wanting to do so, be particularly prone in certain circumstances to provide information that may be unreliable, misleading or self-incriminating. Special care should always be taken when questioning such a person, and the appropriate adult should be involved if there is any doubt about a person's mental state or capacity. Because of the risk of unreliable evidence, it is important to obtain corroboration of any facts admitted whenever possible.

E3 Because of the risks referred to in Note E2, which the presence of the appropriate adult is intended to minimise, officers of superintendent rank or above should exercise their discretion to authorise the commencement of an interview in the appropriate adult's absence only in exceptional cases, if it is necessary to avert an immediate risk of serious harm. See paragraphs 11.1, 11.18 to 11.20

APPENDIX 4

Home Office Circular 66/90, extracts

[3 September 1990]

PROVISION FOR MENTALLY DISORDERED OFFENDERS

[1.] The purpose of this circular is to draw the attention of the courts and those services responsible for dealing with mentally disordered persons who commit, or are suspected of committing, criminal offences to

(a) the legal powers which exist; and
(b) the desirability of ensuring effective co-operation between agencies to ensure that the best use is made of resources and that mentally disordered persons are not prosecuted where this is not required by the public interest.

* * * * *

POLICE

4. The first point of contact between the criminal justice system and a mentally disordered person is often the police, who may be called to intervene in incidents involving a mentally disordered person. There are a range of powers which are available to the police, and it is important that they establish close working relationships with local health, probation, and social services to assist them in exercising their powers:

(i) section 136 of the Mental Health Act 1983 provides a constable with a power to remove to a place of safety a person found in a place to which the public have access and who appears to be suffering from mental disorder within the meaning of the Act and in immediate need of care or control if the constable thinks it is necessary to do so in the interests of that person or for the protection of others. The person may be detained for a maximum of 72 hours. The power in this section may be used in relation to persons who have not committed an offence, and to those who have (or are suspected of having) committed an offence, but where it is not considered necessary in the public interest to arrest that person for the offence. Agreement should be reached with local hospitals and local social services departments so that persons detained under section 136 are assessed by a psychiatrist and interviewed by an Approved Social Worker as soon as possible for the purpose of making any necessary arrangements for the person's treatment or care. It is desirable that, wherever possible, the place of safety in which the person might be detained should be a hospital and not a police station. Guidance on the use of section 136 is contained in Chapter 10 of the Department of Health Code of Practice on the implementation of the Mental Health Act 1983 (a copy is attached at Annex A);
(ii) Section 135 of the 1983 Act empowers a justice of the peace – on information on oath laid by an Approved Social Worker – to issue a warrant authorising any

constable to enter specified premises to remove to a place of safety – which should normally be a hospital – a person believed to be suffering from mental disorder who has been, or is being, ill-treated, neglected or not kept under proper control, or who is living alone and unable to care for himself. The warrant will authorise the person's detention in a place of safety for a maximum of 72 hours. The initiative in seeking a warrant will normally rest with an Approved Social Worker. The warrant may apply to any premises within the justice's jurisdiction, including private property to which the police powers under section 136 do not extend;

(iii) where it is suspected that a mentally disordered person may have committed an offence, consideration should be given – in consultation with the Crown Prosecution Service, where appropriate – to whether any formal action by the police is necessary, particularly where it appears that prosecution is not required in the public interest in view of the nature of the offence. If the suspect is able to meet the requirements for a caution to be administered, he might be cautioned. If the criteria for a caution are not met, the police should consider whether any action need be taken against the suspect. In some cases the public interest might be met by diverting mentally disordered persons from the criminal justice system and finding alternatives to prosecution, such as admission to hospital under sections 2 or 3 or to guardianship under section 7 of the 1983 Act or informal support in the community by social services departments. The development of effective liaison with health and social services authorities will play an essential role in developing satisfactory arrangements to respond constructively in such cases;

(iv) the questioning of mentally disordered persons suspected of committing offences is subject to the Code of Practice for the Detention, Treatment and Questioning of Persons by Police Officers issued under section 66 of the Police and Criminal Evidence Act 1984. (Annex E of the Code summarises the provisions relating to mentally ill and mentally handicapped persons.) Paragraph 9.2 requires the custody officer immediately to call a police surgeon if a person brought to a police station or already detained there appears to be suffering from a mental disorder. In urgent cases the person must be sent to hospital. These requirements apply even if the person makes no request for medical attention. In the case of mentally disordered persons, chief officers of police may find it helpful to arrange with their local health authorities for psychiatrists to fill the role of police surgeon. Chief officers will be aware that even with the protection afforded by the Police and Criminal Evidence Act 1984, some mentally disordered suspects may make confessions which are untrue, and therefore it is always advisable to seek other evidence which may support or reject the suspect's story;

(v) where it is decided that the public interest requires the prosecution of a mentally disordered person for an offence it should be borne in mind that he has the same right as other suspects to bail after charge. If his mental state or other factors, such as homelessness, give rise to difficulties in releasing him on bail, arrangements should be made with the health, probation, and social services to ensure that appropriate support can be provided, such as admission to hospital, where his mental condition warrants it, or to a hostel, if the managers agree. Police bail cannot, of course, be subject to conditions of residence or medical treatment, but satisfactory arrangements to provide for these on a voluntary basis may enable the police to release the suspect on bail rather than to detain him pending his appearance before the magistrates' court;

(vi) after a mentally disordered person has been charged, wherever possible arrangements should be made with the health, probation, and social services for his assessment with a view to ensuring that he receives any medical treatment that may be necessary, and that the Crown Prosecution Service and court can be advised of any particular bail conditions or, after conviction, disposal that may be appropriate to his circumstances. At annex B to this circular is a note outlining court psychiatric assessment arrangements which have been established at certain central London and at Peterborough magistrates' courts to secure expert medical advice when required. Chief officers of police may wish to explore with their local chief probation officers and health authorities the possibility of setting up similar arrangements to ensure that suspects who are thought to be mentally disordered and in need of medical assessment should be seen by a psychiatrist as soon as possible.

* * * * *

CROWN PROSECUTION SERVICE

6. Where proceedings are instituted against a person by the police, the papers will be referred to the Crown Prosecution Service which will review the sufficiency of the evidence and consider carefully whether or not the public interest requires a prosecution in accordance with the Code for Crown Prosecutors. Any information provided by the police with the papers regarding that person's mental condition, or discussions held with other agencies to consider the advisability of diverting him from court, will be taken into account. It will be important to distinguish between those forms of mental disorder which are made worse by the institution of criminal proceedings and those forms of mental disorder which come about by reason of the institution of criminal proceedings. Where the Service is satisfied that the probable effect upon a person's mental health outweighs the interests of justice in the particular case, it will consider discontinuing the proceedings. Where the form of mental disorder is present without there being any indication that proceedings will have an adverse effect, the Crown Prosecutor will take account of the public interest in attempting to ensure that the offence will not be repeated as well as having regard to the welfare of the person in question.

MAGISTRATES' COURTS

7. Mentally disordered persons have the same rights as other persons, including a right to bail. A mentally disordered person should never be remanded to prison simply to receive medical treatment or assessment. It is desirable for the court to receive professional advice at as early a stage as possible on facilities which may be available to assist it with mentally disordered persons. Annex B to this circular describes court psychiatric assessment arrangements at certain central London and at Peterborough magistrates' courts. These enable the courts to receive speedy medical advice and to ensure that, where appropriate, arrangements can be made quickly to admit a mentally disordered person to hospital, for example as a condition of bail or, with the agreement of the hospital managers, under section 35 of the Mental Health Act 1983 following conviction. Where neither of these courses is applicable but the accused person nevertheless requires admission to hospital for assessment or treatment, the health and social services can be asked to consider using their civil powers of admission under sections 2 or 3 of the Act.

* * * * *

18. When a mentally disordered person is arrested and charged, the probation service should play its part in diverting him or her from custodial remand. They can do this in several ways. If there is a bail information scheme, the probation officer will visit the accused in police custody to interview him and obtain information which, if verified, can be passed on to the Crown Prosecution Service to inform the bail decision. Mentally disordered persons may be particularly at risk of being remanded in custody, because their circumstances and way of life may be unstable. Good liaison between the bail information scheme, the police, the health service and

social services will therefore be particularly important. If in-patient treatment is not warranted, the probation officer may be able to identify suitable accommodation in a bail hostel or lodging scheme organised by the probation service, or by the social services. Intervention at this stage can prevent unnecessary remands to prison establishments.

* * * * *

CONCLUSION

25. It is the government's policy to divert mentally disordered persons from the criminal justice system in cases where the public interest does not require their prosecution. Where prosecution is necessary it is important to find suitable non-penal disposals wherever appropriate and the police, courts, and probation service are asked to work together with their local health and social services to make effective use of the provisions of the Mental Health Act 1983 and of the services which exist to help the mentally disordered. They are also asked to ensure that all their officers are aware of this circular, and to consider any training which is necessary to equip them in their contacts with mentally disordered persons.

APPENDIX 5

PCMH form

The Crown Court

CC Case Number D1 ☐

Date of trial ☐

Fixed ☐
Warned ☐

Plea and Case Management Hearing

Advocates Questionnaire

■ Parties must complete this form.

■ This form is to be used at all Crown Court Centres, without local variation.

There is an electronic version of the form which contains answer boxes that expand. The form is at:
http://www.hmcourts-service.gov.uk/HMCSCourtFinder

1

Date of PCMH	PTI URN
Judge	**Estimated length of trial**

2 Parties' details

	Parties name	Age	Remand status	CTL expires	Instructed Advocate	PCMH Advocate (if not the Instructed Advocate)
P						
D1			C ☐ B ☐			

3 Contact details

3.1 Parties

P	Office	Name	Phone
		Email	
	Advocate	Name	Phone
		Email	
D1	Solicitor	Name	Phone
		Email	
	Advocate	Name	Phone
		Email	

5122 Plea and Case Management Hearing, Criminal Procedure Rules 2006 (12.06) HMCS

3.2

Case progression officers

P	Name	Phone
	Email	
D1	Name	Phone
	Email	
Court	Name	Phone
	Email	

4 Which orders made at the magistrates' court have not been complied with?

5

D1 Has the defendant been advised that he or she will receive credit for a guilty plea? ☐ No ☐ Yes

6

D1 Has the defendant been warned that the case may proceed in his or her absence? ☐ No ☐ Yes

7 What plea(s) is / are the defendant(s) offering?

D1

8 Should the case be referred to the Resident Judge for a trial judge to be allocated? ☐ No ☐ Yes

9 Give details of any issues relating to the fitness to plead or to stand trial.

D1

10

10.1 Has the prosecution made statutory disclosure?

P

D1

10.2 Has a defence statement been served?

D1

10.3 Does it comply with the statutory requirements?

P

10.4 If not clear from the defence statement, what are the real issues?

D1

10.5

D1 Has / will the defence made / make an application in writing under section 8 of the Criminal Procedure and Investigations Act 1996? ☐ No ☐ Yes

11 What further evidence is to be served by the prosecution? By when is it reasonably practicable to serve this?

P

12

12.1 Give details of any expert evidence likely to be relied upon, including why it is required and by when it is reasonably practicable to serve this.

P

D1

12.2 Is a note of agreement / disagreement required?

13

13.1

D1 Has the defence completed the Witness List (see **36**)? ☐ No ☐ Yes

13.2 Is any witness summons necessary?

13.3
D1 Is a timetable for the calling of witnesses required (see **30**)? ☐ No ☐ Yes

14
14.1
D1 Is a certificate for a litigator sought? ☐ No ☐ Yes

14.2 If **Yes**, why and for how long?
D1

For 15 to 35, answer the relevant questions only

15 Admissions, schedules etc.

What matters can usefully be admitted or put into schedules, diagrams, visual aids etc.?

16 Case summary

P Is it proposed to serve a case summary or note of opening? ☐ No ☐ Yes

17 Special measures

17.1 Give details of any special measures application to be made.

17.2
Can any order be made now? ☐ No ☐ Yes

17.3 What other arrangements are needed for any young / vulnerable / intimidated witness?

18 Young defendants

Are any arrangements needed for any young defendant?

D1

19 Reporting restrictions

State type and grounds of any reporting restriction sought.

P

D1

20 Third party material

20.1 What third party material is sought, from whom, and why?

P

D1

20.2 If the material can be obtained without a court order, by whom and by when?

P

D1

20.3 Should any person adversely affected by an order be notified?

21 Defendant's interview(s)

21.1 Is there an issue in relation to the accuracy of the transcript / admissibility of the defendant's interview?

D1

21.2 What proposals are made for any editing required?

D1

21.3 What proposals are made to summarise the interview(s)?

D1

22 Video Evidence

22.1 Is there video evidence of any young / vulnerable / intimidated witness yet to be served?

22.2 Has each video been transcribed?

22.3 Is there an issue in relation to the accuracy / admissibility / quality of any video or transcript?

23 Witness interview(s)

23.1 Are there any videos / audio tapes of witness interviews which, if they meet the disclosure test, are yet to be disclosed as unused material?

23.2 If so, is any application made for that video / audio tape to be transcribed and, if so, why?

24 CCTV evidence

24.1 Are there any outstanding issues in relation to service disclosure of CCTV footage? *If the material is in the possession of a third party, complete **20** instead.*

24.2 Is an edited version to be served / used?

25 Electronic equipment

25.1 Give details of any special equipment (e.g. CCTV, live link, audio recordings, DVD) required in the trial courtroom.

P

D1

25.2 Is the evidence in its present form compatible with the equipment in court?

26 Cross-examination on sexual history

If an application has not already been made, does the defence intend to make an application under section 41 of the Youth Justice and Criminal Evidence Act 1999 to cross-examine a witness about his or her sexual history?

D1

27 Bad character

Are any directions necessary in relation to bad character applications? Are there to be any further applications?

P

D1

28 Hearsay

Are any directions necessary in relation to hearsay applications? Are there to be any further applications?

P

D1

29 Admissibility and legal issues

What points on admissibility / other legal issues are to be taken? Is it necessary for any to be resolved before trial?

P

D1

30 Timetable of trial

Are there matters which need to be determined on the day of trial, which may affect the timetable of trial? If so, when will (1) the jury and (2) the witnesses be required?

P

31 Public interest immunity

Is any 'on notice' public interest immunity application to be made?

P

32 Jury bundle

What proposals do the prosecution make for a jury bundle?

P

33 Concurrent family proceedings

Give details of any concurrent family proceedings.

34 Other special arrangements

Give details of any special arrangements (e.g., interpreter, intermediary, wheelchair access, hearing loop system) needed for anyone attending the trial.

35 Linked criminal proceedings

Are there other criminal proceedings against the defendant or otherwise linked?

36 Witness List

The defence should indicate here which prosecution witnesses are required to give evidence at trial. The attendance of any witness is subject to the judge's direction.

Name of witness	Page No.	**Type of witness:** *Provide specific details of the type of witness. For example: eye witness, police officer, firearms expert, continuity*	Required by

APPENDIX 6

CPS Code for Crown Prosecutors, extracts

* * * * *

5 THE FULL CODE TEST

5.1 The Full Code Test has two stages. The first stage is consideration of the evidence. If the case does not pass the evidential stage it must not go ahead no matter how important or serious it may be. If the case does pass the evidential stage, Crown Prosecutors must proceed to the second stage and decide if a prosecution is needed in the public interest. The evidential and public interest stages are explained below.

The evidential stage

5.2 Crown Prosecutors must be satisfied that there is enough evidence to provide a 'realistic prospect of conviction' against each defendant on each charge. They must consider what the defence case may be, and how that is likely to affect the prosecution case.

5.3 A realistic prospect of conviction is an objective test. It means that a jury or bench of magistrates or judge hearing a case alone, properly directed in accordance with the law, is more likely than not to convict the defendant of the charge alleged. This is a separate test from the one that the criminal courts themselves must apply. A court should only convict if satisfied so that it is sure of a defendant's guilt.

5.4 When deciding whether there is enough evidence to prosecute, Crown Prosecutors must consider whether the evidence can be used and is reliable. There will be many cases in which the evidence does not give any cause for concern. But there will also be cases in which the evidence may not be as strong as it first appears. Crown Prosecutors must ask themselves the following questions:

CAN THE EVIDENCE BE USED IN COURT?

(a) Is it likely that the evidence will be excluded by the court? There are certain legal rules which might mean that evidence which seems relevant cannot be given at a trial. For example, is it likely that the evidence will be excluded because of the way in which it was gathered? If so, is there enough other evidence for a realistic prospect of conviction?

IS THE EVIDENCE RELIABLE?

(b) Is there evidence which might support or detract from the reliability of a confession? Is the reliability affected by factors such as the defendant's age, intelligence or level of understanding?

(c) What explanation has the defendant given? Is a court likely to find it credible in the light of the evidence as a whole? Does it support an innocent explanation?
(d) If the identity of the defendant is likely to be questioned, is the evidence about this strong enough?
(e) Is the witness's background likely to weaken the prosecution case? For example, does the witness have any motive that may affect his or her attitude to the case, or a relevant previous conviction?
(f) Are there concerns over the accuracy or credibility of a witness? Are these concerns based on evidence or simply information with nothing to support it? Is there further evidence which the police should be asked to seek out which may support or detract from the account of the witness?

5.5 Crown Prosecutors should not ignore evidence because they are not sure that it can be used or is reliable. But they should look closely at it when deciding if there is a realistic prospect of conviction.

The public interest stage

5.6 In 1951, Lord Shawcross, who was Attorney General, made the classic statement on public interest, which has been supported by Attorneys General ever since: 'It has never been the rule in this country – I hope it never will be – that suspected criminal offences must automatically be the subject of prosecution'. (House of Commons Debates, volume 483, column 681, 29 January 1951.)

5.7 The public interest must be considered in each case where there is enough evidence to provide a realistic prospect of conviction. Although there may be public interest factors against prosecution in a particular case, often the prosecution should go ahead and those factors should be put to the court for consideration when sentence is being passed. A prosecution will usually take place unless there are public interest factors tending against prosecution which clearly outweigh those tending in favour, or it appears more appropriate in all the circumstances of the case to divert the person from prosecution (see section 8 below).

5.8 Crown Prosecutors must balance factors for and against prosecution carefully and fairly. Public interest factors that can affect the decision to prosecute usually depend on the seriousness of the offence or the circumstances of the suspect. Some factors may increase the need to prosecute but others may suggest that another course of action would be better.

The following lists of some common public interest factors, both for and against prosecution, are not exhaustive. The factors that apply will depend on the facts in each case.

SOME COMMON PUBLIC INTEREST FACTORS IN FAVOUR OF PROSECUTION

5.9 The more serious the offence, the more likely it is that a prosecution will be needed in the public interest. A prosecution is likely to be needed if:

(a) a conviction is likely to result in a significant sentence;
(b) a conviction is likely to result in a confiscation or any other order;
(c) a weapon was used or violence was threatened during the commission of the offence;
(d) the offence was committed against a person serving the public (for example, a police or prison officer, or a nurse);
(e) the defendant was in a position of authority or trust;

(f) the evidence shows that the defendant was a ringleader or an organiser of the offence;
(g) there is evidence that the offence was premeditated;
(h) there is evidence that the offence was carried out by a group;
(i) the victim of the offence was vulnerable, has been put in considerable fear, or suffered personal attack, damage or disturbance;
(j) the offence was committed in the presence of, or in close proximity to, a child;
(k) the offence was motivated by any form of discrimination against the victim's ethnic or national origin, disability, sex, religious beliefs, political views or sexual orientation, or the suspect demonstrated hostility towards the victim based on any of those characteristics;
(l) there is a marked difference between the actual or mental ages of the defendant and the victim, or if there is any element of corruption;
(m) the defendant's previous convictions or cautions are relevant to the present offence;
(n) the defendant is alleged to have committed the offence while under an order of the court;
(o) there are grounds for believing that the offence is likely to be continued or repeated , for example, by a history of recurring conduct;
(p) the offence, although not serious in itself, is widespread in the area where it was committed; or
(q) a prosecution would have a significant positive impact on maintaining community confidence.

SOME COMMON PUBLIC INTEREST FACTORS AGAINST PROSECUTION

5.10 A prosecution is less likely to be needed if:

(a) the court is likely to impose a nominal penalty;
(b) the defendant has already been made the subject of a sentence and any further conviction would be unlikely to result in the imposition of an additional sentence or order, unless the nature of the particular offence requires a prosecution or the defendant withdraws consent to have an offence taken into consideration during sentencing;
(c) the offence was committed as a result of a genuine mistake or misunderstanding (these factors must be balanced against the seriousness of the offence);
(d) the loss or harm can be described as minor and was the result of a single incident, particularly if it was caused by a misjudgement;
(e) there has been a long delay between the offence taking place and the date of the trial, unless:

- the offence is serious;
- the delay has been caused in part by the defendant;
- the offence has only recently come to light; or
- the complexity of the offence has meant that there has been a long investigation;

(f) a prosecution is likely to have a bad effect on the victim's physical or mental health, always bearing in mind the seriousness of the offence;
(g) the defendant is elderly or is, or was at the time of the offence, suffering from significant mental or physical ill health, unless the offence is serious or there is real possibility that it may be repeated. The Crown Prosecution Service, where necessary, applies Home Office guidelines about how to deal with mentally disordered offenders. Crown Prosecutors must balance the desirability of diverting a defendant

who is suffering from significant mental or physical ill health with the need to safeguard the general public;

(h) the defendant has put right the loss or harm that was caused (but defendants must not avoid prosecution or diversion solely because they pay compensation); or

(i) details may be made public that could harm sources of information, international relations or national security.

5.11 Deciding on the public interest is not simply a matter of adding up the number of factors on each side. Crown Prosecutors must decide how important each factor is in the circumstances of each case and go on to make an overall assessment.

THE RELATIONSHIP BETWEEN THE VICTIM AND THE PUBLIC INTEREST

5.12 The Crown Prosecution Service does not act for victims or the families of victims in the same way as solicitors act for their clients. Crown Prosecutors act on behalf of the public and not just in the interests of any particular individual. However, when considering the public interest, Crown Prosecutors should always take into account the consequences for the victim of whether or not to prosecute, and any views expressed by the victim or the victim's family.

5.13 It is important that a victim is told about a decision which makes a significant difference to the case in which they are involved. Crown Prosecutors should ensure that they follow any agreed procedures.

* * * * *

APPENDIX 7

Practice Direction (Criminal Proceedings: Consolidation), para. III.30

III.30 TREATMENT OF VULNERABLE DEFENDANTS

(III.30.1) This direction applies to proceedings in the Crown Court and in magistrates' courts on the trial, sentencing or (in the Crown Court) appeal of (a) children and young persons under 18 or (b) adults who suffer from a mental disorder within the meaning of the Mental Health Act 1983 or who have any other significant impairment of intelligence and social function.[1] In this direction such defendants are referred to collectively as 'vulnerable defendants'. The purpose of this direction is to extend to proceedings in relation to such persons in the adult courts procedures analogous to those in use in youth courts.

(III.30.2) The steps which should be taken to comply with paragraphs III.30.3 to III.30.17 should be judged, in any given case, taking account of the age, maturity and development (intellectual, social and emotional) of the defendant concerned and all other circumstances of the case.

The overriding principle

(III.30.3) A defendant may be young and immature or may have a mental disorder within the meaning of the Mental Health Act 1983 or some other significant impairment of intelligence and social function such as to inhibit his understanding of and participation in the proceedings. The purpose of criminal proceedings is to determine guilt, if that is in issue, and decide on the appropriate sentence if the defendant pleads guilty or is convicted. All possible steps should be taken to assist a vulnerable defendant to understand and participate in those proceedings. The ordinary trial process should, so far as necessary, be adapted to meet those ends. Regard should be had to the welfare of a young defendant as required by section 44 of the Children and Young Persons Act 1933, and generally to Parts 1 and 3 of the Criminal Procedure Rules (the overriding objective and the court's powers of case management).

Before the trial, sentencing or appeal

(III.30.4) If a vulnerable defendant, especially one who is young, is to be tried jointly with one who is not, the court should consider at the plea and case management hearing, or at a case management hearing in a magistrates' court, whether the vulnerable defendant should be tried on his own and should so order unless of the opinion that a joint trial would be in accordance with Part 1 of the Criminal Procedure Rules (the overriding objective) and in the interests of justice. If a vulnerable defendant is tried jointly with one who is not, the court should consider whether any of the modifications set out in this direction should apply in the circumstances of the joint trial and so far as practicable make orders to give effect to any such modifications.

(III.30.5) At the plea and case management hearing, or at a case management hearing in a magistrates' court, the court should consider and so far as practicable give directions on the matters covered in paragraphs III.30.9 to III.30.17.

(III.30.6) It may be appropriate to arrange that a vulnerable defendant should visit, out of court hours and before the trial, sentencing or appeal hearing, the courtroom in which that hearing is to take place so that he can familiarise himself with it.

(III.30.7) If any case against a vulnerable defendant has attracted or may attract widespread public or media interest, the assistance of the police should be enlisted to try and ensure that the defendant is not, when attending the court, exposed to intimidation, vilification or abuse. Section 41 of the Criminal Justice Act 1925 prohibits the taking of photographs of defendants and witnesses (among others) in the court building or in its precincts, or when entering or leaving those precincts. A direction informing media representatives that the prohibition will be enforced may be appropriate.

(III.30.8) The court should be ready at this stage, if it has not already done so, where relevant to make a reporting restriction under section 39 of the Children and Young Persons Act 1933 or, on an appeal to the Crown Court from a youth court, to remind media representatives of the application of section 49 of that Act. Any such order, once made, should be reduced to writing and copies should on request be made available to anyone affected or potentially affected by it.

The trial, sentencing or appeal hearing

(III.30.9) Subject to the need for appropriate security arrangements the proceedings should, if practicable, be held in a courtroom in which all the participants are on the same or almost the same level.

(III.30.10) A vulnerable defendant, especially if he is young, should normally, if he wishes, be free to sit with members of his family or others in a like relationship, and with some other suitable supporting adult such as a social worker, and in a place which permits easy, informal communication with his legal representatives. The court should ensure that a suitable supporting adult is available throughout the course of the proceedings.

(III.30.11) At the beginning of the proceedings the court should ensure that what is to take place has been explained to a vulnerable defendant in terms he can understand, and at trial in the Crown Court it should ensure in particular that the role of the jury has been explained. It should remind those representing the vulnerable defendant and the supporting adult of their responsibility to explain each step as it takes place, and at trial to explain the possible consequences of a guilty verdict. Throughout the trial the court should continue to ensure, by any appropriate means, that the defendant understands what is happening and what has been said by those on the bench, the advocates and witnesses.

(III.30.12) A trial should be conducted according to a timetable which takes full account of a vulnerable defendant's ability to concentrate. Frequent and regular breaks will often be appropriate. The court should ensure, so far as practicable, that the trial is conducted in simple, clear language that the defendant can understand and that cross-examination is conducted by questions that are short and clear.

(III.30.13) A vulnerable defendant who wishes to give evidence by live link in accordance with section 33A of the Youth Justice and Criminal Evidence Act 1999 may apply for a direction to that effect. Before making such a direction the court must be satisfied that it is in the interests of justice to do so, and that the use of a live link would enable the defendant to participate more effectively as a witness in the proceedings. The direction will need to deal with the practical arrangements to be made, including the room from which the defendant will give evidence, the identity of the person or persons who will accompany him, and how it will be arranged for him to be seen and heard by the court.

(III.30.14) In the Crown Court robes and wigs should not be worn unless the court for good reason orders that they should. It may be appropriate for the court to be robed for sentencing in a grave case even though it has sat without robes for trial. It is generally desirable that those responsible for the security of a vulnerable defendant who is in custody, especially if he is young, should not be in uniform, and that there should be no recognisable police presence in the courtroom save for good reason.

(III.30.15) The court should be prepared to restrict attendance by members of the public in the court room to a small number, perhaps limited to those with an immediate and direct interest in the outcome. The court should rule on any challenged claim to attend.

(III.30.16) Facilities for reporting the proceedings (subject to any restrictions under section 39 or 49 of the Children and Young Persons Act 1933) must be provided. But the court may restrict the number of reporters attending in the courtroom to such number as is judged practicable and desirable. In ruling on any challenged claim to attend in the court room for the purpose of reporting the court should be mindful of the public's general right to be informed about the administration of justice.

(III.30.17) Where it has been decided to limit access to the courtroom, whether by reporters or generally, arrangements should be made for the proceedings to be relayed, audibly and if possible visually, to another room in the same court complex to which the media and the public have access if it appears that there will be a need for such additional facilities. Those making use of such a facility should be reminded that it is to be treated as an extension of the court room and that they are required to conduct themselves accordingly.

(III.30.18) Where the court is called upon to exercise its discretion in relation to any procedural matter falling within the scope of this practice direction but not the subject of specific reference, such discretion should be exercised having regard to the principles in paragraph III.30.3.

1 This reflects the wording used in section 33A of the Youth Justice and Criminal Evidence Act 1999, as inserted by section 47 of the Police and Justice Act 2006.

APPENDIX 8

Checklists

Listed below are a number of prompts to assist in taking instructions from a mentally disordered offender. Note that the checklists in *Defending Suspects at Police Stations*, Ed Cape (LAG, 2006) which cover all other questions that should be asked in the police station.

1. Mental disorder

   - Diagnosis, for example, schizophrenia, depression
   - Length of illness
   - Symptoms of illness
   - Dates of previous admissions to psychiatric hospital
   - Admissions as inpatient or outpatient
   - Detained voluntarily or on section
   - Civil (s.2, s.3, s.17A – CTO) or criminal section (ss.37–41)
   - Date of last discharge from hospital
   - Name, address and telephone number of most recent hospital
   - Treatment including name of current medication
   - Care in the community, e.g. supported hostel, day centre
   - Name/telephone numbers of (C)RC, social worker, AMHP, key nurse, CPN, etc.
   - GP – name, address and telephone number
   - Name, address and telephone number of nearest relative
   - Consent to talk to:
     - Medical professionals
     - Other professionals
     - Nearest relative

2. Learning disability

   - Form of disability
     - Particular difficulties e.g. limited language ability (expression and/or understanding), memory recall, description of events
   - IQ score (if known)
   - Reading or writing difficulties
   - Name and address of any special school attended
   - Education Act statement by local authority
   - Name/telephone of (C)RC, social worker, key worker, care coordinator, etc.
   - Dates of previous admissions to psychiatric hospital
   - Admissions as inpatient or outpatient
   - Detained voluntarily or on section
   - Name and address of hospital
   - Date of last discharge from hospital
   - Civil (s.2, s.3, s.17A – CTO) or criminal section (ss.37–41)

- Name, address and telephone number of nearest relative
- Consent of client to talk to:
  - Medical professionals
  - Other professionals
  - Nearest relative

APPENDIX 9

Criminal Procedure (Amendment) Rules 2009 (SI 2009/2087), Sched. 5

SCHEDULE 5

PART 33 EXPERT EVIDENCE

Contents of this Part

[Note. *For the use of an expert report as evidence, see section 30 of the Criminal Justice Act 1988.*]

Reference to expert

33.1. A reference to an 'expert' in this Part is a reference to a person who is required to give or prepare expert evidence for the purpose of criminal proceedings, including evidence required to determine fitness to plead or for the purpose of sentencing.

[Note. *Expert medical evidence may be required to determine fitness to plead under section 4 of the Criminal Procedure (Insanity) Act 1964. It may be required also under section 11 of the Powers of Criminal Courts (Sentencing) Act 2000, under Part III of the Mental Health Act 1983 or under Part 12 of the Criminal Justice Act 2003. Those Acts contain requirements about the qualification of medical experts.*]

Expert's duty to the court

33.2. (1) An expert must help the court to achieve the overriding objective by giving objective, unbiased opinion on matters within his expertise.

(2) This duty overrides any obligation to the person from whom he receives instructions or by whom he is paid.

(3) This duty includes an obligation to inform all parties and the court if the expert's opinion changes from that contained in a report served as evidence or given in a statement.

Content of expert's report

33.3. (1) An expert's report must –

(a) give details of the expert's qualifications, relevant experience and accreditation;

(b) give details of any literature or other information which the expert has relied on in making the report;

(c) contain a statement setting out the substance of all facts given to the expert which are material to the opinions expressed in the report, or upon which those opinions are based;

(d) make clear which of the facts stated in the report are within the expert's own knowledge;

(e) say who carried out any examination, measurement, test or experiment which the expert has used for the report and –

(i) give the qualifications, relevant experience and accreditation of that person,

(ii) say whether or not the examination, measurement, test or experiment was carried out under the expert's supervision, and

(iii) summarise the findings on which the expert relies;

(f) where there is a range of opinion on the matters dealt with in the report –

(i) summarise the range of opinion, and

(ii) give reasons for his own opinion;

(g) if the expert is not able to give his opinion without qualification, state the qualification;

(h) contain a summary of the conclusions reached;

(i) contain a statement that the expert understands his duty to the court, and has complied and will continue to comply with that duty; and

(j) contain the same declaration of truth as a witness statement.

(2) Only sub-paragraphs (i) and (j) of rule 33.3(1) apply to a summary by an expert of his conclusions served in advance of that expert's report.

[Note. *Part 27 contains rules about witness statements. Declarations of truth in witness statements are required by section 9 of the Criminal Justice Act 1967 and section 5B of the Magistrates' Courts Act 1980. A party who accepts another party's expert's conclusions may admit them as facts under section 10 of the Criminal Justice Act 1967. Evidence of examinations etc. on which an expert relies may be admissible under section 127 of the Criminal Justice Act 2003.*]

Service of expert evidence

33.4. (1) A party who wants to introduce expert evidence must –

(a) serve it on –

(i) the court officer, and
(ii) each other party;

(b) serve it –

(i) as soon as practicable, and in any event
(ii) with any application in support of which that party relies on that evidence; and

(c) if another party so requires, give that party a copy of, or a reasonable opportunity to inspect –

(i) a record of any examination, measurement, test or experiment on which the expert's findings and opinion are based, or that were carried out in the course of reaching those findings and opinion, and
(ii) anything on which any such examination, measurement, test or experiment was carried out.

(2) A party may not introduce expert evidence if that party has not complied with this rule, unless –

(a) every other party agrees; or
(b) the court gives permission.

[Note. *Under section 81 of the Police and Criminal Evidence Act 1984, and under section 20(3) of the Criminal Procedure and Investigations Act 1996, rules may –*

(a) require the disclosure of expert evidence before it is introduced as part of a party's case; and

(b) prohibit its introduction without the court's permission, if it was not disclosed as required.]

Expert to be informed of service of report

33.5. A party who serves on another party or on the court a report by an expert must, at once, inform that expert of that fact.

Pre-hearing discussion of expert evidence

33.6. (1) This rule applies where more than one party wants to introduce expert evidence.
(2) The court may direct the experts to –

(a) discuss the expert issues in the proceedings; and
(b) prepare a statement for the court of the matters on which they agree and disagree, giving their reasons.

(3) Except for that statement, the content of that discussion must not be referred to without the court's permission.
(4) A party may not introduce expert evidence without the court's permission if the expert has not complied with a direction under this rule.

[Note. *At a pre-trial hearing, a court may make binding rulings about the admissibility of evidence and about questions of law under section 7 of the Criminal Justice Act 1987; sections 31 and 40 of the Criminal Procedure and Investigations Act 1996; and section 45 of the Courts Act 2003.*]

Court's power to direct that evidence is to be given by a single joint expert

33.7. (1) Where more than one defendant wants to introduce expert evidence on an issue at trial, the court may direct that the evidence on that issue is to be given by one expert only.

(2) Where the co-defendants cannot agree who should be the expert, the court may –

(a) select the expert from a list prepared or identified by them; or
(b) direct that the expert be selected in another way.

Instructions to a single joint expert

33.8. (1) Where the court gives a direction under rule 33.7 for a single joint expert to be used, each of the co-defendants may give instructions to the expert.

(2) When a co-defendant gives instructions to the expert he must, at the same time, send a copy of the instructions to the other co-defendant(s).

(3) The court may give directions about –

(a) the payment of the expert's fees and expenses; and
(b) any examination, measurement, test or experiment which the expert wishes to carry out.

(4) The court may, before an expert is instructed, limit the amount that can be paid by way of fees and expenses to the expert.

(5) Unless the court otherwise directs, the instructing co-defendants are jointly and severally liable for the payment of the expert's fees and expenses.

Court's power to vary requirements under this Part

33.9. (1) The court may –

(a) extend (even after it has expired) a time limit under this Part;
(b) allow the introduction of expert evidence which omits a detail required by this Part.

(2) A party who wants an extension of time must –

(a) apply when serving the expert evidence for which it is required; and
(b) explain the delay.

APPENDIX 10

Criminal Justice and Public Order Act 1994 (as amended), extracts

Inferences from accused's silence

34 Effect of accused's failure to mention facts when questioned or charged

(1) Where, in any proceedings against a person for an offence, evidence is given that the accused –

- (a) at any time before he was charged with the offence, on being questioned under caution by a constable trying to discover whether or by whom the offence had been committed, failed to mention any fact relied on in his defence in those proceedings; or
- (b) on being charged with the offence or officially informed that he might be prosecuted for it, failed to mention any such fact,

being a fact which in the circumstances existing at the time the accused could reasonably have been expected to mention when so questioned, charged or informed, as the case may be, subsection (2) below applies.

(2) Where this subsection applies –

- (a) a magistrates' court inquiring into the offence as examining justices;
- (b) a judge, in deciding whether to grant an application made by the accused under –
  - (i) section 6 of the Criminal Justice Act 1987 (application for dismissal of charge of serious fraud in respect of which notice of transfer has been given under section 4 of that Act); or
  - (ii) paragraph 5 of Schedule 6 to the Criminal Justice Act 1991 (application for dismissal of charge of violent or sexual offence involving child in respect of which notice of transfer has been given under section 53 of that Act);
- (c) the court, in determining whether there is a case to answer; and
- (d) the court or jury, in determining whether the accused is guilty of the offence charged,

may draw such inferences from the failure as appear proper.

(2A) Where the accused was at an authorised place of detention at the time of the failure, subsections (1) and (2) above do not apply if he had not been allowed an opportunity to consult a solicitor prior to being questioned, charged or informed as mentioned in subsection (1) above.

(3) Subject to any directions by the court, evidence tending to establish the failure may be given before or after evidence tending to establish the fact which the accused is alleged to have failed to mention.

(4) This section applies in relation to questioning by persons (other than constables) charged with the duty of investigating offences or charging offenders as it applies in relation to questioning by constables; and in subsection (1) above 'officially informed' means informed by a constable or any such person.

(5) This section does not –

- (a) prejudice the admissibility in evidence of the silence or other reaction of the accused in the face of anything said in his presence relating to the conduct in respect of which he is charged, in so far as evidence thereof would be admissible apart from this section; or
- (b) preclude the drawing of any inference from any such silence or other reaction of the accused which could properly be drawn apart from this section.

(6) This section does not apply in relation to a failure to mention a fact if the failure occurred before the commencement of this section.

(7) . . .

35 Effect of accused's silence at trial

(1) At the trial of any person . . . for an offence, subsections (2) and (3) below apply unless –

- (a) the accused's guilt is not in issue; or
- (b) it appears to the court that the physical or mental condition of the accused makes it undesirable for him to give evidence;

but subsection (2) below does not apply if, at the conclusion of the evidence for the prosecution, his legal representative informs the court that the accused will give evidence or, where he is unrepresented, the court ascertains from him that he will give evidence.

(2) Where this subsection applies, the court shall, at the conclusion of the evidence for the prosecution, satisfy itself (in the case of proceedings on indictment with a jury, in the presence of the jury) that the accused is aware that the stage has been reached at which evidence can be given for the defence and that he can, if he wishes, give evidence and that, if he chooses not to give evidence, or having been sworn, without good cause refuses to answer any question, it will be permissible for the court or jury to draw such inferences as appear proper from his failure to give evidence or his refusal, without good cause, to answer any question.

(3) Where this subsection applies, the court or jury, in determining whether the accused is guilty of the offence charged, may draw such inferences as appear proper from the failure of the accused to give evidence or his refusal, without good cause, to answer any question.

(4) This section does not render the accused compellable to give evidence on his own behalf, and he shall accordingly not be guilty of contempt of court by reason of a failure to do so.

(5) For the purposes of this section a person who, having been sworn, refuses to answer any question shall be taken to do so without good cause unless –

(a) he is entitled to refuse to answer the question by virtue of any enactment, whenever passed or made, or on the ground of privilege; or
(b) the court in the exercise of its general discretion excuses him from answering it.

(6) ...

(7) This section applies –

(a) in relation to proceedings on indictment for an offence, only if the person charged with the offence is arraigned on or after the commencement of this section;
(b) in relation to proceedings in a magistrates' court, only if the time when the court begins to receive evidence in the proceedings falls after the commencement of this section.

36 Effect of accused's failure or refusal to account for objects, substances or marks

(1) Where –

(a) a person is arrested by a constable, and there is –

(i) on his person; or
(ii) in or on his clothing or footwear; or
(iii) otherwise in his possession; or
(iv) in any place in which he is at the time of his arrest,

any object, substance or mark, or there is any mark on any such object; and

(b) that or another constable investigating the case reasonably believes that the presence of the object, substance or mark may be attributable to the participation of the person arrested in the commission of an offence specified by the constable; and
(c) the constable informs the person arrested that he so believes, and requests him to account for the presence of the object, substance or mark; and
(d) the person fails or refuses to do so,

then if, in any proceedings against the person for the offence so specified, evidence of those matters is given, subsection (2) below applies.

(2) Where this subsection applies –

(a) a magistrates' court inquiring into the offence as examining justices;
(b) a judge, in deciding whether to grant an application made by the accused under –

(i) section 6 of the Criminal Justice Act 1987 (application for dismissal of charge of serious fraud in respect of which notice of transfer has been given under section 4 of that Act); or
(ii) paragraph 5 of Schedule 6 to the Criminal Justice Act 1991 (application for dismissal of charge of violent or sexual offence involving child in respect of which notice of transfer has been given under section 53 of that Act);

(c) the court, in determining whether there is a case to answer; and
(d) the court or jury, in determining whether the accused is guilty of the offence charged,

may draw such inferences from the failure or refusal as appear proper.

(3) Subsections (1) and (2) above apply to the condition of clothing or footwear as they apply to a sub-stance or mark thereon.

(4) Subsections (1) and (2) above do not apply unless the accused was told in ordinary language by the constable when making the request mentioned in subsection (1)(c) above what the effect of this section would be if he failed or refused to comply with the request.

(4A) Where the accused was at an authorised place of detention at the time of the failure or refusal, sub-sections (1) and (2) above do not apply if he had not been allowed an opportunity to consult a solicitor prior to the request being made.

(5) This section applies in relation to officers of customs and excise as it applies in relation to constables.

(6) This section does not preclude the drawing of any inference from a failure or refusal of the accused to account for the presence of an object, substance or mark or from the condition of clothing or footwear which could properly be drawn apart from this section.

(7) This section does not apply in relation to a failure or refusal which occurred before the commencement of this section.

(8) . . .

37 Effect of accused's failure or refusal to account for presence at a particular place

(1) Where –

- (a) a person arrested by a constable was found by him at a place at or about the time the of-fence for which he was arrested is alleged to have been committed; and
- (b) that or another constable investigating the offence reasonably believes that the presence of the person at that place and at that time may be attributable to his participation in the commission of the offence; and
- (c) the constable informs the person that he so believes, and requests him to account for that presence; and
- (d) the person fails or refuses to do so,

then if, in any proceedings against the person for the offence, evidence of those matters is given, subsection (2) below applies.

(2) Where this subsection applies –

- (a) a magistrates' court inquiring into the offence as examining justices;
- (b) a judge, in deciding whether to grant an application made by the accused under–
  - (i) section 6 of the Criminal Justice Act 1987 (application for dismissal of charge of serious fraud in respect of which notice of transfer has been given under section 4 of that Act); or
  - (ii) paragraph 5 of Schedule 6 to the Criminal Justice Act 1991 (application for dismissal of charge of violent or sexual offence involving child in respect of which notice of transfer has been given under section 53 of that Act);
- (c) the court, in determining whether there is a case to answer; and
- (d) the court or jury, in determining whether the accused is guilty of the offence charged,

may draw such inferences from the failure or refusal as appear proper.

(3) Subsections (1) and (2) do not apply unless the accused was told in ordinary language by the con-stable when making the request mentioned in subsection (1)(c) above what the effect of this section would be if he failed or refused to comply with the request.

(3A) Where the accused was at an authorised place of detention at the time of the failure or refusal, sub-sections (1) and (2) do not apply if he had not been allowed an opportunity to consult a solicitor prior to the request being made.

(4) This section applies in relation to officers of customs and excise as it applies in relation to constables.

(5) This section does not preclude the drawing of any inference from a failure or refusal of the accused to account for his presence at a place which could properly be drawn apart from this section.

(6) This section does not apply in relation to a failure or refusal which occurred before the commencement of this section.

(7) . . .

APPENDIX 11

Coroners and Justice Act 2009, extracts

52 Persons suffering from diminished responsibility (England and Wales)

(1) In section 2 of the Homicide Act 1957 (c. 11) (persons suffering from diminished responsibility), for subsection (1) substitute –

'(1) A person ("D") who kills or is a party to the killing of another is not to be convicted of murder if D was suffering from an abnormality of mental functioning which –

(a) arose from a recognised medical condition,

(b) substantially impaired D's ability to do one or more of the things mentioned in subsection (1A), and

(c) provides an explanation for D's acts and omissions in doing or being a party to the killing.

(1A) Those things are –

(a) to understand the nature of D's conduct;

(b) to form a rational judgment;

(c) to exercise self-control.

(1B) For the purposes of subsection (1)(c), an abnormality of mental functioning provides an explanation for D's conduct if it causes, or is a significant contributory factor in causing, D to carry out that conduct.'

(2) In section 6 of the Criminal Procedure (Insanity) Act 1964 (c. 84) (evidence by prosecution of insanity or diminished responsibility), in paragraph (b) for 'mind' substitute 'mental functioning'.

Partial defence to murder: loss of control

54 Partial defence to murder: loss of control

(1) Where a person ('D') kills or is a party to the killing of another ('V'), D is not to be convicted of murder if –

(a) D's acts and omissions in doing or being a party to the killing resulted from D's loss of self-control,
(b) the loss of self-control had a qualifying trigger, and

(c) a person of D's sex and age, with a normal degree of tolerance and self-restraint and in the circumstances of D, might have reacted in the same or in a similar way to D.

(2) For the purposes of subsection (1)(a), it does not matter whether or not the loss of control was sudden.

(3) In subsection (1)(c) the reference to 'the circumstances of D' is a reference to all of D's circumstances other than those whose only relevance to D's conduct is that they bear on D's general capacity for tolerance or self-restraint.

(4) Subsection (1) does not apply if, in doing or being a party to the killing, D acted in a considered desire for revenge.

(5) On a charge of murder, if sufficient evidence is adduced to raise an issue with respect to the defence under subsection (1), the jury must assume that the defence is satisfied unless the prosecution proves beyond reasonable doubt that it is not.

(6) For the purposes of subsection (5), sufficient evidence is adduced to raise an issue with respect to the defence if evidence is adduced on which, in the opinion of the trial judge, a jury, properly directed, could reasonably conclude that the defence might apply.

(7) A person who, but for this section, would be liable to be convicted of murder is liable instead to be convicted of manslaughter.

(8) The fact that one party to a killing is by virtue of this section not liable to be convicted of murder does not affect the question whether the killing amounted to murder in the case of any other party to it.

55 Meaning of 'qualifying trigger'

(1) This section applies for the purposes of section 54.

(2) A loss of self-control had a qualifying trigger if subsection (3), (4) or (5) applies.

(3) This subsection applies if D's loss of self-control was attributable to D's fear of serious violence from V against D or another identified person.

(4) This subsection applies if D's loss of self-control was attributable to a thing or things done or said (or both) which –

(a) constituted circumstances of an extremely grave character, and
(b) caused D to have a justifiable sense of being seriously wronged.

(5) This subsection applies if D's loss of self-control was attributable to a combination of the matters mentioned in subsections (3) and (4).

(6) In determining whether a loss of self-control had a qualifying trigger –

(a) D's fear of serious violence is to be disregarded to the extent that it was caused by a thing which D incited to be done or said for the purpose of providing an excuse to use violence;

(b) a sense of being seriously wronged by a thing done or said is not justifiable if D incited the thing to be done or said for the purpose of providing an excuse to use violence;
(c) the fact that a thing done or said constituted sexual infidelity is to be disregarded.

(7) In this section references to 'D' and 'V' are to be construed in accordance with section 54.

56 Abolition of common law defence of provocation

(1) The common law defence of provocation is abolished and replaced by sections 54 and 55.

(2) Accordingly, the following provisions cease to have effect –

(a) section 3 of the Homicide Act 1957 (c. 11) (questions of provocation to be left to the jury);
(b) section 7 of the Criminal Justice Act (Northern Ireland) 1966 (c. 20) (questions of provocation to be left to the jury).

Infanticide

57 Infanticide (England and Wales)

(1) Section 1 of the Infanticide Act 1938 (c. 36) (offence of infanticide) is amended as follows.

(2) In subsection (1) –

(a) for 'notwithstanding that' substitute 'if', and
(b) after 'murder' insert 'or manslaughter'.

(3) In subsection (2) –

(a) for 'notwithstanding that' substitute 'if', and
(b) after 'murder' insert 'or manslaughter'.

104 Examination of accused through intermediary

(1) After section 33B of the Youth Justice and Criminal Evidence Act 1999 (c. 23) insert –

'33BA Examination of accused through intermediary

(1) This section applies to any proceedings (whether in a magistrates' court or before the Crown Court) against a person for an offence.

(2) The court may, on the application of the accused, give a direction under subsection (3) if it is satisfied –

(a) that the condition in subsection (5) is or, as the case may be, the conditions in subsection (6) are met in relation to the accused, and

(b) that making the direction is necessary in order to ensure that the accused receives a fair trial.

(3) A direction under this subsection is a direction that provides for any examination of the accused to be conducted through an interpreter or other person approved by the court for the purposes of this section ("an intermediary").

(4) The function of an intermediary is to communicate –

(a) to the accused, questions put to the accused, and

(b) to any person asking such questions, the answers given by the accused in reply to them, and to explain such questions or answers so far as necessary to enable them to be understood by the accused or the person in question.

(5) Where the accused is aged under 18 when the application is made the condition is that the accused's ability to participate effectively in the proceedings as a witness giving oral evidence in court is compromised by the accused's level of intellectual ability or social functioning.

(6) Where the accused has attained the age of 18 when the application is made the conditions are that –

(a) the accused suffers from a mental disorder (within the meaning of the Mental Health Act 1983) or otherwise has a significant impairment of intelligence and social function, and

(b) the accused is for that reason unable to participate effectively in the proceedings as a witness giving oral evidence in court.

(7) Any examination of the accused in pursuance of a direction under subsection (3) must take place in the presence of such persons as Criminal Procedure Rules or the direction may provide and in circumstances in which –

(a) the judge or justices (or both) and legal representatives acting in the proceedings are able to see and hear the examination of the accused and to communicate with the intermediary,

(b) the jury (if there is one) are able to see and hear the examination of the accused, and

(c) where there are two or more accused in the proceedings, each of the other accused is able to see and hear the examination of the accused.

For the purposes of this subsection any impairment of eyesight or hearing is to be disregarded.

(8) Where two or more legal representatives are acting for a party to the proceedings, subsection (7)(a) is to be regarded as satisfied in relation to those representatives if at all material times it is satisfied in relation to at least one of them.

(9) A person may not act as an intermediary in a particular case except after making a declaration, in such form as may be prescribed by Criminal Procedure Rules, that the person will faithfully perform the function of an intermediary.

(10) Section 1 of the Perjury Act 1911 (perjury) applies in relation to a person acting as an intermediary as it applies in relation to a person lawfully sworn as an interpreter in a judicial proceeding.

33BB Further provision as to directions under section 33BA(3)

(1) The court may discharge a direction given under section 33BA(3) at any time before or during the proceedings to which it applies if it appears to the court that the direction is

no longer necessary in order to ensure that the accused receives a fair trial (but this does not affect the power to give a further direction under section 33BA(3) in relation to the accused).

(2) The court may vary (or further vary) a direction given under section 33BA(3) at any time before or during the proceedings to which it applies if it appears to the court that it is necessary for the direction to be varied in order to ensure that the accused receives a fair trial.

(3) The court may exercise the power in subsection (1) or (2) of its own motion or on an application by a party.

(4) The court must state in open court its reasons for –

(a) giving, varying or discharging a direction under section 33BA(3), or

(b) refusing an application for, or for the variation or discharge of,

a direction under section 33BA(3), and, if it is a magistrates' court, it must cause those reasons to be entered in the register of its proceedings.'

(2) In the heading of Chapter 1A of Part 2 of that Act, after 'LIVE LINK' insert 'AND INTERMEDIARY'.

Index